The Curiosities of Heraldry
by
M. A. Lower

**A facsimile copy produced and privately printed by
The Armorial Register Limited
2016**

First Published in 2016
by
The Armorial Register Limited
All rights reserved

ISBN: 978-0-9568157-8-1

British Library Cataloguing-in-Publication Data
A catalogue record of this book is available on request from the
British Library

Cover image:
17c Belgian stone carving of what may be a boar's head –
but is it?

THE

CURIOSITIES OF HERALDRY.

WITH

Illustrations from Old English Writers.

BY

MARK ANTONY LOWER,

AUTHOR OF "ENGLISH SURNAMES," ETC.

WITH NUMEROUS WOOD ENGRAVINGS,

From Designs by the Author.

LONDON:

JOHN RUSSELL SMITH,

4, OLD COMPTON STREET, SOHO.

MDCCCXLV.

C. AND J. ADLARD, PRINTERS, BARTHOLOMEW CLOSE.

PREFACE.

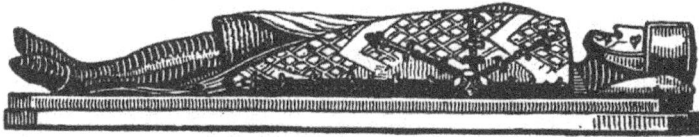

LITTLE need be said to the lover of antiquity in commendation of the subject of this volume; and I take it for granted that every one who reads the history of the Middle Ages in a right spirit will readily acknowledge that Heraldry, as a system, is by no means so contemptible a thing as the mere utilitarian considers it to be. Yet, notwithstanding, how few are there who have even a partial acquaintance with its principles. To how many, even of those who find pleasure in archæological pursuits, does the charge apply:

"— neque enim clypei cælamina norit."

Two hundred years ago, when the study of armory was much more cultivated than at present, this general ignorance of our 'noble science' called forth the cen-

sure of its admirers. Master Ri. Brathwait, lamenting
it, says of some of his contemporaries :

> " They weare theire grandsire's signet on their thumb,
>   Yet aske them whence their crest is, they are *mum;*"

and adds :

> " Who weare gay *coats,* but can no *coat* deblaze,
>   Display'd for *gulls,* may bear *gules* in their face !"[1]

This invective is perhaps a little too severe, yet it is
mildness itself when compared with that of Ranulphus
Holme, son of the author of the 'Academy of Armory,'
who declares that unless the reader assents to what is
contained in his father's book he is

> "neither Art's nor Learning's friend,
>   But an ignorant, empty, brainless sot,
>   Whose chiefest study is the *can* and *pot !*"

Now, though I would by no means place the objector
to Heraldry upon the same bench with the devotee of
Bacchus, nor even upon the stool of the dunce, yet I
hope to make it appear that the study is worthy of
more attention than is generally conceded to it.[2] At
the same time I wish it to be distinctly understood
that I do not over-rate its importance. " The benefit
arising from different pursuits will differ, of course, in

---

[1] Yorke's ' Union of Honour.'

[2] The general ignorance of Heraldry even among the well-educated may be
illustrated by the fact that not many months since the Commissioners of Assessed
Taxes decided that a person who sealed his letters with a Thistle surrounded by
the words ' 𝔇inna 𝔉orget,' was liable to the charge for armorial bearings,
albeit the device contained neither shield, helmet, wreath, nor any other *necessary*
element of heraldric insignia !

degree, but nothing that exercises the intellect can be useless, and in this spirit it may be possible to study even conchology without degradation."

Many persons regard arms as nothing more than a set of uncouth and unintelligible emblems by which families are distinguished from one another; the language by which they are described as an antiquated "jargon;" and both as little worthy of an hour's examination as astrology, alchemy or palmistry. This is a mistake; and such individuals are guilty, however unintentionally, of a great injustice to a lordly, poetical, and useful science.

That Heraldry is a *lordly* science none will deny; that it is also a *poetical* science I shall shortly attempt to prove; but there are some sour spirits who know not how to dissever the idea of lordliness from that of tyranny, and who "thank the gods for not having made them poetical." These, therefore, will be no recommendations of our subject to *such* readers; but should I be able to show that it is a *useful* science, what objections can those cavillers then raise?

I purpose to give a short dissertation on the utility of Heraldry, but first let me say a few words on the *poetry* of the subject. Do not the 'Lion of England,' the 'Red-Cross Banner,' the 'White and Red Roses,' the 'Shamrock of Ireland,' and 'Scotia's barbed Thistle' occupy a place in the breast of every patriot? and what are they but highly poetical expressions? Do not the poetry of Chaucer and Spenser and Shakspeare, not to mention our old heroic ballads and the pleasant legends

of a Scott, abound with heraldrical allusions? Tasso
is minute, though inaccurate, in the description of the
banners of his Christian heroes; he was far from
despising blazon as a poetical accessory. And, lastly,
see how nobly the stately Drayton makes the 'jargon'
of Heraldry chime in with his glorious numbers:

> " Upon his surcoat valiant *Neville* bore
>   A SILVER SALTIRE upon martial red;
>   A LADIE'S SLEEVE high-spirited *Hastings* wore;
>   *Ferrers* his tabard with rich VAIRY spred,
>   Well known in many a warlike match before;
>   A RAVEN sate on *Corbet's* armed head;
>   And *Culpeper* in SILVER ARMS enrailed
>   Bore thereupon a BLOODIE BEND ENGRAILED;
>   The noble *Percie* in that dreadful day
>   With a BRIGHT CRESCENT in his guidhomme came;
>   In his WHITE CORNET *Verdon* doth display
>   A FRET OF GULES," &c.
>
> Barons' War, B. 1, 22, 23.

I now proceed to show that Heraldry is a *useful*
science. It has already been said that nothing which
calls into exercise the intellectual powers can be useless. But it may be said that there is an abundance of
studies calculated more profitably to exercise them.
Granted: but it should be remembered that, as there is
a great diversity of tastes, so there is a great disparity
in the mental capacities of mankind. Heraldry may
therefore be recommended as a study to those who are
not qualified to grasp more profound subjects, and as a
source of amusement to those who wish to relieve their

minds in the intervals of graver and more important pursuits. To either class a very brief study will give an insight into the theory of heraldry, and a competent knowledge of the terms it employs.

The nomenclature of Heraldry is somewhat repulsive to those who casually look into a treatise on the subject, and often deters even the unprejudiced from entering upon the study; but what science is there that is not in a greater or less degree liable to the same objection?

A recent writer observes: "The language of Heraldry is occasionally barbarous in sound and appearance, but it is always peculiarly expressive ; and a practice which involves habitual conciseness and precision in their utmost attainable degree, and in which tautology is viewed as fatally detrimental, may insensibly benefit the student on other more important occasions."[1]

But Heraldry is useful on higher grounds than these, and particularly as an aid to the right understanding of that important period of the history of Christendom, the reign of feudalism. An eminent French writer, Victor Hugo, declares that " for him who can decipher it, Heraldry is an *algebra, a language*. The whole history of the second half of the middle ages is written in blazon, as that of the preceding period is in the

---

[1] Woodham's 'Application of Heraldry to the Illustration of various University and Collegiate Antiquities ;' Nos. 4 and 5 of the publications of the Cambridge Antiq. Soc.—an interesting essay, which would be none the worse if divested of a few remarks on "church principles," "conventicles," "Cobbett," and the "Morning Chronicle,"—subjects as irrelevant as the whims of old Morgan, or any other heraldric writer of the sixteenth or seventeenth century.

symbolism of the Roman church." To the student of history, then, Heraldry is far from useless.

The sculptured stone or the emblazoned shield often speaks when the written records of history are silent. A grotesque carving of coat or badge in the spandrel of some old church-door, or over the portal of a decayed mansion, often points out the stock of the otherwise forgotten patron or lord. "A dim-looking pane in an oriel window, or a discoloured coat in the dexter corner of an old Holbein may give not only the name of the benefactor or the portrait, but also identify him personally by showing his relation to the head of the house, his connexions and alliances."[1] The antiquary and the local historian, then, possess in Heraldry a valuable key to many a secret of other times.

To the genealogist a knowledge of Heraldry is indispensable. Coats of arms in church windows, on the walls, upon tombs, and especially on seals, are documents of great value. Many persons of the same name can now only be classed with their proper families by an inspection of the arms they bore. In Wales, where the number of surnames is very limited, families are much better recognized by their arms than by their names.[2]

The painter, in representing the gaudy scenes of the courts and camps of other days, can by no means dispense with a knowledge of our science; and the archi-

---

[1] Woodham.   [2] Grimaldi. Orig. Gen. p. 82.

tect who should attempt to raise some stately Gothic fane, omitting the well-carved shield, the heraldric corbel, and the blazoned grandeur of

"rich windows that exclude the light,"

would inevitably fail to impart to his work one of the greatest charms possessed by that noblest of all styles of building, and produce a meagre, soulless, abortion! Heraldry is, then, in the eyes of every man of any pretensions to taste, a useful, because an indispensable, science.

Now for an argument far stronger than all : Heraldry has been known to further the ends of *justice*. "I know three families," says Garter Bigland, "who have acquired estates by virtue of preserving the arms and escutcheons of their ancestors." I repeat, therefore, without the fear of contradiction, that Heraldry is a *useful* science. Q. E. D.

With respect to the sheets now submitted to the reader a few observations may be necessary. In the first place, I wish it to be understood that I have avoided, as much as possible, the technicalities of blazon : it was not my wish to supersede (even had I been competent to do so) the various excellent treatises on the subject already extant. The sole motive I entertained in writing this volume was a desire to render the science of Heraldry more intelligible to the general reader, and to present it in aspects more interesting and attractive than those writers can possibly

do who treat of blazon merely as an art, and to make
him acquainted with its origin and progress by means
of brief historical and biographical sketches, and by
inquiries into the derivation and meaning of armorial
figures.   In such an antient and well-explored field
there has been but little scope for original discovery;
but if I have succeeded in concentrating, and placing
in a somewhat new light, old and well-known truths,
my labour has not been lost, and my wish to render
popular a too-much neglected study has been in some
measure realized.

~ The references at the foot of nearly every page
render acknowledgments to the authors whose works
I have consulted almost unnecessary.   It is, however,
but justice to confess my obligations to Dallaway and
Montagu for the general subject, to Noble for the
notices of the heralds, and to Moule for the biblio-
graphy.   For the illustrations and extracts I am principally indebted to the Boke of St. Albans, Leigh,
Bossewell, Ferne, Guillim, Morgan, Randle Holme, and
nearly all the writers of the antient school; whose
works are rarely met with in an ordinary course of
reading.   From all these, both antient and modern, it
has been my aim to select such points as appeared
likely to interest both those who have some acquaintance with the subject and those who are confessedly
ignorant of it.

Besides the authors of acknowledged reputation
named above, I have consulted many others of comparatively little importance and value, convinced with

Pliny, "nullum esse librum tam malum ut non aliquâ parte posset prodesse." Should a small proportion only of the reading public peruse my 'Curiosities of Heraldry' on the same principle, I shall not want readers!

My thanks are due to William Courthope, Esq. Rouge-Croix pursuivant of arms, for several obliging communications from the records of the Heralds' Office, as well as for the great courtesy and promptitude with which he has invariably attended to every request I have had occasion to make during the progress of the work.

For the notice of the interesting relic discovered at Lewes (Appendix E), I am indebted to the kindness of W. H. Blaauw, Esq., M.A., author of the 'Barons' War,' some remarks from whom on the subject were read at the late meeting of the Archæological Association at Canterbury, where the relic itself was exhibited.

The reader is requested to view the simple designs which illustrate these pages with all the candour with which an amateur draughtsman is usually indulged. Every fault they exhibit belongs only to myself, not to Mr. Vasey, the engraver, who, unlike Sir John Ferne's artist,[1] must be acknowledged to have "done *his* duety" in a very creditable manner.

---

[1] Vide p. 254.

It is not unlikely that I may be called upon to justify the orthography of several words of frequent occurrence in this work. I will therefore anticipate criticism by a remark or two, premising that I am too thoroughly imbued with the spirit of antiquarianism to make innovations without good and sufficient reason. The words to which I allude are *antient, lyon, escocheon,* and, particularly, *heraldric.* The first three cannot be regarded as innovations, as they were in use centuries ago. For ‘*antient,*’ apology is scarcely necessary, as many standard writers have used it; and it must be admitted to be quite as much like the low Latin *antianus* as *ancient* is. ‘Lyon’ looks *picturesque,* and seems to be in better keeping with the form in which the monarch of the forest is pourtrayed in heraldry than the modern spelling: an antiquarian predilection is all that I can urge in its defence. I would never employ it except in heraldry. ‘Escocheon’ is used by many modern writers on heraldry in preference to *escutcheon,* not only as a more elegant orthography, but as a closer approximation to the French *écusson,* from which it is derived.

For ‘HERALDRIC’ more lengthened arguments may be deemed necessary, as I am not aware that it occurs in any English dictionary. This adjective is *almost* invariably spelt without the R—heraldic; and that orthography, though sometimes correct, is still oftener false. I contend that two spellings are necessary, because *two totally different words* are required in different senses,—to wit,

I. Heraldic, belonging to a herald; and

II. Heraldric, belonging to heraldry.

I will illustrate the distinction by an example or two.

(I) "The office of Garter is the 'ne plus ultra' of *heraldic* ambition," i. e., it is the height of the herald's ambition ultimately to arrive at that honour. The word here has no relation whatever to proficiency in the science of coat-armour or heraldry, since it is possible that a herald or pursuivant may entertain the desire of gaining the post, *causâ honoris*, without any particular predilection for the study. Again,

"Queen Elizabeth was a staunch defender of *heraldic* prerogatives;" in other words, she defended the rights and privileges of her *officers* of arms; not the prerogatives of *coats* of arms, for to what prerogatives can painted ensigns lay claim?

(II) "A. B. is engaged in *heraldric* pursuits;" that is, in the study of armorial bearings; not in the pursuits of a herald, which consist in the proclamation of peace or war, the attendance on state ceremonials, the *granting* of arms, &c. To say that A. B., who has no official connexion with the College of Arms, is a herald, would be an obvious misnomer, although he may be quite equal in *heraldrical* skill to any gentleman of the tabard.

"The so-called arms of the town of Guildford have

nothing *heraldric* about them," that is, they are not framed in accordance with the laws of blazon. To say that they are not *heraldic*, would be to say that they do not declare war, attend coronations, wear a tabard, or perform any of the functions of a herald— a gross absurdity.

A literary friend, who objects to my reasoning, thinks that the *one word, heraldic*, answers every purpose for both applications. That it has done so, heretofore, is not certainly a reason why it should after the distinction has been pointed out. Besides, my doctrine is not unsupported by analogy. We have a case precisely parallel in the words *monarchal* and *monarchical;* and he who would charge me with innovation must, to be consistent with himself, expunge *monarchical* from his dictionary as a useless word.

Lewes; Dec. 1844.

Contents.

Appendix.

ERRATA.

Page 15, line 6, *for* pays? *read* pays!
20, — 15, for *preterea* read *præterea*.

The distinction between the *supports* and *tenans* of French heraldry made at page 144 is erroneous. The true distinction is that human figures and angels, when employed to support the shield, are called *tenans*, while quadrupeds, fishes, or birds engaged in the same duty are styled *supports*.

THE

CURIOSITIES OF HERALDRY.

CHAPTER I.

Fabulous History of Heraldry.

"You had a maister that hath fetched the beginning of Gentry from Adam, and of Knighthood from Olybion." *Ferne's Blazon of Gentrie.*

"Gardons nous de mêler le douteux au certain, et le chimérique avec le vrai." *Voltaire, Essai sur les Mœurs.*

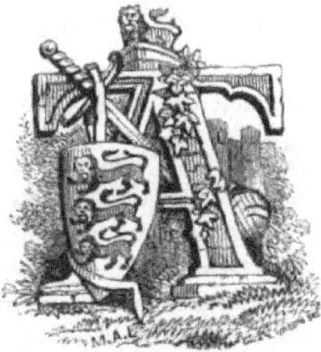

NTIQUITY has, in a greater or less degree, charms for all; and it is supposed to stamp such a value on things as nothing else can confer. This feeling, unexceptionable in itself, is liable to great abuse; especially in relation to historical matters. In States and in Families, Antiquity implies greatness,

1

strength, and those other attributes which command vene-
ration and respect.   Hence the first historians of nations
have uniformly endeavoured to carry up their annals to periods far beyond the limits of probability, thus rendering the
earlier portions of their works a tissue of absurdity deduced
from the misty regions of tradition, conjecture, and song.[1]

This reverence for antiquity has extended itself to genealo-
gists, and to those who have recorded the history of sciences
and inventions.   Thus has it been with the earliest writers
on 𝔥𝔢𝔯𝔞𝔩𝔡𝔯𝔭, a system totally unknown till within the last
thousand years; but which in the fancies of its zealous admirers has been presumed to have existed, not merely in the
first ages of the world, but at a period

> " Ere Nature was, or Adam's dust
> Was fashioned to a man !"

We are gravely assured by a writer of the fifteenth century
that heraldric ensigns were primarily borne by the ' hierarchy
of the skies.'   "*At hevyn*," says the author of the Boke of
St. Albans, "*I will begin;* where were V orderis of aungelis,
and now stand but IV, in *cote armoris* of knawlege, en-
crowned ful hye with precious stones, where Lucifer with
mylionys of aungelis, owt of hevyn fell into hell and odyr

---

[1] Some curious specimens (for example) of this kind of history occur in the
writings of John Rous of Warwick, temp. Edw. IV.   His *History of England* is
compiled indiscriminately *from the Bible* and from monastic writers.   Moses, he
tells us, does not mention all the cities founded before the deluge, but Barnard
de Breydenback, dean of Mayence, does !   With the same taste he acquaints us,
that, though the book of Genesis says nothing of the matter, Giraldus Cambrensis
writes, that Caphera or Cesera, Noah's niece, being apprehensive of the deluge,
set out for Ireland, where, with three men and fifty women, she arrived safe with
one ship, the rest perishing in the general destruction !   Vide Walpole's Historic
Doubts.

places, and ben holdyn ther in bondage; and all [the remaining angels] were erected in hevyn of gentill nature!"

Thus, in one short sentence, the origin both of nobility and
of its external symbols is summarily disposed of. When *proofs*
are not to be adduced, how can we regret that it is no longer?

But to descend a little lower, let us quote again the
poetical language of this indisputable authority: "Adam,
the begynnyng of mankind, was as a stocke unsprayed and
unfloreshed,"—having neither boughs nor leaves—"and in
the braunches is knowledge wich is rotun and wich is grene;"
that is, if I rightly understand it, (for poetry is not always
quite intelligible,) both the gentle and the ungentle, the earl
and the churl, are descended from one progenitor; *omnes
communem parentem habent;* a truth which, it is presumed,
will not be called in question.

The *gentility* of the great ancestor of our race is stoutly
contended for, and, that his claim to that distinction might
not want support, Morgan, an enthusiastic armorist of the
seventeenth century, has assigned him *two coats of arms;*
one as borne in Eden—when he neither used nor needed
either *coat* for covering or *arms* for defence—and another
suited to his condition after the fall. The first was a plain
red shield, described in the language of modern heraldry as
'gules,' while the arms of Eve, a shield of white, or 'argent,'
were borne upon it as an 'escocheon of pretence,' she being
an heiress! The arms of Abel were, as a matter of course,
those of his father and mother borne 'quarterly,' and ensigned
with a crosier, like that of a bishop, to show that he was a
'shepheard.'[1]

Sir John Ferne, a man of real erudition, was so far carried
away by extravagant notions of the great antiquity of heraldric

---

[1] Morgan. Adam's Shield, p. 99.

insignia, as seriously to deduce the use of furs in heraldry from the ' coats of skins' which the Creator made for Adam and Eve after their transgression. This, independently of its absurdity, is an unfortunate idea; for coats of arms are as certainly marks of honour as these were badges of disgrace; and as Morgan says, ' innocens was Adam's best gentility.'[1] The second coat of Adam, says this writer, was '*paly tranche,* divided every way and tinctured of every colour.' Cain, also, after *his* fall, changed his armorials " by ingrailing and *indented* lines—to show, as the preacher saith, There is a generation whose *teeth* are as swords, and their jaw-*teeth* as knives to devour the poor from the earth." He was the first, it is added, who desired to have his arms changed—' So God set a mark upon him !'[2]

This ante-diluvian heraldry is expatiated upon by our author in a manner far too prolix for us to follow him through all his grave statements and learned proofs. I shall therefore only observe, *en passant,* that arms are assigned to the following personages, viz. : Jabal, the inventor of tents, *Vert, a tent argent,* (a white tent in a green field !) Jubal, the primeval musician, *Azure, a harp, or, on a chief argent three rests gules;*[3] Tubal-Cain, *Sable, a hammer argent, crowned or,*

[1] Morgan. Adam's Shield, p. 100.

[2] " God himselfe set a marke upon Cain. But you perhaps will say, that was Stigma, and not Digma, a brand, not an ornament." Bolton's Armories.

[3] ' Three *rests* gules.' A difference of opinion exists as to what this charge represents. Some blazon it a *horseman's rest,* and assert that it was the *rest* in which the tilting-spear was fixed. Others contend that it was a wind instrument called the Clarion or Claricorde; while " Leigh and Boswell will have them to be *sufflues,* instruments which transmit the wind from the bellows to the organ." Lastly, Minshen advises those who blazon them *rests,* to call them brackets or *organ-rests;* and this is evidently the sense implied by Morgan.

and Naamah, his sister, the inventress of weaving, *In a lozenge gules, a carding-comb argent.*

Noah, according to the Boke of St. Albans, "came a *gentilman* by kynde . . . . and had iij sonnys begetyn by kinde . . . . yet in theys iij sonnys gentilness and ungentilnes was fownde." The sin of Ham degraded him to the condition of a churl; and upon the partition of the world between the three brethren Noah pronounced a malediction against him. "Wycked kaytiff," says he, "I give to thee the north parte of the worlde to draw thyne habitacion, for ther schall it be, where sorow and care, cold and myschef, as a churle thou shalt live in the thirde parte of the worlde wich shall be calde Europe, that is to say, *the contre of churlys !*"

"Japeth," he continues, "cum heder my sonne, thou shalt have my blessing dere . . . . I make the a gentilman of the west parte of the world and of Asia, that is to say, *the contre of gentilmen.*" He then in like manner creates Sem a gentleman, and gives him Africa, or "*the contre of tempurnes.*"[1]

"Of the offspryng of the gentleman Japheth come Habraham, Moyses, Aron, and the profettys, and also the kyng of the right lyne of Mary, of whom that gentilman Jhesus . . . kyng of the londe of Jude and of Jues, gentilman by his modre Mary prynce[ss] of cote-armure !" . . . . "Jafet made the first target and therin he made a ball in token of all the worlde."

Morgan's researches do not seem to have furnished him with the arms of Abraham, Isaac, and Jacob, but those of the twelve patriarchs are given by him and others. Joseph's

[1] The correctness of these extracts, historically and etymologically considered, needs no comment.

"coat of many colours," Morgan, by a strange oversight, makes to consist of two tinctures only, viz. black, chequered with white—in the language of heraldry, *chequy sable and argent*,—to denote the lights and shadows of his history.

The pathetic predictions and benedictions pronounced by the dying patriarch Jacob to his sons, furnished our old writers with one of their best pretences for giving coat-armour to persons in those remote ages. The standards ordered to be set up around the Israelitish camp in the desert[1] are likewise adduced in support of the notion that regular heraldry was then known. The arms of the twelve tribes are given by Morgan in the following hobbling verses :[2]

> " Judah bare Gules, a lion[a] couchant or ;
> Zebulon's black Ship's[b] like to a man of war ;
> Issachar's asse[c] between two burthens girt ;
> As Dan's[d] sly snake lies in a field of vert ;
> Asher with *Azure* a Cup[e] of gold sustains ;
> And Nephtali's Hind[f] trips o'er the flow'ry plains ;
> Ephraim's strong Ox lyes with the couchant Hart ;
> Manasseh's Tree its branches doth impart ;
> Benjamin's Wolfe in the field gules resides ;
> Reuben's field argent and blew bars wav'd glides ;
> Simeon doth beare his Sword ; and in that manner
> Gad, having pitched his Tent, sets up his Banner."

The same authority gives as the arms of Moses a *cross*, because he preferred "taking up the cross," and suffering

---

[1] Numb. ii. 2. "Every man shall pitch by his own standard, with the ensign of his father's house."

[2] Gen. xlix. [a] He couched as a lion..... [b] Zebulon shall be for an haven of ships..... [c] Issachar is a strong ass couching down between two burdens..... [d] Dan shall be a serpent by the way..... [e] He shall yield royal dainties .... [f] Naphtali is a hind let loose ..... &c. &c. &c.

the lot of his brethren to a life of pleasure and dignity in the court of Pharaoh. The 'parfight armory of Duke Joshua,' given by Leigh, is *Partie bendy sinister, or and gules, a backe displayed sable.* The arms of Gideon were *Sable, a fleece argent, a chief azure gutté d'eau,*[1] evidently a 'composition' from the miracle recorded in the Book of Judges. To Samson is ascribed, *Gules, a lion couchant or, within an orle argent, semée of bees sable,* an equally evident allusion to a passage in the bearer's history. David, as a matter of course, bore *a golden harp in a field azure.*[2]

But it is not alone to the worthies of sacred history that these honourable insignia are ascribed—the heroes of classical story, too, had their 'atchievements.' Hector of Troy, for example, bore, *Sable, ij lyons combatand or.*[3] Here again our great authority, Dame Julyan Berners,[4] may be cited. "Two thousand yere and xxiiij," says she, "before thyncarnation of Christe, **Cote=Armure** was made and figurid at the sege of Troye, where in gestis troianorum it tellith that the first begynnyng of the lawe of armys was ; the which was effygured and begunne before any lawe in the world bot the lawe of nature, and before the X commaundementis of God."

I have been favoured with the following curious extract

---

[1] Sprinkled with drops of water.

[2] Morgan gives the preamble of the Letters Patent of King David *for the warrant of a pedigree.* It commences with "Omnibus, &c. David, Dei gratiâ Rex Juda et Israel, universis et singulis," &c.!!

[3] Leigh's Accedens of Armory.

[4] Boke of St. Alb. It will be seen in this extract that the origin of arms is referred to other times than those mentioned in the former quotations. Several similar discrepancies occur in the work, proving it to have been a compilation from different and conflicting authorities.

from a MS. at the College of Arms,[1] which also refers the origin of arms to the siege of Troy. I believe it has never been printed.

" 𝔚𝔥𝔞𝔱 𝔄𝔯𝔪𝔢𝔰 𝔟𝔢, 𝔞𝔫𝔡 𝔴𝔥𝔢𝔯𝔢 𝔱𝔥𝔢𝔶 𝔴𝔢𝔯𝔢 𝔣𝔦𝔯𝔰𝔱𝔢 𝔦𝔫𝔟𝔢𝔫𝔱𝔢𝔡. As kinges of Armes record, the begynynge of armes was fyrste founded at the great sege of Troye wthin the Cytie and wthout, for the doughtines of deades don on bothe partyes and for so mouche as thier were soo many valliaunt knights on bothe sydes wch did soo great acts of Armes, and none of them myght be knowen from other, the great Lords on both p'ties by thier dyscreate advice assembled together and accorded that every man that did a great acte of armes shoulde bere upon him a marke in token of his doutye deades, that the pepoell myght have the bet^r knowledge of him, and if it were soo that suche a man had any chylderen, it was ordeyned that they should also bere the same marke that their father did wth dyvers differences, that ys to saye, Theldeste as his father did wth a labell, the secounde wth a cressente, the third wth a molett, the fourth a marlet, the vth an annellet, the vjth a flewer delisse. And if there be anye more than sixe the rest to bere suche differences as lyketh the herauld to geve them. And when the said seige was ended ye lordes went fourth into dyvers landes to seke there adventures, and into England came Brute and [his] knights wth there markes and inhabited the land; and after, because the name of MERKES was rewde, they terned the same into ARMES, for as mouche *as that name was far fayerer,* and becausse that markes were gotten through myght of armes of men."

The humour of Alexander the Great must have been some-

[1] Miscellaneous Collection.

what of the quaintest when he assumed the arms ascribed to
him by Master Gerard Leigh, to wit, *Gules a* GOLDEN LYON
SITTING IN A CHAYER and holding *a battayle-axe of silver.*[1]
The 'atchievement' of Cæsar was, if we may trust the same
learned armorist, *Or, an eagle displayed with two heads
sable.*[2]

[1] See vignette at the head of this chapter.

[2] Those who wish for other examples of this fictitious heraldry may find in
Ferne's 'Blazon of Gentrie,' the arms of Osyris king of Egypt, Hercules king of
Lybia, Macedonus, Anubis, Minerva, Semiramis, Tomyris, Delborah (Judge of
Israell), Jahel the Kenite, and Judith. These six last mentioned, together with
the Empress Maud, Elizabeth of Arragon, and Joan of Naples, constitute the
"nine worthies amongst women." Ferne, 220 et seq., where their arms are
engraved.

Upon the accession of James VI of Scotland to the throne of England, a controversy arose between the heralds of the two nations respecting the priority of
right to the first quarter in the British achievement. The Scottish officers maintained that as Scotland was the older sovereignty, its tressured lion should take
precedence of the three lions-passant, or, as they called them, the *leopards*, of
England. This was an indignity which the English heralds could not brook, and
they employed Sir William Segar to investigate the antiquity of our national
ensigns. Segar's treatise on this subject, dedicated to his majesty, contains some
fine examples of fictitious heraldry. He begins with the imaginary story of Brutus,
king of Britain, a thousand years before the Christian era, and his division of the
island between his three sons. To Locheren, the eldest, he gave that portion
afterwards called England, with arms 'Or, a Lion passant-guardant, gules.' To
his second son, Toalknack, he assigned Albania, or Scotland, with 'Or, a Lion
rampant, gules,' which, says he, with the addition of the double tressure, continue
the arms of Scotland. And to his youngest son he gave Cambria, with 'Argent,
three Lions passant-guardant, gules,' which the princes of Wales used for a long
time. Vide Nisbet's Essay on Arm. p. 162.

Bolton (Elements of Armories, 1610, p. 14,) gives the arms of Caspar and
Balthasar, two of the three kings who, guided by the 'Star in the East,' came to
worship our Saviour at Bethlehem. He admits, indeed, that there is no 'canonicall
proofe' of them, yet appears to think that a painting "in the mother church of

Arms are also assigned to King Arthur, Charlemagne, Sir Guy of Warwick, and other heroes, who, though belonging to much more recent periods, still flourished long before the existence of the heraldric system, and never dreamed of such honours.

That these pretended armorials were the mere figments of the writers who record them, no one doubts. In these ingenious falsehoods we recognize a principle similar to that which produced the 'pious frauds' of enthusiastic churchmen, and to that which led self-duped alchemists to deceive others. In their zeal for the antiquity of arms—a zeal of so glowing a character that no one who has not read their works can estimate it—they imagined that they must have existed from the beginning of the world. Then, throwing the reins upon the neck of their fancy, they ascribed to almost every celebrated personage of the earliest ages, the ensigns they deemed the most appropriate to his character and pursuits. The feeling inducing such a procedure originated in a mistake as to the antiquity of chivalry, of which heraldry was part and parcel. Feelings unknown before the existence of this institution are attributed to the heroes of antiquity. '*Duke* Joshua' is presumed to have been only another Duke William of Normandy, influenced in war by similar motives and surrounded by the same social circumstances in time of peace. Chaucer talks of classical heroes as if they were knights of some modern order; and Lydgate, in his 𝕋𝕣𝕠𝕡 𝔹𝕠𝕜𝕖 invests the heroes of the Iliad with the costume of his own times, carrying emblazoned shields and fighting under feudal banners :

Canterburie, upon a wal, on the left hand, as you enter the north ile of the first quire," is pretty respectable authority! It was a favourite crotchet with this writer, that heraldry did not owe its origin to any particular period or nation, but that it sprang from the light of nature.

"And to behold in the knights shields
The fell beastes.

"Where that he saw,
In the shields hanging on the hookes,
The beasts rage.

"The which beastes as the storie leres
Were wrought and bete upon their banners
Displaied brode, when they schould fight."[1]

The fabulous history of the science might be fairly deduced to the eleventh century, as the Saxon monarchs up to
that date are all represented to have borne arms. Yet as
there are not wanting, even in our day, those who admit the
authenticity of those bearings, their claims will be briefly
referred to in the next chapter.

In justice to the credulous and inventive armorists of the
' olden tyme,' the reader should be reminded that warriors
did, in very antient times, bear various figures upon their
shields. These seem in general to have been engraved in,
rather than painted upon, the metal of which the shield was
composed. The French word *escu* and *escussion*, the Italian
scudo, and the English *escocheon*, are evident derivations from
the Latin *scutum*, and the equivalent word *clypeus* is derived
from the Greek verb γλυφειν, TO ENGRAVE. But those sculptured devices were regarded as the peculiar ensigns of one
individual, who could change them at pleasure, and did not
descend hereditarily like the modern coat of arms.

A few references to the shields here alluded to may not be
unacceptable. Homer describes the shield of Agamemnon

---

[1] Story of Thebes, p. 2.

as being ornamented with the Gorgon, his peculiar badge;
and Virgil says of Aventinus,[1] the son of Hercules—

> "Post hos insignem palmâ per gramina currum,
>   Victoresque ostentat equos, satus Hercule pulchro
>   Pulcher Aventinus : clypeoque, *insigne paternum*,
>   Centum angues, cinctamq : gerit serpentibus *hydram*."
>
> *Æneid.* vii, 655.

> "Next Aventinus drives his chariot round
>   The Latian plains, with palms and laurels crowned;
>   Proud of his steeds he smokes along the field,
>   His father's *hydra* fills his ample shield."
>
> *Dryden,* vii, 908.

The Greek dramatists describe the symbols and war-cries
placed upon their shields by the seven chiefs, in their expedition against the city of Thebes.   As an example, Capaneus
is represented as bearing the figure of a giant with a blazing
torch, and the motto, "*I will fire the city !*"   Such ensigns
seem to have been the peculiar property of the valiant and
well-born, and so far they certainly resembled modern heraldry.   Virgil, speaking of Helenus, whose mother had been
a slave, says,

> "Slight were his arms—a sword and silver shield;
>   No *marks of honour* charged its empty field."[2]

Several of our more recent writers, while they disclaim all
belief of the existence of armorial bearings in earlier times,

[1] Romulus.

[2] Vide Donaldson on the Connexion between Heraldry and Gothic Architecture, &c. &c. &c.

The far-renowned shield of Achilles was covered with so great a number of
figures *pictorially disposed*, that it resembled modern heraldry still less than those
above alluded to.

still think they find traces of these distinctions in the days of the Roman commonwealth. The family of the Corvini are particularly cited as having hereditarily borne a raven as their crest; but this device was, as Nisbet has shown,[1] merely an ornament bearing allusion to the apocryphal story of an early ancestor of that race having been assisted in combat by a bird of this species. The *jus imaginum* of the Romans is also adduced. In every condition of civilized society distinctions of rank and honour are recognized. Thus the Romans had their three classes distinguished as *nobiles, novi,* and *ignobiles.* Those whose ancestors had held high offices in the state, as Censor, Prætor, or Consul, were accounted nobiles, and were entitled to have statues of their progenitors executed in wood, metal, stone, or wax, and adorned with the insignia of their several offices, and the trophies they had earned in war. These they usually kept in presses or cabinets, and on occasions of ceremony and solemnity exhibited before the entrances of their houses. He who had a right to exhibit his own effigy only, was styled *novus,* and occupied the same position with regard to the many-imaged line as the upstart of our own times, who bedecks his newly-started equipage with an equally new coat of arms, does to the head of an antient house with a shield of forty quarterings. The ignobiles were not permitted to use any image, and therefore stood upon an equality with modern plebeians, who bear no arms but the two assigned them by the heraldry of nature.

The patricians of our day to a certain extent carry out the *jus imaginum* of antiquity, only substituting painted canvas for sculptured marble or modelled wax ; and there is no sight

---

[1] Essay on Armories. p. 4.

better calculated to inspire respect for dignity of station than the gallery of some antient hall hung with a long series of family portraits; in which, as in a kind of physiognomical pedigree, the speculative mind may also find matter of agreeable contemplation. The *jus imaginum* doubtless originated in the same class of feelings that gave birth to heraldry, but there is no further connexion or analogy between the two. It is to hereditary shields and hereditary banners we must limit the true meaning of heraldry, and all attempts to find these in the classical era will end in a disappointment as inevitable as that which accompanies the endeavour to gather " grapes of thorns or figs of thistles."

CHAPTER II.

Authentic History of Heraldry.

[John Talbot, Earl of Shrewsbury, temp. Hen. VI,
in his surcoat or coat of arms.][1]

"Vetera quæ nunc sunt fuerunt olim *nova*."

"L'histoire du blazon ! mais c'est l'histoire tout entière de notre pays ?"
Jouffroy d'Eschavannes.

HAVING given some illustrations of the desire of referring the heraldric system to times of the most remote
antiquity, and shown something of the misapplication of learning to prove what was incapable of proof, let us now leave the
obscure byways of those mystifiers of truth and fabricators of
error, and emerge into the more beaten path presented to us
in what may be called the historical period, which is confined
within the last eight centuries. The history of the sciences,

[1] From a contemporary picture at Castle-Ashby, engraved in Pennant's Journey
from Chester to London.

like that of nations, generally has its fabulous as well as its historical periods, and this is eminently the case with heraldry; yet in neither instance is there any exact line of demarcation by which the former are separable from the latter. This renders it the duty of a discriminating historian to act with the utmost caution, lest, on the one hand, truths of a remote date should be sacrificed because surrounded by the circumstances of fiction, and lest, on the other, error should be too readily admitted as fact, because it comes to us in a less questionable shape; and I trust I shall not be deemed guilty of misappropriation if I apply to investigations like the present, that counsel which primarily refers to things of much greater import, namely, "Prove all things; hold fast that which is good."

The *germ* of that flourishing tree which eventually ramified into all the kingdoms of Christendom, and became one of the most striking and picturesque features of the feudal ages, and the most gorgeous ornament of chivalry, and which interweaves its branches into the entire framework of mediæval history, is doubtless to be found in the banners and ornamented shields of the warriors of antiquity. Standards, as the necessary distinctions of contending parties on the battle-field, must be nearly or quite as antient as war itself; and every such mark of distinction would readily become a national cognizance both in war and peace.[1] But it was reserved for later ages to apply similar marks and symbols to the purpose of distinguishing different commanders on the same side, and even after this became general it was some

---

[1] It is scarcely necessary to remind the reader that all early nations had their national emblems, for the ox of the Egyptians, the owl of the Athenians, the eagle of the Romans, and the white horse of the Saxons (retained in the arms of Saxony and of Kent), must occur to the recollection of every one.

time ere the hereditary transmission of such ensigns was resorted to as a means of distinguishing families, which in the lapse of ages—the warlike idea in which they had their origin having vanished—has become almost the only purpose to which they are now applied.

The standards used by the German princes in the centuries immediately preceding the Norman Conquest, are conjectured to have given rise to Heraldry, properly so called. Henry l'Oiseleur (the Fowler), who was raised to the throne of the West in 920, advanced it to its next stage when, in regulating the tournaments—which from mismanagement had too often become scenes of blood—he ordered that all combatants should be distinguished by a kind of mantles or livery composed of lists or narrow pieces of stuff of opposite colours, whence originated the pale, bend, &c.—the marks now denominated 'honourable ordinaries.'[1]

If the honour of inventing heraldry be ascribed to the Germans, that of reducing it to a system must be assigned to France. To the French belong "the arrangement and combination of tinctures and metals, the variety of figures effected by the geometrical positions of lines, the attitudes of animals, and the grotesque delineation of monsters."[2] The art of describing an heraldric bearing in proper terms is called blasonry, from the French verb *blasonner*, whence also we derive our word *blaze* in the sense of to proclaim or make known.

"The heavens themselves *blaze* forth the death of princes." *Shak.*

"But he went out and began to publish it much, and to *blaze* abroad the matter." *St. Mark.*

"'Tis still our greatest pride,
To *blaze* those virtues which the good would hide." *Pope.*

---

[1] Vide the next chapter, where a *rationale* of these figures is attempted.

[2] Dallaway, p. 9.

The verb seems to have come originally from the German
blaſen, to blow a horn.   At the antient tournaments the
attendant heralds proclaimed with sound of trumpet the dignity of the combatants, and the armorial distinctions assumed
by them; and hence the application of the word to the scientific description of coat armour.[1]   The arrangement of the
tinctures and charges of heraldry into a system may be regarded as the third stage in the history of the science. This,
as we have just seen, was achieved by the French: and hence
the large admixture of old French terms with words of native
growth in our heraldric nomenclature.

Speed and other historians give the arms of a long line of
the Anglo-Saxon and Danish monarchs of England up to the
period of the Norman Conquest; but we search in vain for
contemporary evidence that armorial distinctions were then
known.   The MSS. of those early times which have descended to us are rich in illustrations of costume, but no
representation of these 'ensigns of honour' occurs in any
one of them.   It seems probable that Speed was misled by the
early chroniclers, who in their illuminated tomes often represented events of a much earlier date in the costume of their
own times.   Thus, in a work by Matthew Paris, who flourished in the thirteenth century, Offa, a Danish king of the
tenth, is represented in the habits worn at the first-mentioned date, and bearing an armorial shield according to the
then existing fashion.

At what period the colours and charges of the banner
began to be copied upon the shield is uncertain.   A proof
that regular heraldry was unknown at the era of the Con-

[1] *Blazon* is closely allied to the Anglo-Saxon BLAWAN, to blow. There are
some however who deduce it from the German, *blasse*, a mark.—*Vide Montagu's
Guide*, p. 14.

quest, is furnished by that valuable monument, the Bayeux Tapestry, a pictorial representation of the event, ascribed to the wife of the Conqueror.   In these embroidered scenes neither the banner nor the shield is furnished with proper arms.   Some of the shields bear the rude effigies of a dragon, griffin, serpent or lion, others crosses, rings, and various fantastic devices ;[1] but these, in the opinion of the most learned antiquaries, are mere ornaments, or, at best, symbols, more akin to those of classical antiquity than to modern heraldry.   Nothing but disappointment awaits the curious armorist, who seeks in this venerable memorial the pale, the bend, and other early elements of arms.   As these would have been much more easily imitated with the needle than the grotesque figures before alluded to, we may safely conclude that personal arms had not yet been introduced.[2]

Dallaway asserts that, after the Conquest, William " encou-

---

[1] Planché Hist. Brit. Costume.

[2] Those who contend for the earlier origin of heraldry adduce a certain shield occurring in the Bayeux tapestry, and resembling a modern coat charged with a cross coupée between five roundles ; but whatever may be said of the cross, the roundles are probably only the studs or rivets of the shield.   Again, as there are several shields in which the ornaments are exactly alike, the arms of a family cannot be intended.   They also bring forward the encaustic tiles taken up from the floor of a monastery at Caen by Mr. Henniker, and now in the possession of the Society of Antiquaries, which they presume to have been laid down at the time of the foundation of the abbey in 1064.   The arms upon these, supposed to have been those of benefactors, have been proved to belong to a date considerably posterior.   Among them

(Caen Tile.)

are the arms of England, three lions passant, an ensign which had no existence till the reign of Richard I, upwards of a century later than the foundation of the monastery of Caen.

raged, but under great restrictions, the individual bearing of
arms ;" but, strangely, does not cite the most slender authority for the assertion.   Camden and Spelman agree that arms
were not introduced until towards the close of the eleventh
century, which must have been within a very short time of the
Conqueror's death.   Others again, with more probability,
speak of the second Crusade (A.D. 1147) as the date of their
introduction into this country.   But even at this period the
proofs of family bearings are very scanty.   Traditions, indeed, are preserved in many families, of arms having been
acquired during this campaign, and in a future chapter several
examples will be quoted, rather as a matter of curiosity than
as historical proof; for all tradition, and especially that which
tends to flatter a family by ascribing to it an exaggerated
antiquity, will generally be found to be *vox et preterea nihil.*
The arms said to occur on *seals* in the seventh and eighth
centuries may be dismissed as merely fanciful devices, having
no connexion whatever with the heraldry of the twelfth and
thirteenth.

Towards the close of the twelfth century, and at the
beginning of the thirteenth, A.D. 1189-1230, it was usual for
warriors to carry a miniature escocheon suspended from a
belt, and decorated with the arms of the wearer.[1]

It was in the time of Richard I that heraldry assumed
more of the fixed character it now bears.   That monarch
appears on his great seal of the date of 1189, with a shield
containing two lions combatant; but in his second great
seal (1195) three lions passant occur, as they have ever since
been used by his successors.   Before coming to the throne,
as Earl of Poitou, he had borne lions in some attitude; for,

---

[1] Dallaway.

in an antient poem, cited by Dallaway, William de Barr, a French knight, utters an exclamation to this effect : " Behold

(Rich. I, from his second Great Seal.)

the Count of Poitou challenges us to the field ; see he calls us to the combat ; I know the grinning lions in his shield ;" and in the romance of ' Cuer de Lyon,' we read the following couplet :

" 𝔘pon his shoulders a 𝔖chelde of stele,
   𝔚ith the 'lybbardes'[1] painted wele."

[1] *Lybbardes*—leopards. It has long been a matter of controversy between French and English armorists, whether the charges of our royal arms were originally leopards or lions. Napoleon always derisively called them leopards. The author of the 'Roll of Karlaverok,' described in a future page, speaking of the banner of Edward I, says it contained "three leopards courant of fine gold, set on red, fierce, haughty, and cruel."—*Nicolas' Karlav.* p. 23.

Nisbet, who, as a Scotchman, viewed English heraldry with a somewhat supercilious eye, decides in favour of leopards, and cites the 'Survey of London,' by John Stowe, who quotes a record of the city of London, stating that Frederick, Emperor of Germany, in 1225, sent to Henry III three living leopards, "in token of the regal shield of arms." The same author likewise mentions an order of Edward II to the Sheriff of London, to pay the keeper of the King's leopards in the Tower of London sixpence a day for the sustenance of the leopards.—*Nisbet's Essay on Armories,* p. 163.

The earliest representation of arms upon a seal is of the
date of 1187.[1]   The embellishment of seals was one of the
first as well as one of the most interesting and useful applications of Heraldry.   Seals, at first rude and devoid of ornament, became, in course of time, beautiful pieces of workmanship, elaborately decorated with arms, equestrian figures,
and tabernacle work of gothic architecture.

The Crusades are admitted by all modern writers to have
given shape to heraldry.   And although we cannot give
credit to many of the traditions relating to the acquisition of
armorial bearings by valorous knights on the plains of
Palestine, yet there is no doubt that many of our commonest
charges, such as the crescent, the escallop-shell, the water-
bowget, &c., are derived from those chivalric scenes. Salverte
observes that "the ensigns which adorned the banner of a
knight had not, in earlier times, been adopted by his son,
jealous of honouring, in its turn, the emblem which he himself had chosen.   But this glorious portion of the heritage
of a father or a brother who had died fighting for the cross
was seized with avidity by his successor on the fields of
Palestine; for, in changing the paternal banner, he would have
feared that he should not be recognized by his own vassals
and his rivals in glory.   History expressly tells us that, at this
epoch, many of the chiefs of the crusaders rendered the
symbols which they bore peculiar to their own house."[2]
Dallaway, with his accustomed elegance, remarks, "Those
chiefs who, during the holy war, returned to their own country,
were industrious to call forth the highest admiration of their
martial exploits in the middle ranks.   Ambitious of display-

[1] Dallaway; but Nisbet (Armories, p. 61,) alludes to earlier examples abroad.
[2] Salverte. Essai sur les Noms d'Hommes, (Paris, 1824,) vol. 1, p. 240.

ing the banners they had borne in the sacred field, they procured every external embellishment that could render them either more beautiful as to the execution of the armorial designs, or more venerable as objects of such perilous attainment. The bannerols of this era were usually of silk stuffs, upon which was embroidered the device; and the shields of metal, enamelled in colours, and diapered or diversified with flourishes of gold and silver. Both the arts of encaustic painting and embroidery were then well known and practised, yet of so great cost as to be procured only by the most noble and wealthy. Amongst other pageantries was the dedication of these trophies to some propitiatory Saint, over whose shrine they were suspended, and which introduced armorial bearings in the decoration of churches, frequently carved in stone, painted in fresco upon the walls, or stained in glass in the windows. The avarice of the ecclesiastics in thus adding to their treasures conduced almost as much as the military genius of the age to the more general introduction of arms. So sanctioned, the use of them became indispensable."[1]

[1] Dall. pp. 31-32. The offering of trophies to the Deity is of a much earlier origin, and it was derived from the nations of antiquity. The Old Testament furnishes us with several instances, the classics with many more: "It was very common," says Robinson, "to dedicate the armour of the enemy, and to suspend it in temples."—Vide Homer, Iliad, vii. 81, "I will bear his armour to Troy, and hang it up in the temple of Apollo;" and Virgil, Æn. vii, describes a temple hung round with

———— " helmets, darts and spears,
And captive chariots, axes, shields, and bars,
And broken beaks of ships, *the trophies of their wars*."

Dryden, vii. 252.

But, what is more to our purpose, "It was also customary to dedicate to the

By the time of Edward the First we find that all great commanders had adopted arms, which were at that date really *coats;* the tinctures and charges of the banner and shield being applied to the surcoat, or mantle, which was worn over the armour, while the trappings of horses were decorated in a similar manner.

In the ages immediately subsequent to the Crusades, heraldric ensigns began to be generally applied as architectural decorations. The shields upon which they were first represented were in the form of an isosceles triangle, slightly curved on its two equal sides; but soon afterwards they began to assume that of the gothic arch reversed, a shape probably adopted with a view to such decoration, as harmonising better with the great characteristics of the pointed style. Painted glass, too, in its earliest application, was employed to represent military portraits, and arms with scrolls containing short sentences, from which family mottoes may have originated. Warton[1] places this gorgeous ornament at an era earlier than the reign of Edward II.

Encaustic tiles, also, which were introduced in the early days of heraldry, afforded another means of displaying the insignia of warriors. They are still found in the pavements of many of our cathedrals and old parish churches.

gods their own weapons, when they retired from the noise of war to a private life." (Rob. Archæolog. Græc.) From I Sam. xxi, 9, it appears that David, after his victory over Goliath, had dedicated the Philistine's sword to God as a trophy. "Behold it is here," says the priest, on a subsequent occasion, "wrapped in a cloth behind the ephod." In I Chron. x, 10, we read that the Philistines put the armour of Saul "in the house of their gods, and fastened his head in the temple of Dagon;" and, in xxvi, 27, we are told that "out of the spoils won in battles did they (the Israelites) dedicate to maintain the House of the Lord."

[1] Hist. Poet. i, 302.

Rolls of Arms, which afford, after seals, the best possible
evidence of the ancient tinctures and charges, occur so early
as the time of Henry III. A document of this description,
belonging to that reign, is preserved in the College of Arms,
and contains upwards of 200 coats emblazoned or described
in terms of heraldry differing very little from the modern
nomenclature. In a subsequent chapter I shall have occasion to refer for some facts to this curious and valuable
manuscript.

In the succeeding reigns the science rapidly increased in
importance and utility. The king and his chief nobility
began to have heralds attached to their establishments. These
officials, at a later date, took their names from some badge
or cognizance of the family whom they served, such as
Falcon, Rouge Dragon, or from their master's title, as Hereford, Huntingdon, &c. They were, in many instances, old
servants or retainers, who had borne the brunt of war,[1] and
who, in their official capacity, attending tournaments and
battle-fields, had great opportunities of making collections of
arms, and gathering genealogical particulars. It is to them,
as men devoid of general literature and historical knowledge,
Mr. Montagu ascribes the fabulous and romantic stories
connected with antient heraldry; and certainly they had
great temptations to falsify facts, and give scope to invention when a championship for the dignity and antiquity of
the families upon whom they attended was at once a labour
of love and an essential duty of their office.

The Roll of Karlaberok, the name of which must be
familiar to every reader who has paid any attention to heraldry,

[1] The second book of Upton's treatise, written in the fifteenth century, is entitled
' Of *Veterans*, now called Heralds.'

is a poem in Norman-French, describing the valorous deeds of Edward I and his knights at the siege of the castle of Karlaverok, in Dumfriesshire, in the year 1300. This roll, which is curious on historical grounds, and by no means contemptible as a poem, possesses especial charms for the heraldric student. It describes with remarkable accuracy the banners of the barons and knights who served in the expedition against Scotland, and "affords evidence of the perfect state of the science of heraldry at that early period." It is believed to have been written by Walter of Exeter, a Franciscan friar, further known as the author of the romantic history of Guy, Earl of Warwick. A contemporary copy of this valuable relic exists in the British Museum, and another copy, transcribed from the original, is in the Library of the College of Arms. The latter was published in 1828 by Sir Harris Nicolas, with a translation and memoirs of the personages commemorated by the poet.

The poem commences by stating that, in the year of Grace one thousand three hundred, the king held a great court at Carlisle, and commanded his men to prepare to go together with him against his enemies the Scots. On the appointed day the whole host was ready. "There were," says the chivalrous friar, "many rich caparisons embroidered on silks and satins; many a beautiful penon fixed to a lance, and many a banner displayed.

"And afar off was the noise heard of the neighing of horses; mountains and valleys were everywhere covered with sumpter horses and waggons with provisions, and sacks of tents and pavilions.

"And the days were long and fine [it was Midsummer]. They proceeded by easy journeys arranged in four squadrons; the which I will so describe to you that not one shall be passed over. But first I will tell you of the names and arms of the companions, especially of the banners, if you will listen how."

In truth, by far the greater portion of the composition consists of descriptions of the heraldric insignia borne upon the banners of the commanders, upwards of one hundred in number. The following are quoted as examples :

" 𝔥enri le bon Conte de 𝔑ichole
𝔇e prowesse enbrasse & a cole
𝔈 en son coer le a souberaine
𝔐enans le eschiele primeraine
𝔅aniere ot de un cendall saffrin
𝔒 un lion rampant porprin."

'Henry the good Earl of Lincoln, burning with valour, which is the chief feeling of his heart, leading the first squadron, had a banner of yellow silk with a purple lion rampant.'[1]

" 𝔓rowesse ke avoit fait ami
𝔇e 𝔊uilleme de 𝔏atimier
𝔎e la crois patee de or mier
𝔓ortoit en rouge bien portraite
𝔖a baniere ot cele parte traite."

'Prowess had made a friend of William le Latimer, who

[1] Nicolas' Karlaverok, p. 4.

bore on this occasion a well-proportioned banner, with a
gold cross patée, pourtrayed on red.'[1]

> " 𝔍𝔬𝔥𝔞𝔫𝔰 𝔡𝔢 𝔅𝔢𝔞𝔲𝔠𝔥𝔞𝔪𝔭 𝔭𝔯𝔬𝔭𝔯𝔢𝔪𝔢𝔫𝔱
> 𝔓𝔬𝔯𝔱𝔬𝔦𝔱 𝔩𝔢 𝔟𝔞𝔫𝔦𝔢𝔯𝔢 𝔡𝔢 𝔟𝔞𝔦𝔯
> 𝔄𝔲 𝔡𝔬𝔲𝔷 𝔱𝔢𝔫𝔰 𝔢𝔱 𝔞𝔲 𝔰𝔬𝔟𝔢𝔰𝔱 𝔞𝔦𝔢𝔯."

> ' John de Beauchamp
> Handsomely bore his banner of vair,
> To the gentle weather and south-west air.'[2]

The best authorities are agreed that coat-armour did not
become hereditary until the reign of Henry III and his
successor.   Before that period families "kept no constant
coat, but gave now this, anon that, sometimes their paternal,
sometimes their maternal or adopted coats, a variation caus-
ing much obfuscation in history."[3]   Many of the nobility
who had heretofore borne ensigns consisting of the honor-
able ordinaries, the simplest figures of heraldry, now began
to charge them with other figures.   Some few families,
however, never adopted what are called common charges,
but retained the oldest and simplest forms of bearing, such
as bends, cheverons, fesses, barry, paly, chequy, &c.; and, as
a general rule, such coats may be regarded as the most
antient in existence.   With respect to Welsh heraldry,
Dallaway thinks that the families of that province did not
adopt the symbols made use of by other nations, until its
annexation to the English Crown by Edward I.   Certain it
is that many of the oldest families bear what may be termed

---

[1] Nicolas' Karlaverok, p. 44.   The charge here blazoned, a cross patée, is,
in fact, a cross patonce.

[2] Ibid., Notes, p. 368.

[3] Waterhouse's Discourse, p. 77.

legendary pictures, having little or no analogy to the more systematic armory of England; such, for example, as a wolf issuing from a cave; a cradle under a tree with a child guarded by a goat, &c.

The reigns of Edward III and Richard II were the "palmy days" of heraldry. Then were the banners and escocheons of war refulgent with blazon; the light of every chancel and hall was stained with the tinctures of heraldry; the tiled pavement vied with the fretted roof; every corbel, every vane, spoke proudly of the achievements of the battle-field, and filled every breast with a lofty emulation of the deeds which earned such stately rewards. We, the men of this calculating and prosaic nineteenth century, have, it is probable, but a faint idea of the influence which heraldry exerted on the minds of our rude forefathers of that chivalrous age: but we can hardly refuse to admit that, by diffusing more widely the enthusiasm of martial prowess, it lent a powerful aid to the formation of our national character, and strongly tended to give to England that proud military ascendancy she has long enjoyed among the nations of the earth.[1]

At this period that peculiar species of ordeal, TRIAL BY COMBAT, the prototype of the modern duel, was licensed by the supreme magistrate. When a person was accused by another without any further evidence than the mere *ipse dixit* of the accuser, the defendant making good his own

---

[1] Let it not be understood from this remark that I mean in the slightest degree to advocate war as a means of acquiring national greatness. The war which Edward waged against France was totally unjustifiable; and the desolating civil wars which followed the misgovernment of his pusillanimous grandson Richard, were (as many of our subsequent wars have been) a disgrace to the very name of England.

cause by strongly denying the fact, the matter was referred
to the decision of the sword,[1] and although the old proverb that
" might overcomes right" was frequently verified in these encounters, the vanquished party was adjudged guilty of the
crime alleged against him, and dealt with according to law.
The charge usually preferred was that of treason, though the
dispute generally originated in private pique between the
parties. These combats brought together immense numbers

(Ordeal Combat.)

of people. That between Sir John Annesley and Katrington,
in the reign of Richard II, was fought before the palace at
Westminster, and attracted more spectators than the king's
coronation had done.[2]   All such encounters were regulated
by laws which it was the province of the heralds to enforce.[3]

The TOURNAMENT, though proscribed by churchmen (jealous, as Dallaway observes, of *shows* in which they could
play no part), had nothing in it of the objectionable character attaching to the judicial combat.   Nor will it suffer, in
the judgment of Gibbon, on a comparison with the Olympic
games, " which, however recommended by the idea of classic

[1] Strutt's Roy. and Eccl. Antiq.

[2] Holinshed.

[3] The engraving above is from Royal MS., 14 E. iii. Brit. Mus.

antiquity, must yield to a Gothic tournament, as being, in
every point of view, to be preferred by impartial taste."[1]
Descriptions of tournaments occur in so many popular works
that it is not here necessary to do more than to refer to
them. The vivid picture of one by Sir Walter Scott in
'Ivanhoe' is probably fresh in the reader's memory.

As early heraldry consisted of very simple elements, it
cannot excite surprise that the same bearings were frequently
adopted by different families unknown to each other; hence
arose very violent disputes and controversies, as to whom the
prior right belonged. The celebrated case of Scrope against
Grosvenor in the reign of Richard II, may be cited as an example. The arms *Azure, a bend or,* were claimed by no less than
three families, namely, Carminow of Cornwall, Lord Scrope,
and Sir Robert Grosvenor. On the part of Scrope, it was asserted that these arms had been borne by his family from the
Norman conquest. Carminow pleaded a higher antiquity, and
declared they had been used by *his* ancestors ever since the
days of king Arthur! The trial by combat had been resorted
to by these two claimants without a satisfactory decision,
wherefore it was decreed that both should continue to bear
the coat as heretofore. The dispute between Scrope and
Grosvenor was not so summarily disposed of; a trial, not by
the sword, but by legal process, took place before the high
Constables and the Earl Marshal, and lasted five years. The
proceedings, which were printed in 1831 from the records in
the Tower, occupy two large volumes! The depositions of
many gentlemen bearing arms, touching this controversy,
are given at full length, and present us with some curious
and characteristic features of the times. Among many others

[1] Decline and Fall, v. 6, p. 59.

who gave evidence in support of the claims of Lord Scrope
was the famous Chaucer.   His deposition, taken from the
above records, and printed in Sir Harris Nicolas's elegant
life of the poet, recently published, is interesting, no less from
its connexion with the witness than for its curiosity in
relation to our subject :

   "Geoffrey Chaucer, Esquire, of the age of forty and upwards,
armed for twenty-seven years, produced on behalf of Sir Richard
Scrope, sworn and examined.   Asked, whether the arms *Azure, a
bend or*, belonged, or ought to belong, to the said Sir Richard? Said,
Yes, for he saw him so armed in France, before the town of Retters,[1]
and Sir Henry Scrope armed in the same arms with a white label,
and with a banner; and the said Richard, armed in the entire arms,
' Azure, with a bend or ;' and so he had seen him armed during the
whole expedition, until the said Geoffrey was taken [prisoner.]
Asked, how he knew that the said arms appertained to the said Sir
Richard?   Said, that he had heard say from Old Knights and
Esquires, that they had been reputed to be their arms, as common
fame and the public voice proved; and he also said that they had
continued their possession of the said arms ; and that all his time he
had seen the said arms *in banners, glass, paintings, and vestments,*
and commonly called the arms of Scrope.   Asked, if he had heard
any one say who was the first ancestor of the said Sir Richard, who
first bore the said arms?   Said, No, nor had he ever heard otherwise
than that they were come of antient ancestry and old gentry, and
used the said arms.   Asked, if he had heard any one say how long a
time the ancestors of the said Sir Richard had used the said arms?
Said, No, but he had heard say that it passed the memory of man.
Asked, whether he had ever heard of any interruption or challenge
made by Sir Robert Grosvenor, or by his ancestors, or by any one in

---

[1] Apparently the village of Retiers, near Rennes, in Brittany.

his name, to the said Sir Richard, or to any of his ancestors? Said, No, but he said that he was once in Friday-street in London, and as he was walking in the street he saw hanging a new sign made of the said arms, and he asked what Inn that was that had hung out these arms of *Scrope?* and one answered him and said, No, Sir, they are not hung out for the arms of Scrope, nor painted there for those arms, but they are painted and put there by a knight of the county of Chester, whom men call Sir Robert Grosvenor; and that was the first time he ever heard speak of Sir Robert Grosvenor or of his ancestors, or of any other bearing the name of Grosvenor."[1]

At this date the nobility claimed, and to a considerable extent exercised, the right of conferring arms upon their followers for faithful services in war. A memorable instance is related by Froissart, in which the Lord Audley, a famous general at the battle of Poictiers, rewarded four of his esquires in this manner. When the battle was over, Edward the Black Prince, calling for this nobleman, embraced him and said, " Sir James, both I myself and all others acknowledge you, in the business of the day, to have been the best doer in arms; wherefore, with intent to furnish you the better to pursue the wars, I retain you for ever my knight, with 500 marks yearly revenue, which I shall assign you out of my inheritance in England." This was, at the period, a great estate, and the Lord Audley duly appreciated the generosity of the donation; yet, calling to mind his obligations in the conflict to his four squires, Delves, Mackworth, Hawkeston, and Foulthurst, he immediately divided the Prince's gift among them, giving them, at the same time, permission to bear his own arms, altered in detail, for the

---

[1] De Controversia in Curia Militari inter R. de Scrope and R. Grosvenor, Milites, Rege Ricardo Secundo, 1385-1390. E Recordis in Turre, Lond. Asservatis, vol. i, p. 178.

sake of distinction. When the prince heard of this noble
deed he was determined not to be outdone in generosity,
but insisted upon Audley's accepting a further grant of
600 marks per annum, arising out of his duchy of Cornwall.

The arms of Lord Audley were GULES, FRETTY OR, and
those of the four valiant esquires, as borne for many generations by their respective descendants, in the counties of
Chester and Rutland, as follows:

> DELVES. Argent, a cheveron *gules, fretty or*, between
> three delves or billets sable.
>
> MACKWORTH. Party per pale indented, ermine and
> sable, a cheveron *gules, fretty or*.
>
> HAWKESTONE. Ermine, a fesse, *gules, fretty or*, be-
> tween three hawks. The hawks were in later times
> omitted.
>
> FOULTHURST. *Gules, fretty or*, a chief ermine.[1]

Another interesting instance of the granting of arms to
faithful retainers, occurs in a deed from William, Baron of
Graystock, to Adam de Blencowe, of Blencowe, in Cumberland, who had fought under his banners at Cressy and
Poictiers: "To ALL to whom these presents shall come to
be seen or heard, William, Baron of Graystock, Lord of
Morpeth, wisheth health in the Lord. Know ye that I have
given and granted to Adam de Blencowe, an escocheon
sable, with a bend closetted, argent and azure, with three
chaplets, gules; and with a crest closetted argent and azure
of my arms; *to have and to hold* to the said Adam and his

---

[1] Vide Historical and Allusive Arms; Lond. 1803, p. 43, et seq. Anecdotes of
Heraldry and Chivalry; Worcester, 1795.

heirs for ever; and I, the said William and my heirs will warrant to the said 'Adam the arms aforesaid. In witness whereof, I have to these letters patent set my seal. Written at the castle of Morpeth, the 26th day of February, in the 30th year of the reign of King Edward III, after the Conquest."[1]

The practice of devising armorial bearings by will is as antient as the time of Richard II. In some cases they were also transferred *by deed of gift*. In the 15th year of the same reign Thomas Grendall, of Fenton, makes over to Sir William Moigne, to have and to hold to himself, his heirs and assigns for ever, the arms which had escheated to him (Grendall) at the death of his cousin, John Beaumeys, of Sawtrey.[2]

Notwithstanding the numerous traditions relative to the granting of arms by monarchs in very early times, it seems to have been the *general* practice before the reigns of Richard II and Henry IV for persons of rank to assume what ensigns they chose.[3] But these monarchs, regarding themselves as the true " fountains of honour," granted or took them away by royal edict. The exclusive right of the king to this privilege was long called in question, and Dame Julyan Berners, so late as 1486, declares that " armys bi a

[1] Hutchinson's Cumberland, vol. i, p. 314. The arms borne by a junior branch of the Blencowes are ' Gules, a quarter argent,' the original coat of the family. The baron of Graystock's grant is sometimes borne as a quartering. The arms of his lordship, from which it is borrowed, were ' Barry of six, *argent* and *azure*, over all three *chaplets* gules.' According to a family tradition, Adam de Blencowe was standard-bearer to the Baron. Vide West's Antiquities of Furness, quoted by Hutchinson.

[2] Montagu's Study of Heraldry, Appendix A.

[3] One of the earliest grants of Arms preserved in the Heralds' Coll. is printed in the Appendix. It is of the time of Edward III.

mannys auctorite taken (if an other man have not borne theym afore) be of strength enogh." The same gallant lady boldly challenges the right of heralds : " And it is the opynyon of moni men that an herod of armis may gyve armys. Bot I say if any sych armys be borne . . . . thoos armys be of no more auctorite then thoos armys the wich be taken by a mannys awne auctorite."

So strictly was the use of coat-armour limited to the military profession, that a witness in a certain cause in the year 1408, alleged that, although descended from noble blood, he had no armorial bearings, because neither himself nor his ancestors had ever been engaged in war.[1]

It was in the reign of the luxurious Richard II that heraldric devices began to be displayed upon the civil as well as the military costume of the great ; " upon the mantle, the surcoat and the just-au-corps or boddice, the charge and cognizance of the wearer were profusely scattered, and shone resplendent in tissue and beaten gold."[2] Hitherto the escocheon had been charged with the hereditary (paternal) bearing only, but now the practice of impaling the wife's arms, and quartering those of the mother, when an heiress,

became the fashion. Impalement was sometimes performed by placing the dexter half of the lord's shield in juxta-position with the sinister moiety of his consort's ;[3] but this mode of marshalling occasioned great confusion, entirely de-

---

[1] " Nihil sibi insignii accidisse quia nec ipse nec majores sui in bello unquam descendissent." Waterhouse, quoted by Dallaway.

[2] Dallaway.

[3] This was called *dimidiation*.

stroying the character of both coats,[1] and was soon abandoned in favour of the present mode of placing the full
arms of both parties side by side in the escocheon.
Occasionally the shield was divided horizontally, the husband's coat occupying the chief or upper compartment, and
the wife's the base or lower half; but this was never a
favourite practice, as the side-by-side arrangement was
deemed better fitted to express the equality of the parties in
the marriage relation.

The practice of impaling official with personal arms, for
instance, those of a bishopric with those of the bishop, does
not appear to be of great antiquity. Provosts, mayors, the
kings of arms, heads of houses, and certain professors in
the universities, among others, possess this right; and it is
the general practice to cede the dexter, or more honourable
half of the shield to the coat of office.

Nisbet mentions a fashion formerly prevalent in Spain,
which certainly ranks under the category of ' Curiosities,'
and therefore demands a place here. Single women frequently divided their shield per pale, placing their paternal
arms on the sinister side, and leaving the dexter *blank*, for
those of their husbands, as soon as they should be so fortunate
as to obtain them. This, says mine author, " was the custom

---

[1] The dimidiated coat represented on p. 36, is not the arms of a family, but those
of the corporation of Hastings. Here three demi-lions are conjoined with three
sterns of antient ships—a composition compared with which the griffin, cockatrice,
and every other *hybrid* of a herald's imagination sinks into insignificance. That
this singular shield is a dimidiation of two antient coats cannot be doubted. Three
ships, in all probability, formed the original arms of the town—the dexter-half of
the royal arms of England having been superimposed in commemoration of some
great immunity granted to this antiently important corporation.

for young ladies that were resolved to marry!"[1]   These
were called " Arms of Expectation."[2]

The gorgeous decoration of the male costume with the
ensigns of heraldry soon attracted the attention and excited
the emulation of that sex which is generally foremost in the
adoption of personal ornaments. Yes,
incongruous as the idea appears to
modern dames, the ladies too assumed
the embroidered *coat of arms!* On
the vest or close-fitting garment they
represented the paternal arms, re-
peating the same ornament, if *femmes
soles*, or single women, on the more
voluminous upper robe ; but if married women, this last was occupied by
the arms of the husband, an arrangement not unaptly expressing their
condition as *femmes-covertes*. This
mode of wearing the arms was afterwards laid aside, and the ensigns of
husband and wife were impaled on
the outer garment, a fashion which
existed up to the time of Henry VIII,
as appears from the annexed engraving
of Elizabeth, wife of John Shelley,
Esq.[3] copied from a brass in the parish

---

[1] Query—Might not some of our English maidens, who are verging somewhat
on the *antique*, resort to this mode of advertising for a husband with advantage ?
The odious appellation of " old maids" would then give place to the more courteous
one of " Ladies of the half-blank shield."

[2] Nisbet's Essay on Armories, p. 70.

[3] A lineal ancestor of Sir John Shelley, Bart. The date of the lady's death is 1513.

church of Clapham, co. Sussex. The arms represented are those of Shelley and Michelgrove, otherwise Fauconer; both belonging, it will be seen, to the class called canting or allusive arms; those of Shelley being welk-*shells*, and those of Fauconer, a *falcon*.

Quartering is a division of the shield into four or more equal parts, by means of which the arms of other families, whose heiresses the ancestors of the bearer have married, are combined with his paternal arms; and a shield thus quartered exhibits at one view the ensigns of all the houses of which he is the representative. In modern times this *cumulatio armorum* is occasionally carried to such an extent that upwards of a hundred coats centre in one individual, and may be represented upon his shield.[1] The arms of England and France upon the great seal of Edward III, and those of Castile and Leon in the royal arms of Spain, are early examples of quartering. The first English subject who quartered arms was John Hastings, Earl of Pembroke, in the fourteenth century.

In this century originated the practice of placing the shield between two animals as supporters, for which see a future chapter.

The application of heraldric ornaments to household furniture and implements of war is of great antiquity. I have now before me the brass pommel of a sword on which are three triangular shields, two of them charged with a lion rampant, the other with an eagle displayed. This relic, which was dug up near Lewes castle, is conjectured to be of the reign of Henry III.[2] Arms first occur on coins in one of

---

[1] In the great hall at Fawsley, co. Northampton, the seat of Sir Charles Knightly, Bart., is a shield containing the unprecedented number of 334 quarterings. Vide Baker's Northampton, vol. i, p. 386.

[2] Vide Appendix.

Edmund, King of Sicily, in the thirteenth century; but the first English monarch who so used them was Edward III. The first supporters on coins occur in the reign of Henry VIII, whose 'sovereign' is thus decorated. Arms upon tombs are found so early as 1144.[1]

Among the 'curiosities' of heraldry belonging to these early times may be mentioned *adumbrated* charges; that is, figures represented in outline with the colour of the field showing through; because the bearers, having lost their patrimonies, retained only the *shadow* of their former state and dignity.[2]

Monasteries and other religious foundations generally bore arms, which were almost uniformly those of the founders, or a slight modification of them.[3] Dallaway traces this usage to the knights-templars and hospitallers who were both soldiers and ecclesiastics. The arms assigned to most cities and antient boroughs are borrowed from those of early feudal lords : thus the arms of the borough of Lewes are the chequers of the Earls of Warren, to whom the barony long appertained, with a canton of the lion and cross-crosslets of the Mowbrays, lords of the town in the fourteenth century. Some of the quaint devices which pass for the arms of particular towns have nothing heraldric about them, and seem to have originated in the caprice of the artists who engraved their seals. Such for example is the design which the good

---

[1] In the Temple Church, London. Tomb of Sir Geoffrey de Magnaville. Vide woodcut at the head of the Preface.

[2] Boke of St. A. and Dall.

[3] The arms of the See of Hereford at this day are identical with those of Thomas Cantilupe, who held the episcopate in the thirteenth century, and was canonized as St. Thomas of Hereford, 34° Edward I.

townsmen of Guildford are pleased to call their arms. This consists of a green mount rising out of the water, and supporting an odd-looking castle, whose two towers are ornamented with high steeples, surmounted with balls; from the centre of the castle springs a lofty tower, with three turrets, and ornamented with the arms of England and France. Over the door are two roses, and in the door a key, the said door being guarded by a lion-couchant, while high on each side the castle is a pack of wool gallantly floating through the air! What this assemblage of objects may signify I do not pretend to guess.

Persons of the middle class, not entitled to coat-armour, invented certain arbitrary signs called 𝔐𝔢𝔯𝔠𝔥𝔞𝔫𝔱𝔰' 𝔐𝔞𝔯𝔨𝔰, and these often occur in the stonework and windows of old buildings, and upon tombs. Piers Plowman, who wrote in the reign of Edward III, speaks of " merchauntes' markes ymedeled " in glass. Sometimes these marks were impaled with the paternal arms of aristocratic merchants, as in the case of John Halle, a wealthy woolstapler of Salisbury, rendered immortal by the Rev. Edward Duke in his 'Prolusiones Historicæ.' The early printers and painters likewise adopted similar marks, which are to be seen on their respective works.[1] A rude monogram seems to have been

[1] It is almost unnecessary to observe that the expression 'a merchant's mark' is by no means appropriate; for such devices were employed in a great variety of ways. They appear, primarily, to have been used as signatures by illiterate though wealthy merchants, who could not write their names. At a later date they were employed for *marking* bales of goods. Within the last century, many flockmasters in the South of England used them for marking sheep. Although the illiterate of our own times substitute a + for their proper names, it was far otherwise two centuries ago, when they generally made a rude monogram, or *peculiar* mark, analogous to the merchant's mark of earlier date.

attempted, and it was generally accompanied with a cross, and, occasionally, a hint at the inventor's peculiar pursuit, as in the cut here given, where the staple at the bottom 'refers to the worthy John Halle's having been a merchant of the staple. The heralds objected to such marks being placed upon a shield, for, says the writer of Harl. MS. 2252 (fol. 10), " 𝕮𝕳𝕰𝖄𝖘 𝖇𝖊 𝖓𝖔𝖓𝖊 𝕬𝖗𝖒𝖞𝖘, for every man may take hym a marke, but not armys without a herawde or purcyvaunte ;" and in " The duty and office of an herald," by F. Thynne, Lancaster Herald, 1605, the officer is directed " to prohibit merchants and others to put their names, marks, or devices, in escutcheons or shields, which belong to gentlemen bearing arms and none others."

At the commencement of the fifteenth century considerable confusion seems to have arisen from upstarts having assumed the arms of antient families—a fact which shows that armorial bearings began to be considered the indispensable accompaniment of wealth. So great had this abuse become that, in the year 1419, it was deemed necessary to issue a royal mandate to the sheriff of every county " to summon all persons bearing arms to prove their right to them," a task of no small difficulty, it may be presumed, in many cases. Many of the claims then made were referred to the heralds as commissioners, " but the first regular chapter held by them in a collective capacity was at the siege of Rouen, in 1420."[1]

The first *King of Arms* was William Bruges, created by Henry V. Several grants of arms made by him from 1439 to 1459 are recorded in the College of Arms.

During the sanguinary struggle between the Houses of

[1] Dallaway.

Lancaster and York " arms were universally used, and most religiously and pertinaciously maintained." Sometimes, however, when the different branches of a family espoused opposing interests they varied their arms either in the charges or colours, or both. The antient family of Lower of Cornwall originally bore " . . . . . a cheveron between three *red* roses," but espousing, it is supposed, the Yorkist, or white-rose side of the question, they changed the tincture of their arms to " sable, a cheveron between three *white* roses,"[1] the coat borne by their descendants to this day. The interest taken by the Cornish gentry in these civil dissensions may account for the frequency of the rose in the arms of Cornwall families. The *red rose* in the centre of the arms of Lord Abergavenny was placed there by his ancestor, Richard Neville, Earl of Warwick, " better known as the king-maker," " to show himself the faithful homager and soldier of the House of Lancaster."[2]

The non-heraldric reader will require a definition of what, in the technical phrase of blazon, are called 𝔇𝔦𝔣𝔣𝔢𝔯𝔢𝔫𝔠𝔢𝔰. These are certain marks, smaller than ordinary charges, placed upon a conspicuous part of the shield for the purpose of distinguishing the sons of a common parent from each other. Thus, the eldest son bears a label; the second a crescent; the third a mullet; the fourth a martlet; the fifth an annulet; and the sixth a fleur-de-lis. The arms of the six sons of Thomas Beauchamp, Earl of Warwick, who died 30° Edward III, were, in the window of St. Mary's Church, Warwick, *differenced* in this manner.[3] These distinctions are

---

[1] C. S. Gilbert's Hist. Cornw. vol. i, Introd. to Herald.

[2] Historical and Allusive Arms, p. 347.

[3] Montagu, Study of Heraldry. But this is, perhaps, an isolated instance of such early date, for Dame Julyan Berners, more than a century later, says, " There

carried still further, for the sons of a second son bear the label, crescent, mullet, &c. upon a crescent; those of a third son the same upon a mullet, respectively. In the third generation the mark of cadency is again superimposed upon the two preceding differences, producing, at length, unutterable confusion. Dugdale published a work, in 1682, on the differences of arms, in which he condemns this system, and suggests a return to the antient mode, which consisted in varying the colours and charges of the field, though preserving the general characteristics of the hereditary bearing. For example, Beauchamp of Elmley branched out into four lines; the eldest line bore the paternal arms, *Gules a fess, or*; the other three superadded to this bearing a charge *or*, six times repeated, namely,

II, Beauchamp of Abergavenny, 6 cross-crosslets
III, Beauchamp of Holt,   6 billets, and
IV, Beauchamp of Bletshoe,   6 martlets,

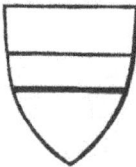  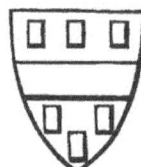 

1.   2.   3.   4.

and among the further ramifications of the family we find

V, Beauchamp of Essex   6 trefoils slipped
VI, Beauchamp of ——   6 mullets
VII, Beauchamp of ——   6 pears,

be vi differences in armys; ij for the excellent and iiij for the nobles; Labelle and Enborduryng for lordis; Jemews, Mollettys, Flowre delyce and Quintfoyles for the nobles," (i. e. gentry).

and upwards of ten other coats, all preserving the field gules and the fess or. The Bassets, according to the Ashmolean MSS.[1] varied their coat 7 times, the Lisles 4, the Nevilles 11, and the Braoses 5.

An interesting example of early differencing is cited by Sir Harris Nicolas, in his ' Roll of Carlaverok.'[2] In the early part of the fourteenth century—

Leicestershire.	Barons.	Alan le Zouche bore Gules, besanté Or		
		William le Zouche, of Haryngworth }	the same with	a quarter ermine
	Knights.	Sir William Zouche		a label azure
		Sir Oliver Zouche		a cheveron erm.
		Sir Amory Zouche		a bend argent
		Sir Thomas Zouche		on a quarter argent, a mullet sable.

Surnames in these early times were in a very unsettled state, for the younger branches of a family, acquiring new settlements by marriage and otherwise, abandoned their patronymics, and adopted new ones derived from the seignories so acquired.[3] Hence it often happens that arms are identical or similar, when the relationship is not recognized by identity of appellation.

Illegitimate children generally bore the paternal ensigns differenced by certain *brizures*. Thus John de Beaufort, eldest natural son of John of Gaunt, bore *Per pale argent and azure* [blue and white being the *colours* of the House of Lancaster] *on a bend gules, three lions passant-guardant or* [the

---

[1] Cited by Dall. p. 127.

[2] Memoirs, p. 287. Cott. MS., Calig. A. xviii.

[3] Vide my English Surnames, 2d edition, p. 194 et seq.

royal arms of England] *in the upper part of the bend a label azure, charged with nine fleur-de-lis or*.[1] The arms borne in the usual manner were often surrounded with a bordure to indicate bastardy; of this mode of differencing several examples are furnished in the arms of existing peers descended from royalty. Some of the descendants of Henry Beaufort, third duke of Somerset, placed the Beaufort arms upon a fesse, and numerous similar instances might be adduced.

The mode of differencing by alterations, or the addition of new charges, however commended by Dugdale and other great names, is certainly exposed to the same objection as the use of the label, crescent, mullet, &c., as tending equally to confusion; for, with the addition of cross-crosslets, billets, &c., to the primary charge of the Beauchamps, no herald will dare assert that the original arms are preserved. It is a canon of heraldry that "Omnia arma arithmeticis figuris sunt simillima, quibus si quid addas vel subtrahas non remanet eadem species." Every alteration, however slight, produces a new coat, and thus the principal advantage of coat armour—its hereditary character—is sacrificed. In fact, a coat of arms is the symbol of a generic, or family, name, and it is not within the compass of the heraldric art to particularize individual branches and members of a family by any additions or changes whatever, at least to any great extent.[2]

---

[1] Montagu, p. 42.

[2] If Heraldry had to be established *de novo*, something of the sort might be done, by giving each family a patent right to a particular ordinary, provided the ordinaries were much more numerous than they are. But as nearly every ordinary and charge is common to many families, Dugdale's system cannot possibly be carried out.

"The numerous class of men who were termed 𝕬𝖗𝖒𝖎𝖌𝖊𝖗𝖎, or gentry of coat-armour," observes Dallaway, " very generally took, with a small variation, the escocheon of that feudal lord whose property and influence extended over that province which they inhabited," and Camden, in his ' Remaines,' says, " Whereas the earles of Chester bare garbes or wheat-sheafes, many gentlemen of that countrey took wheatsheafes. Whereas the old earles of Warwicke bare chequy or and azure, a cheueron ermin, many thereabout tooke ermine and chequy. In Leicestershire and the countrey confining diuers bare cinquefoyles, for that the ancient earles of Leicester bare geules, a cinquefoyle ermine, &c." This was a fertile source of new bearings.

Sometimes, in the absence of other evidence of one family's having been feudally dependent upon another, presumptive proof is furnished by a similarity between the arms. I subjoin an instance. The coat of the baronial family of Echingham of Echingham, co. Sussex, was ' AZURE A FRET ARGENT,' and the crest, ' A DEMI-LION RAMPANT ARGENT.'

The arms of Jefferay, of Chiddingly, in the same county, were ' *Azure fretty or*' (with the addition of a lion passant-

guardant, gules, on a chief argent), and the crest, ' *A lion's head* erased *argent*, ducally crowned azure. The first settlement of the Jefferays was at Betchington, co. Sussex, an estate which had previously belonged to the lords Echingham, but there is no proof of the feudal connexion except that which is furnished by a comparison of the arms.

Richard III greatly promoted the cause of Heraldry in England by the erection of the heralds into the corporate body which still exists under the designation of the 𝕮𝖔𝖑𝖑𝖊𝖌𝖊 𝖔𝖋 𝕬𝖗𝖒𝖘. This epoch may be considered the noonday of the history of armory in England; and as two subsequent chapters of this volume, devoted respectively to the history of that institution, and to notices of celebrated writers on heraldry, will bring down the annals of the science to our own times, " I here make an end " of a chapter which I trust may not have been found totally devoid of interest to any reader who loves to trace the records of the past.

CHAPTER III.

Rationale of Heraldric Charges, etc.

(Arms of the See of Chichester)

" The Formes of the pure celestiall bodies mixt with grosse terrestrials; earthly animals with watery; sauage beasts with tame; whole-footed beasts with diuided; reptiles with things gressible; fowles of prey with home-bred; these again with riuer fowles; aery insecta with earthly; also things naturall with artificiall; arts liberall with mechanicall; military with rusticall; and rusticall with ciuil. Which confused mixture hath not a little discouraged many persons—otherwise well affected to the study of Armory—and impaired the estimation of the profession."

Guillim.

DICTIONARIES of the technical terms employed in heraldry are so common, and the elements of the science so well explained in various popular treatises,[1] that it would be impertinent in an essay like the present to go into all the details

---

[1] Hugh Clark's 'Introduction to Heraldry,' which may be purchased for a few shillings, contains everything necessary to a thorough knowledge of the art of blazon.

4

usually comprised in those useful books of reference. Still
it may interest the general reader, and will, I trust, give no
offence to adepts in the science, if I offer a few observations
on this subject, with illustrations from our old writers, adding some etymological conjectures of my own.

The origin of the expression ‘a coat of arms’ we have
already seen, as also the cause why heraldric ensigns are
borne upon a shield. Shields have been· made of every
imaginable shape according to the taste of the age or the
fancy of the bearer, with these two restrictions, that the
shields of knights-bannerets must be square, and those of
ladies in the form of a lozenge. The most usual, because
the most convenient, shape is that which is technically called
the *heater*-shield——from its resemblance to the heater of an

iron——with some slight variations. Our friend
Sylvanus Morgan, whose ingenuity all must ad-
mire, in defiance of the oft-quoted proverb :

" 𝔚𝔥𝔢𝔫 𝔄𝔡𝔞𝔪 𝔡𝔦𝔤𝔤𝔢𝔡 𝔞𝔫𝔡 𝔈𝔟𝔢 𝔰𝔭𝔞𝔫,
   𝔚𝔥𝔬 𝔴𝔞𝔰 𝔱𝔥𝔢𝔫 𝔱𝔥𝔢 𝔊𝔢𝔫𝔱𝔩𝔢𝔪𝔞𝔫?"

deduces this shape for men, and that of the
lozenge for women, from the *spade* of Adam, and
the *spindle* of Eve !

The ground or field of every coat of arms must be either
of metal, colour, or fur. The METALS of heraldry are, Or = gold,
and argent = silver, and as the shield of war was antiently
of metal, either embossed or enamelled, the retention of the
two precious metals as the field of an escocheon is easily
accounted for. The COLOURS are gules, azure, vert, purpure,
sable, tenne, and sanguine. While some of these terms are
French ; others, though coming to us through that medium,

are originally from other languages. GULES, according to Ducange, is *goulis, guelle, gula* sive *guella*, the red colour of the mouth or throat of an animal. Mackenzie derives it from the Hebrew *gulude*, a piece of red cloth, or from the Arabic *gule*, a red rose. *Ghul* in the Persian signifies rose-coloured, and *Ghulistan* is 'the country of roses.' It is probably one of those importations from the East which the Crusades introduced, both into the elements of armory and the nomenclature of the science. It was sometimes called *vermeil*[1] (vermilion) and *rouget*. An antient knight is represented as bearing a plain red banner without any charge :

> " Mais Eurmenions de la Brette
> La baniere eut *toute rougecte*." [2]

The barbarous term *blodius* was likewise occasionally used to express this colour.

AZURE=light-blue, is a French corruption of the Arabic word *lazur* or *lazuli*. The lapis lazuli is a copper ore, very compact and hard, which is found in detached lumps, of an elegant blue colour, and to it the artist is indebted for his beautiful ultra-marine. This colour, still one of the dearest of pigments, was antiently in great request, and called 'beyond-sea azure.'[3] The lapis lazuli is found in Persia, Bucharia, and China.

VERT (French) is light green. This word was applied at

---

[1] Spenser uses this word :
> " How the red roses flush up in her cheeks,
> And the pure snow with goodly *vermeil* stain."

[2] Roll of Karlaverok, p. 26.

[3] In the 'Secretes of Master Alexis of Piedmont' are many recipes for making this article.

an early period " to every thing," says Cowell, " that grows
and bears a *green* leaf within the forest that may cover and
hide a deer." Vert and venison, in the vocabulary of woodcraft, were as inseparable as shadow and substance. *To vert*
signified to enter the forest, as in an old song of the thirteenth century:

> " Sumer is i-cumen in,
> Lhude sing cuccu ;
> Groweth sed and bloweth med,
> And springeth the wde nu.
>
> 𝔖ing 𝕮uccu, 𝕮uccu!
>
> Awe bleteth after lomb,
> Lhouth after calvé cu,
> Bulluc sterteth,
> Bucke VERTETH,
>
> 𝔐urie sing 𝕮uccu," etc.

This colour was antiently called *synople*, and in the Boke
of St. Albans *synobylt*, a word which Colombiere derives from
the Latin *sinopis*, a dyeing mineral,[1] or from Synople, a
town in the Levant, whence a green dye was procured.

Of SABLE the derivation is very uncertain. It seems unlikely to have been taken from the colour of the diminutive
animal now known by this name, first, because it would

---

[1] There is an extraordinary difference of opinion respecting the Mediæval Latin,
Sinopis. Ducange, with the authorities quoted above, make its colour green ; but
the *sinoper*, or ruddle of commerce, is of a dark red or purplish hue. In one of
the Cottonian MSS. Nero, c. vi, fol. 156, is the following account of it : " Sinopim,
colorem videlicet illum cujus tres sunt species, videlicet *rubea, subrubea, et* inter
has media, invenerunt primitus, ut scribit Ysidorus viri regionis Ponticæ in urbe
eorum quam solent ipsi Sinopem vocitare."

then rank under the category of *furs* ; and, secondly, because that animal is far from black. Indeed, the best sable is of a light brown or sand colour. Dallaway quotes a line, however, which might be adduced in support of this derivation :

> " Sables, ermines, vair et gris."

Guillim derives it from *sabulum,* gross sand or gravel, but this seems very improbable, although I have nothing better to substitute. It is curious that ' sable' and ' azure' should have been selected from the ' jargon' of heraldry for poetical use, to the exclusion of other similar terms :

> " By this the drooping daylight 'gan to fade,
> And yield his room to sad succeeding night,
> Who with her *sable* mantle 'gan to shade
> The face of earth, and ways of living wight."
>
> *Faerie Queen.*

> " Thus replies
> Minerva, graceful, with her *azure* eyes."
>
> *Pope.*

PURPURE (purple) is not common in English armory: still less so are the *stainant* or disgraceful colours, TENNY (orange) and MURREY, which Dr. Johnson defines as " darkly red," deriving it through the French *morée,* and the Italian *morello.* The fine cherry designated by this last word is, when ripe, of the exact colour intended by murrey. Bacon says, " Leaves of some trees turn a little *murrey,* or reddish ;" and " a waistcoat of *murrey*-coloured satin" occurs in the writings of Arbuthnot.

By these terms were the arms of gentlemen described; but for the arms of nobility they were not sufficiently lofty. These were blazoned by the precious stones, as *topaz* for yellow, *ruby* for red, &c. For the arms of princes it was necessary to go a step higher, namely, to the heavenly bodies, *Sol, Luna, Mars*, &c. Sir John Ferne enumerates several other sets of terms, in all thirteen, which he classifies thus: 1, planets; 2, precious stones; 3, vertues; 4, celestiall signes; 5, months; 6, days of the week; 7, ages of man; 8, flowers; 9, elements; 10, sesons of the yeer; 11, complexions; 12, numbers; 13, mettailes. What would those who are disgusted with the 'jargon' of our science say to such blazon as the following?—

> He beareth *Sunday*, a lion rampant *Tuesday*.
> He beareth *Faith*, a wolf salient *Loyalty*.
> He beareth *Marigold*, a bear passant, *Blue Lily*, muzzled
>   *White Rose*.
> He beareth, *Infancy*, three grasshoppers *Virility*.
> He beareth, *Melancholy*, three asses' heads, *Flegmatique!*

I must confess that, in the course of my heraldric reading, I have never met with blazon of this singular description, but Ferne assures his reader that it may be his fortune " to light upon such phantasticall termes," and he gives an historical and philosophical account of their origin. So recently as the last century the planets and gems were used in royal and noble armory, but of late good taste has limited blazon to the first-mentioned and most simple set of terms in all cases.

The *furs* are ermine, ermines, erminois, erminites, pean,

vair, and potent counter-potent. They are all said to be in-
dicative of dignity. In armorial painting their effect is very
rich. ERMINE, which may be taken as the type of the five
first mentioned, is represented by three spots placed triangu-
larly, and three hairs in black upon a white ground. It is
intended to represent the black tail of a species of weasel
fixed upon the white skin of the animal. Guillim[1]
gives a coat, containing six *whole ermines*, as
represented in the margin. Sir G. Mackenzie
informs us that "the first user of this fur in
arms was Brutus, the son of Silvius, who having
by accident killed his father, left that unhappie ground, and
travelling in Bretaigne in France, fell asleep, and when he
awoke he found this little beast upon his shield, and from
that time wore a shield ermine!" This fur is said to have
been introduced into England by Alan, Earl of Richmond,
so created by William the Conqueror. The ermine (*mustela
erminea*) is found in all the northern regions of the old continent, and as far southward as Persia and China. It was
originally brought into western Europe from Armenia, then
called *Ermonie*, whence its name. Chaucer employs *ermin*
for the adjective Armenian. VAIRE is composed of miniature shields of blue and white alternately placed. According
to Mackenzie it represents the skin of a small quadruped
called *varus*, the back of which is of a bluish grey, and the
belly white; and Guillim adds that when the head and feet
of the animal are cut off from the skin, the latter resembles
the figure of vaire used in heraldry. The costly fur so much
spoken of by our old poets under the name of *miniver* is derived by Dallaway from the French *menu vair*, on account of

[1] Page 205.

its smallness and delicacy.   The old French *vairon* signifies anything of two colours, and may possibly be the etymon of *vaire.*

(Temp. Edw I.)   (Arms of Sackville.

POTENT - COUNTER - POTENT, literally "crutch - opposite-crutch," resembles the tops of crutches counter-placed. What the origin of this figure may have been does not appear, although the word potent, in the sense of crutch, was common in the days of Chaucer.

> "When luste of youth wasted be and spent,
>   Then in his hand he takyth a *potent.*"

And again,

> "So eld she was that she ne went
>   A foote, but it were by potent."

> *Romaunt of the Rose.*

Having thus taken a glance at the field, or ground of the heraldric shield, let us next briefly notice what are called the honourable ordinaries, one or other of which occurs in the great majority of arms, viz., the CHIEF, BEND, BEND-SINISTER, FESSE, PALE, CROSS, SALTIRE, CHEVERON, and PILE. The 𝕮𝖍𝖎𝖊𝖋 is a fifth part of the shield nearest the top; *unde nomen.* In the primitive bearings, which were literally coats, or rather mantles of arms, the chief might be formed by turning the upper part of the garment back in form of a collar, thus exposing the lining, which doubtless was often of a different colour from the mantle itself. A knight who might chance at a tournament to wear a scarlet mantle lined with white, would in this manner acquire as arms, ' Gules, a chief argent.' The 𝖇𝖊𝖓𝖉 is a stripe passing diagonally across the shield from the dexter corner; (and the 𝖇𝖊𝖓𝖉-𝖘𝖎𝖓𝖎𝖘𝖙𝖊𝖗, the contrary way,) and is, etymologically, the same word with

(" Gules, a bend argent ")

the French *bande* and Saxon band.[1] This ordinary evidently represents a band or scarf worn over one shoulder, and pass-

---

[1] It is a prevailing error that the bend sinister is a mark of dishonour, as betokening illegitimacy; this seems to have arisen from its having been confounded with the baton, which bearing differs from it both in being much narrower, and in being cut off from the borders of the escocheon.

ing under the opposite arm, and is well exemplified in the
white belt worn by a soldier over his red coat. Of a similar
origin is the *fesse*, a horizontal stripe across the middle of
the shield, which represents a sash or military girdle.   The
term is evidently derived from the Latin *fascia*, through the
French *fasce*.   The *pale* is like the fesse, except that its
direction is perpendicular.   From its name it has been supposed to represent the *pales*, or palisades of a camp, and in
support of this origin it has been remarked that, in antient
warfare, every soldier was obliged to carry a pale, and to fix
it as the lines were drawn for the security of the camp. This
hypothesis seems to be one of those *after-thoughts* with
which heraldric theories abound.   There is no doubt that
most armorial *forms* existed long before the invention of
blazon, and that when it was found necessary to give every
figure its distinctive appellation, the real origin of many
bearings had been lost sight of, and the names assigned
them were those of objects they were *conjectured* to represent.

It is far more probable that this ordinary originated in
the insertion of a perpendicular stripe of a different colour
from the mantle itself, an idea which is supported by the
fact that the pale occupies in breadth a third of the escocheon. Two breadths of blue cloth divided by one of yellow,
would produce a blazonable coat, ' *Azure, a pale or.*' When
a shield is divided into several horizontal stripes of alternate
colours it is called *barry*; when the stripes run perpendicularly it is said to be *paly*; and when they take a diagonal
direction it is styled *bendy*.   The love of a striking contrast
of colours in costume is characteristic of a semi-barbarous
state of society, and the shawls and robes of the orientals of
the present day afford a good illustration of the origin of

these striped bearings.[1] Such vestments were not peculiar to the military, with whom we must always associate the heraldry of the earliest times; for, so lately as the time of Chaucer, they were the favourite fashion of civilians. This author, in his 'Parson's Tale,' makes that worthy ecclesiastic complain of the "sinful costly array of clothing in the embrouding, the disguising, indenting or *barring*, ounding, *paling*, winding or *bending*, and semblable waste of cloth in vanity."[2]

Arms divided into two compartments by a horizontal line are said to be *parted per fesse*; when the line is perpendicular, *parted per pale*; and so of the others. Ridiculous as it may seem, our ancestors, from the reign of Edward II to that of Richard II, affected this kind of dress. In a contemporary illumination, John of Gaunt is represented in a long robe divided exactly in half, one side being blue, the other white, the colours of the House of Lancaster. Chaucer's Parson, just now quoted, inveighs against the "wrappings of their hose which are departed of two colours, white and red, white and blue, or black and red," making the wearers seem as though "the fire of St. Anthony or other such mischance had consumed one half of their bodies." "These party-coloured hose," humorously remarks Mr. Planché, "render uncertain the fellowship of the legs, and the common term *a pair* perfectly inadmissible." But to return to the honourable ordinaries. The 𝕮𝕽𝕺𝕾𝕾. It would not be difficult to

---

[1] Among the sovereign states whose armorial ensigns are formed of such stripes are Cyprus, Hungary, Saxony, Austrasia, Burgundy, Arragon, and Germany under the descendants of Louis the Debonaire. The private families who bear armories so formed are innumerable.—*Brydson*, p. 66.

[2] These, as Mr. Planché (Hist. Brit. Costume, p. 151,) observes, are mostly heraldric terms. Ounding, or *undeing*, signifies a waved pattern or edge.

fill a volume with disquisitions upon this bearing, forming, as it does, a prominent feature in the heraldry of all Christendom; but I must content myself with a general view, without entering much into detail. The cross, as the symbol of Christianity, naturally engaged the reverent and affectionate regard of the early Christians, a feeling which lapsed first into superstition, and eventually into idolatry. In those chivalrous but ill-directed efforts of the princes and armies of Christian Europe to gain possession of the Holy Land, the cross was adopted as the sign or mark of the common cause; it floated upon the standard, was embroidered upon the robes, and depicted on the shields of the enthusiastic throng whose campaigns hence took the designation of *Croisades*, or *Crusades*. On subsequent occasions the cross was employed in this general manner, especially when the interests of the church were concerned, as, for instance, at the battle of Lewes in 1264, when the soldiers of the baronial army marked themselves with a white cross for the purpose of distinguishing each other from the king's forces.[1] The plain cross, or cross of St. George, is the most antient form of this bearing; it differed, however, from the form now in use in having the horizontal bar placed higher than the centre of the upright. The alteration was doubtless a matter of convenience to allow the common charges of the field, when any occurred, a more equal space. But the cross has been so modified by the varying tastes of different ages, that Dame Juliana Berners, at a time when armory was comparatively simple, declares that " crossis innumerabull are borne dayli." The principal and most usual varieties of this ordinary are described in the 'Boke of St. Albans.' One of the

---

[1] Blaauw's Barons' War.

most interesting forms is the *cross fitchée*, or ' fixibyll,' because being sharpened at the lower end it could be fixed into the ground, like the little crosses in Catholic cemeteries. It probably originated in the cross antiently carried by pilgrims, which answered the purpose of a walking-staff, and served, when occasion required, for the use of devotion. Next to this may be reckoned the *cross patée*, the *crosscrosslet*, the *cross patonce*, and the *cross moline*, called in the Boke a " mylneris cros," " for it is made to the similitude of a certain instrument of yrne in mylnys, the which berith the

| Crosslet fitchee | patee | patonce | moline | Calvary |

mylneston."[1] The plain cross *corded*, or entwined with ropes, was borne, according to the same authority, in the " armys of a nobull man, the which was some tyme a crafty man (handicraftsman), a *roper* as he himself said." These crosses are fully described in the larger treatises on heraldry, together with numerous others. Berry's Encyclopædia Heraldica enumerates no less than THREE HUNDRED AND EIGHTY-FIVE varieties.

The 𝖘𝖆𝖑𝖙𝖎𝖗𝖊, popularly called St. Andrew's cross, is formed like two bends crossing each other in the centre of the escocheon. A great variety of opinions has existed as to its origin. Some authors take it for an antient piece of harness attached to the saddle of a horse to enable the rider,

---

[1] Mylneris, miller's ; yrne, iron ; mylnys, mills ; mylne-ston, mill-stone.

sauter dessous, to jump down.[1] Others derive it from an instrument used *in saltu,* in the forest, for the purpose of taking wild beasts ; but neither of these hypotheses seems very probable. Leigh says, "This in the old tyme, was of ye height of a man, and was borne of such as used to scale the walls [*saltare in muros*] of towns. For it was driven full of pinnes necessary to that purpose. And walles of townes were *then* but lowe as appeared by the walls of Rome, whiche were suche that Remus easelye leaped over them. Witnesseth also the same the citie of Winchester whose walls were over-looked of Colbrande, chieftaine of the Danes, who were slayne by Guye, Erle of Warwike." The **cheveron,** which resembles a pair of rafters, is likewise of very uncertain origin. It has generally been considered as a kind of architectural emblem. Leigh, speaking of a coat containing three cheveronels, or little cheverons, says, "The ancestour of this cote hath builded iij greate houses in one province," and this remark applies with some truth to the Lewkenors of Sussex, who bore similar arms, though whether assumed from such a circumstance I cannot ascertain. The **pile** is a wedge-like figure based upon the edge of the shield, and having its apex inwards. The following etymons have been suggested : 1, *pilum,* Lat. the head of an arrow ; the Spaniards and Italians call this ordinary *cuspis.* 2, *pile,* French, a strong pointed timber driven into boggy ground to make a firm foundation. 3, *pied,* French, the foot ; in French armory it is called *pieu.* I cannot admit any of these derivations, though perhaps my own etymon may not be deemed less irrelevant, viz. *pellis,* the skin of a beast, whence our English terms pell, pelt, poultry, &c. The skin of a wild beast, deprived of the head

---

[1] Furetiere, quoted by Dall.

and fore legs, and fastened round the neck by the hinder ones, would form a rude garment, such as the hunter would consider an honourable trophy of his skill, and such as the soldier of an unpolished age would by no means despise; and it would resemble, with tolerable exactness, the pile of heraldry. The QUARTER is, as the word implies, a fourth part of the field, differing in tincture from the remainder; and the CANTON, a smaller quadrangular figure in the dexter, or sinister, chief of the escocheon, so called from the French *cantoné*, cornered.

The following figures rank as sub-ordinaries, viz. *Flasques, Flanches*, the *Fret, Border, Orle, Tressure, Gyron*, &c.

FLASQUES, always borne in pairs, are two pieces hollowed out at each side of the shield: FLANCHES and VOIDERS are modifications of this bearing. The last, says Leigh,[1] is the reward of a gentlewoman for service by her done to the prince or princess." It is not improbable that it was bor-

rowed from a peculiar fashion in female costume which pre-vailed temp. Richard II. Chaucer uses the word *voided* in

[1] Accid. fol. 121.

the sense of removed, made empty, and this is probably the origin of the term.

When a shield is divided into eight acute-angled triangles, by lines drawn perpendicularly, horizontally, and diagonally through the centre, it is blazoned by the phrase ' *gyronny* of eight,' and so of any other number of equal partitions of the same form. If one of these triangles occur singly it is termed a *gyron*. For this term the nomenclature of heraldry is indebted to the Spanish language, in which it means a gore, gusset, or triangular piece of cloth. The family of Giron, subsequently ennobled as Dukes of Ossona, bear three such figures in their arms, from the following circumstance. Alphonso VI, king of Spain, in a battle with the Moors, had his horse killed under him, when, being in great personal danger, he was rescued and remounted by Don Roderico de Cissneres, who, as a memorial of the event, cut three triangular pieces from his sovereign's mantle, which being afterwards exhibited to the king, he bestowed on his valiant follower an adequate reward, and gave him permission to bear three gyrons as his arms. The English family of Gurr, whose surname was probably derived from the village of Gueures, near Dieppe, bear ' gyronny . . . . and . . . .' as a ' canting' or allusive coat. Some derive this species of bearing from a kind of patchwork mantle of various colours. Hence, doubtless, also arose that picturesque species of bearing called *chequy*, consisting of alternate squares of different tinctures. Chaucer and Spenser use the word *checkelatoun;* probably in this sense :

> " His robe was *cheque-latoun*."
>
> *Knight's Tale.*

> " But in a jacket, quilted richly rare
> Upon *checklaton*, was he richly dight."
>
> *Faerie Queen.*

The chequered dress of the Celtic nations, still retained in the Highland plaid or tartan, may, in some way, have originated the chequered coat of heraldry. At all events, this is a more probable source than the chess-board, from which some writers derive it.

Most of the ordinaries have their diminutives, as the bendlet, the pallet, the cheveronel, &c. These are usually bounded by straight lines; but the ordinaries themselves admit of a variety of modifications of outline, as follows : 1. *Indented*, like the teeth of a saw. According to Upton, this line represents the teeth of wild beasts, but Dallaway derives it from a moulding much employed in Saxon architecture. 2. *Crenelle*, or embattled, like the top of a castle, (Lat. *crena*, a notch.) The ' licentia crenellare' of the middle ages was the sovereign's permission to his nobles to embattle or fortify their mansions. 3. *Nebuly* (nebulosus,) from its resemblance to clouds. 4. *Wavy*, or undulated. 5. *Dancette*, like indented, but larger, and consisting of only three pieces. 6. *Engrailed*, a number of little semi-circles connected in a line, the points of junction being turned outward. Johnson derives this word from the French ' grêle,' hail, marked or indented as with hailstones. And 7. *Invecked*, the same as the last, but reversed.

ROUNDLES are charges, as their name implies, of a circular form. The first idea of bearing them as charges in heraldry may have been suggested by the studs or knobs by which the parts of an actual buckler were strengthened and held together. As soon as blazon was introduced they received distinctive names, according to their tinctures. The bezant (or) was supposed to represent a gold coin, in value about a ducat, struck at Constantinople (Byzantium) in the times of the Crusades. Leigh, however, assigns it a much

5

greater value, and calls it a talent weighing 104 lbs. troy,
and worth 3750*l.* "Of these beisaunts you shall rede
dyversly in Scripture, as when Salomon had geuen unto
Hiram xx cities, he again gave vnto Salomon 120 *beisaunts*
of gold, whereof these toke their first name," (' obeisance ?')
The *plate* (argent) was probably some kind of silver coin.
The *torteaux* (red) called in the Boke of S. A. " tortellys, or
litill cakys," are said to be emblematical of plenty, and to
represent a cake of bread.   The modern French ' torteau '
is applied more exclusively to a kind of oil-cake of an oblong
form used as food for cattle.   ' Tortilla,' in Spanish, is a
cake compounded of flour and lard.   Dame J. Berners says
it should be called *wastel.* ' Wastel-brede' is defined in the
glossary to Chaucer, as bread made of the finest flour, and
derived from the French ' gasteau.'   Chaucer represents
his Prioresse as keeping small hounds

" that she fedde
With rosted flesh, and milk and *wastel brede.*"

Prol. Cant. Tales.

Pommes (green), says Dallaway, are berries; but if etymology
is worth anything, they must be apples, and such Leigh
calls them. *Hurts* (blue) the same authority considers berries,
and most heralds have taken them to be those diminutive
things, whortleberries, or as they are called in Sussex,
Cornwall, and Devonshire, ' hurts.'   But I am rather inclined with Leigh to consider them representations of the
' black and *blue*' contusions resulting from the " clumsy
thumps" of war. *Pellets* or *Ogresses* (black) are the ' piletts '
or leaden knobs forming the heads of blunt arrows for killing
deer without injuring the skin.[1] *Golpes* (purple) are wounds,

[1] By a statute of temp. Edw. II. (apud Winton) every person not having a
ual revenue in land than 100 pence, was compelled to have in his pos-

and when they stand five in a shield may have a religious allusion to the five wounds of Christ. *Oranges* (tenne) speak for themselves; and *Guzes*, Leigh says, are eyeballs; but as their colour is sanguine, or dull red, this seems unlikely.

The *Annulet* seems to have been taken from the ring armour, much in use about the period of the Norman Conquest. The *Orle*, or false escocheon, is merely a band going round the shield at a short distance from the edge: it was probably borrowed from an antient mode of ornamenting a shield, serving as a kind of frame to the principal charge. Animals or flowers disposed round the escocheon in the same form, are also termed an orle. The *bordure*, or border, explains itself. Like the orle, it was primarily designed as an ornament. The *lozenge*, derived by Glover from the quarry, or small pane of glass of this shape, Dallaway thinks originated in the diamond-shaped cushions which occur on tombs to support the heads of female effigies, as helmets do those of men. The *mascle* is taken for the mesh of a net. When many are

session a bow and arrows, with other arms both offensive and defensive; but all such as had no possessions (in land), but could afford to purchase arms, were commanded to have a bow with sharp arrows if they resided without the royal forests, and a bow with round-headed arrows if their habitation was within the forests. The words of the statute are, "Ark et setes hors de foreste, et en foreste ark et *piles*." The word pile is supposed to be derived from the Latin 'pila,' a ball; and Strutt supposes this kind of missile to have been used to *prevent* the owners from killing the king's deer. In the following reign archery, as a pastime of the common people, began to be neglected, which occasioned the king to send a letter of complaint to the sheriffs of London, desiring them to see that the leisure time upon holidays was spent in the use of the bow. In the thirty-ninth year of this reign, 1365, the penalty incurred by offenders was imprisonment at the king's pleasure. The words of the letter are, "arcubus et sagittis, vel *pilettis* aut boltis," with bow and arrows, or piles or bolts. *Vide Strutt's Sports and Pastimes. Edit. Hone*, pp. 54, 55.

united the arms are blazoned *masculy*, and then represent a
rich network thrown over the armour. At the siege of
Carlaverok a certain knight is described as having his armour
and vestments 'masculy or and azure:'

> "Son harnois et son attire
> Avoit masclé de or et de azure."

Billets have been conjectured to be representations of oblong
camps, but from the name they would seem to be *letters*.
They may have been originally assigned to bearers of important despatches. *Guttée* is the term applied to a field or
charge sprinkled over with drops of gold, silver, blood, tears, &c.
according to the tincture. This kind of bearing is said to
have originated with the Duke of Anjou, King of Sicily, who,
after the loss of that island, appeared at a tournament with
a black shield sprinkled with drops of water, to represent
tears, thus indicating both his grief and his loss.[1] A warrior
returning victorious from battle, with his buckler sprinkled
with blood, would, in the early days of heraldry, readily have
adopted the bearing afterwards called 'guttée de sang.' In
those times the besiegers of a fortress were often assailed with
boiling pitch, poured by the besieged through the machico-
lations of the wall constructed for such purposes. Splashes
of this pitch falling upon some besieger's shield, in all probability gave the first idea of 'guttée de poix.' The *fusil* is
like the lozenge, but narrower. Whatever the charge may
mean, the name is evidently a corruption of the Fr. *fuseau*, a
spindle. The *fret* may have been borrowed from the
architectural ornaments of the interior of a roof, or more
probably, from a knotted cord. It is sometimes called

---

[1] Nisbet.

Harington's Knot, though it is not peculiar to the arms
of that family, for it was also borne by the baronial races
of Echingham, Audley, and Verdon, and by many other
families.[1]

My purpose being not to describe all the charges or figures
occurring in heraldry, but merely to assign a reasonable
origin for those which appear to the uninitiated to have
neither propriety nor meaning, I pass by many others, and
come to those to which a symbolical sense is more readily
attachable, as the heavenly bodies, animals, vegetables,
weapons of war, implements of labour, &c. &c. Here I shall
merely offer some general remarks, for it is less my object to
gratify curiosity on this subject than to excite that attention
to it which it really deserves, and therefore I must say, with
gentle Dame Julyan, " Bot for to reherce all the signys that
be borne in armys it were too long a tarying, nor I can not
do hit : *ther be so mony!*"

The heavenly bodies occur frequently in heraldry, and in-
clude the Sun, 'in his glory,' or 'eclipsed;' the Moon,
'incressant,' 'in her complement,' 'decressant,' and 'in her
detriment,' or eclipse; stars and comets. The *crescent* was
the standard of the Saracens during the crusades, as it is of
their successors, the Turks, at this day. As one of the
antient laws of chivalry enacted that the vanquisher of a
Saracen gentleman should assume his arms, it is not remarkable that the crescent was, in the latter Crusades, often transferred to the Christian shield; although we must reject the
notion that the infidels bore regular heraldric devices. It is
probable, however, that their bucklers were ornamented in
various ways with their national symbol. Several authentic

[1] Vide p. 47, Arms of Echingham, &c.

instances of arms with crescents borne by English families
from that early date, are to be found.   Most of the families
of Ellis, of this country, bear a cross with four or more
crescents, derived from Sir Archibald Ellis, of Yorkshire, who
went to the Holy Land.   From a miraculous event said to
have happened during the Crusade under Rich. I. to Sir
Robert Sackville, the noble descendants of that personage
still bear an *estoile*, or star, as their crest.

The ELEMENTS also furnish armorial charges, as flames of fire,
rocks, stones, *islands*, thunderbolts, clouds, rainbows, water,
and fountains.   These last are represented by azure roundles
charged with three bars wavy argent.   In the arms of Sykes,
of Yorkshire, they are called *sykes*—that being a provin-
cialism for little pools or springs.   The antient family of
Gorges bore a *gurges*, or whirlpool, an unique instance, I
believe, of that bearing.

If we derive heraldry from the standards of antient nations,
then, undoubtedly, ANIMALS are the very oldest of armorial
charges, since those standards almost invariably exhibited
some animal as their device.   Familiar examples present
themselves in the Roman *eagle* and the Saxon *horse*.   Of
QUADRUPEDS the lion occupies the first place, and is far more
usual than any other animal whatever.   The king of beasts
is found in the heraldric field in almost every variety of posture, and tinctured with every hue recognized by the laws of
blazon.   It may be remarked here, that in the early days of
heraldry animals were probably borne of their 'proper' or
natural colour, but as, in process of time, the use of arms
became more common, and the generous qualities of the lion
rendered him the object of general regard as an armorial
ensign, it became absolutely necessary to vary his attitudes
and colours, for the purposes of distinction.   The same remark

applies, in a greater or less degree, to other animals and objects. As the emblem of courage the lion has been represented and misrepresented in a thousand forms. A well-drawn heraldric lion is a complete caricature of the animal; and hence the ire displayed by the country herald-painter when shown the lions in the Tower is very excusable: "What!" said the honest man, "tell me that's a lion; why I've painted lions rampant and lions passant, and all sorts of lions these five and twenty years, and for sure I ought to know what a lion's like better than all that!"

The circumstance of the royal arms of England containing three lions and those of Scotland one, has rendered this animal a special favourite with British armorists. Leigh and Guillim, particularly, are very minute in their remarks upon him. The French heralds object to the representation of the lion *guardant*, that is, with his face turned full upon the spectator, and declare that this posture is proper to the leopard, "wherein," says Guillim, "they offer great indignity to that *roiall beast*, in that they will not admit him, as saith Upton, to show his full face, the sight whereof doth terrifie and astonish all the beasts of the field, and wherein consisteth his chiefest majesty, 'quia omnia animalia debent depingi et designari in suo feroriore actu.' The French still allude derisively to our national charge as only a leopard. That one of these dissimilar animals could be mistaken for the other affords singular evidence of the rudeness with which arms in the middle ages were delineated.

(Lyon rampant. Guillim.)

The *leopard*, as an heraldric charge, has been treated with more obloquy than he deserves, from the erroneous notion that he was a bigene-

rous animal, bred between the lion and the female panther.
The *bear* is generally borne muzzled and 'salient,' leaping,
or rather jumping, the posture of the animal most familiar
to our ancestors, who greatly delighted in his uncouth danc-
ing. The *elephant*, the *wolf*, one of the most elegant of
heraldric devices, the *fox*, the *rabbit*, the *squirrel*, the *monkey*,
the *beaver*, the *porcupine*, the *cat-a-mountain*, and many
other wild animals borne in arms, need no comment.

The *heraldric tiger* furnishes another proof of the ignorance
of our ancestors in the natural history of foreign animals.
It is represented thus :

Among the domestic animals borne in arms are the *horse*,
the *ass*, the *camel*, the *bull*, the *ox*, the *greyhound*, the *talbot*
or mastiff, the *ram*, the *lamb*, the *hog*, &c.

The horse, from his associations with chivalry and war, has
ever been a favourite charge. The lamb, as commonly represented, with the nimbus round its head and the banner
of the cross, is termed a *holy lamb*. The *alant* or wolf-dog,
an extinct species, is of rare occurrence in arms.

> "Abouten his char ther wenten white *alauns*,
>   Twenty and mo as gret as any stere,
>   To hunten at the leon or the dere."
>   *Chaucer.*

The *alant* was the supporter of Fynes, Lord Dacre.

Most of the above were probably borne emblematically, but the *stag, deer, boar,* &c., seem to be trophies of the chase, especially when their heads only occur. The heads and other parts of animals are represented either as *couped,* cut off smoothly, or *erased,* torn off as it were with violence, leaving the place of separation jagged and uneven. The boar's head may have been derived from the old custom of serving up a boar's head at the tables of feudal nobles. This practice is still observed in the hall of Queen's College, Oxford, on Christmas-day, when an antient song or carol, appropriate enough to the ceremony, though not very well befitting the time and the place, is sung. It begins thus:

> " The boar's head in hand bear I,
> Bedeck'd with bays and rosemary,
> And I pray you, my masters, be merry,
> Quot estis in convivio.
> 𝕮aput aprí ðefero
> 𝕽eððens lauðes 𝕯omíno."

The presentation of a boar's head forms the condition of several feudal tenures in various parts of the country. As an heraldric bearing, and as a sign for inns, it is of very antient date. Of its latter application the far-famed hostelry in Eastcheap affords one among many examples; while its use in armory was familiar to the father of English poesy, who, describing the equipments of Sir Thopas, says,

> " His sheld was all of gold so red
> And therin was a *bore's hed,*
> A charboncle beside.

The annexed singular bearing, ' a cup with a boar's head erect,' evidently alludes to some obsolete custom or tenure.

It may be remarked here that many of the terms of heraldry, when applied to the parts and attitudes of ' beastes of venerie and huntyng,' are identical with the expressions used by learned *chasseurs* of the ' olden tyme,' and which are fully elucidated by Dame Julyan, Manwood, Blundeville, and other writers on woodcraft and the chase; a *science*, by the way, as systematic in the employment of terms as heraldry itself. This remark applies equally to the technical words in falconry used in describing falcons, hawks, &c., when they occur in armory.

When antient armorists had so far departed from the propriety of nature as to paint swans red and tigers green, it was not difficult to admit still greater monstrosities. Double-headed and double-tailed lions and eagles occur at an early date; but these are nothing when compared with the double and triple-*bodied* lions figured by Leigh.[1] It would be a mere waste of time to speculate upon the origin of such bearings, which owe their birth to "the rich exuberance of a Gothick fancy"—the fertile source of the chimerical figures noticed in the next chapter.

Among BIRDS, the *eagle* holds the highest rank. The lyon was the royal beast—this the imperial bird. He is almost uniformly exhibited in front, with expanded wings, and blazoned by the term ' displayed.' The *falcon, hawk,*

---

[1] ' *Gules*, a tri-corporated lyon issuant out of the three corners of the field, and meeting under one head in fesse, *or*,' was the coat-armour of Edmund Crouchback, second son of Henry III. This is the earliest specimen of *differencing* I have met with.

moor-cock, swan, cock, owl, stork, raven, turkey, peacock, swallow, and many others of the winged nation are well known to the most careless observer of armorial ensigns. The *Cornish chough,* a favourite charge, is curiously described by Clarke as " a *fine blue or purple black-bird,* with red beak and legs," and said to be " a noble bearing of antiquity, being accounted the *king of crows !*"

The *pelican* was believed to feed her young with her own blood, and therefore represented " vulning herself," that is, pecking her breast for a supply of the vital fluid.[1]   The wings are usually indorsed or thrown upwards; " but this," says Berry, " is unnecessary in the blazon, as that is the only position in which the pelican is represented in coat-armour." This may be true of modern heraldry, but antiently this bird was borne ' close,' that is, with the wings down.   The pelicans in the arms of the family of Pelham, resident at Laughton, co. Sussex, temp. Henry IV, were represented in this manner, as appears from a shield in one of the spandrels of the western door of Laughton church, and from some painted glass in the churches of Waldron and Warbleton.   In a carving of the fifteenth century, among the ruins of Roberts-bridge Abbey, the pelicans have their wings slightly raised,

---

[1] This is the usual notion of the old armorists, but Bossewell gives a different statement: " The pellicane feruently loueth her [young] byrdes. Yet when thei ben haughtie, and beginne to waxe hote, they smite her in the face and wounde her, and she smiteth them againe and sleaeth (kills) them.   And after three daies she mourneth for them, and then striking herself in the side till the bloude runne out, she sparpleth it upon theire bodyes, and by vertue thereof they quicken againe." —Armorie of Honour, fol. 69.   On the brass of Wm. Prestwick, dean of Hastings, in Warbleton church, co. Sussex, there is a representation of a pelican feeding her young with her blood, and the motto on a scroll above,

' 𝔖𝔦𝔠 𝔈𝔭𝔲𝔰 𝔟𝔦𝔩𝔢𝔯𝔦𝔱 𝔫𝔬𝔰,'—' Thus hath Christ loved us.'

and in the modern arms of Pelham they are indorsed, as
shown below.

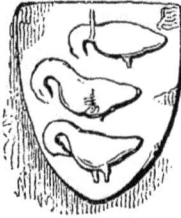

Laughton Church.   Robertsbridge Abbey.   Modern Arms.

Fishes, as borne in arms, have recently been made the
subject of an able, most interesting, and beautifully illustrated
volume.[1]   In my *en passant* survey of the ensigns of armory
it will suffice to remark that the *dolphin* takes the same rank
among heraldric fishes as the lion occupies among quadrupeds,
and the eagle among birds ; after him the *pike, salmon, barbel,*
and *trout* hold an honourable place, and even the *herring* and
sprat are not deemed too mean for armory.   Neither have
shell-fish been overlooked : the *escallop* in particular, from
its religious associations, has always been a special favourite.

AMPHIBIA, REPTILES, and INSECTS sometimes occur, particularly *toads, serpents, adders, tortoises, scorpions, snails,*
grasshoppers, spiders, ants, bees, and *gad-flies.*   It is singular
that such despised and noxious creatures as the scorpion and
the toad should have been adopted as marks of honour ; yet
such, in former times, was the taste for *allusive* arms that
the Botreuxes, of Cornwall, relinquished a simple antient coat
in favour of one containing three toads, because the word
' botru ' in the Cornish language signified a toad !

The HUMAN FIGURE and its parts are employed in many

---

[1] The Heraldry of Fish, by Thomas Moule, Esq.   London, 1842.

arms. The arms pertaining to the bishopric of Salisbury contain a representation of "our blessed Lady, with her son in her right hand and a sceptre in her left." The arms of the see of Chichester are the most singular to be found in the whole circle of church heraldry. They are blazoned thus: 'Azure, *Prester-John* hooded, sitting on a tomb-stone; in his sinister hand an open book ; his dexter hand extended, with the two fore-fingers erect, all or ; *in his mouth* a sword, fessewise, gules, hilt and pommel or, the point to the sinister.'[1] Prester or Presbyter-John, the person here represented, was a fabulous person of the middle ages, who was imagined to sway the sceptre of a powerful empire *somewhere* in the East, and who must have been a very long-lived personage, unless he was *reproduced* from time to time like the phœnix of antiquity. Many writers, during the thirteenth, fourteenth, and fifteenth centuries, make mention of him. Sir John Maundevile describes his territory, which, however, he did not visit. That country, according to his statement, contained rocks of adamant,[2] which attracted all the ships that happened to come near them, until the congeries appeared like a forest, and became a kind of floating island. It also abounded in popinjays or parrots as "plentee as gees," and precious stones large enough to make "plateres, dissches, and cuppes." "Many other marveylles been there," he adds, "so that it were to cumbrous and to long to putten it in scripture of bokes." He describes the Emperor himself as "cristene," and believing "wel in the Fadre, in the Sone, and in the Holy Gost," yet, in some minor points, not quite sound in the faith. As to his imperial state, he possessed

---

[1] Vide cut at the head of this chapter. [2] Loadstone.

72 provinces, over each of which presided a king; and he
had so great an army that he could devote 330,000 men to
guard his standards, which were " 3 crosses of gold, fyn, grete
and hye, fulle of precious stones." It is related of Columbus
that he saw on one of the islands of the West Indies, which
he then apprehended to be a part of the continent of Asia,
a grave and sacred personage whom he at first believed to be
Prester-John. This incident serves to show that the existence of this chimerical being was credited even so lately as
the close of the fifteenth century, although Roger Bacon, in
the thirteenth, doubted many of the tales related of him—
" de quo tanta fama solebat esse, et multa falsa dicta sunt et
scripta."[1] The best account of him is to be found in the
work of Matthew Paris, the monk of St. Albans, who wrote
before the year 1250. Marco Polo also mentions him in his
travels.[2] Porny places him in Abyssinia under the title of
Preter cham, or ' prince of the worshippers,' while Heckford[3]
considers him a priest and one of the followers of Nestorius,
patriarch of Constantinople in the fifth century.

Kings and *bishops* occur as charges; but rarely. The
heads of Moors and Saracens are more common, and belong
to the category of trophies, having originated, for the most
part, during the Crusades. The arms of the Welsh family of
Vaughan are ' a cheveron between three children's heads ...
enwrapped about the necks with as many snakes proper.'
" It hath beene reported," saith old Guillim, " that some one
of the ancestors of this family was borne with a snake about
his necke : *a matter not impossible*, but yet very unprobable!"
Besides heads, the armorial shield is sometimes charged with

---

[1] Op. Maj. edit. Jebb. 232.

[2] Halliwell's Sir John Maundevile, p. 319.

[3] Succinct Account of Religions and Sects, sect. 4, No. 42.

arms and legs, naked, vested, or covered with armour, hands, feet, eyes, hearts, winged and unwinged, &c. The coat of Tremaine exhibits three arms (et tres manus!) and that of the Isle of Man, three legs, as here represented. Of the

former, Guillim remarks, "these armes and hands conjoyned and clenched after this manner may signify a treble offer of revenge for some notable injurie." If we might be jocular upon so grave a subject as armory, we should consider the second coat a happy allusion to the geographical position of the island between the three kingdoms of England, Ireland, and Scotland, as if it had run away from all three, and were kicking up its heels in derision of the whole empire![1]

The VEGETABLE KINGDOM has furnished its full quota of charges. We have whole trees, as the *oak, pine, pear-tree,* &c.; parts of trees, as *oak-branches,* and *starved* (*i.e.* dead) *branches,* trunks of trees, generally raguly or knobbed; leaves, as *laurel, fig, elm, woodbine, nettle,* and *holly;* fruit, as *pomegranates, apples, pears, pine-apples, grapes, acorns,* and *nuts;* flowers, as the *rose, lily, columbine, gilliflower,* &c.; corn, as stalks of wheat and rye, and particularly *garbs* (*Fr.* gerbes)

[1] Some of the Greek coins of Sicily bear an impress of three legs conjoined, exactly similar to this fanciful charge, except that they are naked, and have at the point of conjunction a Mercury's head.

or wheatsheaves ; to which some add *trefoils, quatrefoils,* and *cinquefoils,* and the bearing familiar to all in the arms of France, and called the *Fleur-de-lis.*

Respecting the *trefoil,* there can be little doubt, as Mr. Dallaway observes, that it was borrowed from the foliated ornaments of antient coronets, which again were imitations of the natural wreath. The shamrock, which is identical with the trefoil, is the national badge of Ireland. Of the quatre and cinquefoils "almost any conjecture would be weakly supported. Amongst the very early embellishments of Gothic architecture are quatrefoils, at first inserted simply in the heads of windows, between or over the incurvated or elliptical points of the mullions, and afterwards diversified into various ramifications, which were the florid additions to that style."[1] These terms are common to both architecture and heraldry, but from which of the two the other adopted them must remain in doubt.

The non-heraldric reader will be surprised to learn that the identity of the *fleur-de-lis* with the iris or ' royal lily' has ever been called in question; yet it has been doubted, with much reason, whether an ornamented spear-head or sceptre be not the thing intended. The Boke of S. A. informs us that the arms of the king of France were " certainli sende by an awngell from heuyn, that is to say iij flowris in maner of swerdis in a felde of asure, the wich certan armys ware geuyn to the forsayd kyng of fraunce in sygne of euerlasting trow-bull, and that he and his successaries all way with bataill and swereddys (swords) shulde be punyshid !" Those who imagine the bearing to be a play upon the royal name of Loys or Louis decide in favour of the flower. Upton calls

[1] Dallaway.

it '𝖋𝖑𝖔𝖘 𝖌𝖑𝖆𝖉𝖎𝖔𝖑𝖎.'[1] Perhaps it was made a flower for the purpose of assimilating it to the English rose; certainly all our associations, historical and poetical, would tell in favour of its being such; and such it was undoubtedly understood to be in the time of Chaucer, who says of Sire Thopas,

"Upon his crest he bare a tour (tower),
And therein stiked a *lily flour*."

Leigh seems to entertain no doubt of its belonging to the vegetable kingdom; for in his notice of this charge he particularly describes the flower and the root of the iris. Mr. Montagu, in his recent 'Guide to the Study of Heraldry,' thinks the arguments of M. de Menestrier "in favour of the iris so strong as *almost* to set the question at rest."[2]

Those who advocate the spear-head view of the question, bring forward the common heraldric bearing, *a leopard's head jessant de lis*, i. e. thrust through the mouth with a fleur-de-lis, which passes through the skull as represented in the above cut. "There cannot," as Dallaway says, " be a more absurd combination than that of a leopard's head producing a lily, while the idea that it was typical of the triumph after

[1] The flower of the 'sword-grass, a kind of sedge.' *Dict.*

[2] A work on the Fleur-de-Lis, in 2 vols. 8vo (!), was published in France in 1837.

6

the chase, when the head of the animal was thrust through
with a spear and so carried in procession," seems perfectly
consistent. Still the query may arise 'how is it that the
head of no other animal, the wolf or boar for instance, is
found represented in a similar manner?'

The little band surrounding the *pieces* of which the fleur-
de-lis of heraldry is composed is analogous to nothing whatever in the flower, while it does strongly resemble the forril
of metal which surrounds the insertion of a spear-head into
its staff or pole. After an attentive consideration of both
hypotheses, I have no hesitation in affirming that the fleur-
de-lis is *not* the lily. This is shown, not from the occurrence
of lilies in their proper shape in some coats, and that of the
heraldric *lis* in others, (for such a varia-
tion might have been accidentally made
by the incorrect representations of un-
skilful painters,) but from the fact that
both lilies and lis are found in one and the
same coat—that of Eton College.[1]

The Tressure surrounding the lion in the royal arms of

---

[1] The following jest on the *fleur-de-lis* may amuse some readers. Sir William
Wise " having lente to the King (Henry VIII) his signet to seale a letter, who
having powdred eremites engrayl'd in the seale, [qy. ermine?—Several families
of Wise bear this fur:] ' Why, how now, Wise,' quoth the King, ' What? hast thou
lice here?' ' And if it like your Majestie,' quoth Sir William, ' a *louse* is a rich
coate, for, by giving the louse, I part armes with the French King, in that he
giveth the *floure de lice.*' Whereat the king heartily laugh'd, to heare how
pretily so byting a taunt (namely, proceeding from a Prince,) was so sodaynely
turned to so pleasaunte a conceyte." (Stanihurst's Hist. of Ireland in Holinshed's
Chron.) Nares thinks that Shakspeare, who is known to have been a reader of
Holinshed, took his conceit of the '*white lowses*,' which ' do become an old coat
well,' in the Merry Wives of Windsor, from this anecdote. (Heraldic Anom.
vol. i, p. 204.)

Scotland is blazoned 'fleury and counter-fleury,' that is, having fleurs-de-lis springing from it, both on the outer and inner sides. The fabulous account of the tressure is that it was given by Charlemagne to Achaius, king of Scotland in the year 792, in token of alliance and friendship. Nisbet says, "The Tressure Flowcrie encompasses the Lyon of Scotland, to show that he should defend the Flower-de-lisses, and *these to continue a defence to the Lion.*"[1]

Now, although we must discard this early existence of the Scottish ensigns, it is by no means improbable that the addition of the tressure was made in commemoration of some alliance between the two crowns at a later date. But the *defence* which a bulwark of lilies could afford the king of beasts would be feeble indeed! Yet, upon the supposition that the fleur-de-lis is intended for a spear-head, such an addition would be exceedingly appropriate, as forming a kind of chevaux-de-frise[2] around the animal.

This doubtful charge may serve as a turning point between 'things naturall' and 'things artificiall.' Among the latter, crowns, sceptres, orbs, caps of maintenance, mantles of state, and such-like insignia may be first named. According to Dame Julyan Berners, *crowns* formed part of the arms of King Arthur—"iij dragonys and over that an other sheelde of iij crownys." Mitres, crosiers, &c. occur principally, though not exclusively, in church heraldry. From attention in the first instance to the 'arts liberall' came such charges as books, pens, ink-horns, text-letters, as 𝕬's, 𝕮's and 𝕾's, organ-pipes, hautboys, harps, viols, bells, &c. The 'arts

[1] Essay on Armories, p. 10.

[2] Chevaux-de-frise (in fortification), large joists of wood stuck full of wooden spikes, armed with iron, to stop breaches, or to secure the passes of a camp.— *Bailey's Dict.*

mechanicall' furnish us with implements of agriculture, as ploughs, harrows, scythes, wheels, &c. The *Catherine Wheel* Dallaway takes for a cogged, or denticulated mill-wheel, with reference to some feudal tenure, but it seems rather ungallant to rob the female saint of the instrument of her passion, while St. Andrew and St. George are allowed to retain theirs in undisturbed possession. Manufactures afford the wool-comb, the spindle, the shuttle, the comb, the hemp-break, &c. Among mechanical implements are included pick-axes, mallets, hammers, plummets, squares, axes, nails, &c. Architecture furnishes towers, walls, bridges, pillars,&c. From the marine we have antient ships, boats, rudders, masts, anchors, and sails.   From field-sports come bugle (that is bullock) horns, bows, arrows, pheons or fish-spears, falcons' bells, and lures, fish-hooks, eel-spears, nets of various kinds, and bird-bolts. The bird-bolt was a small blunt arrow, with one, two, or three heads, used with the cross-bow for shooting at birds.   Hence the adage of '𝔗𝔥𝔢 𝔣𝔬𝔬𝔩'𝔰 𝔅𝔬𝔩𝔱 𝔦𝔰 𝔰𝔬𝔬𝔫 𝔰𝔥𝔬𝔱,' applied to the hasty expression or retort of an ignorant babbler.   John Heywood versifies the proverb thus :

"A foole's bolte is soone shot, and fleeth oftymes fer ;
But the foole's bolte and the mark cum few times ner." [1]

From sedentary games are borrowed playing-tables, dice, chess-rooks, &c.

War has naturally supplied heraldry with a numerous list of charges, as banners, spears, beacons, drums, trumpets,

[1] Heywood's Epigrams and Prov. 1566. No. 13.

cannons, or chamber-pieces, 'murthering chain-shot,' burning matches (of rope), portcullises, battering-rams, crossbows, swords, sabres, lances, battle-axes, and scaling-ladders;
also shields, generally borne in threes, helmets, morions,
gauntlets, greaves (leg armour), horse-trappings, bridles,
saddles, spurs, horse-shoes, shackles, *cum multis aliis*. Many
of these, though disused in modern warfare, will require no
explanation, but a few others whose use is less obvious may
be added, as *swepes, caltraps,* and *water-bowgets*.

The *swepe*, sometimes called a *mangonel*, and as such
borne in the canting arms of Magnall, was a war-engine, used
for the purpose of hurling stones into a besieged town or
fortress; a species of balista.

Murthering   Caltrap.   Beacon.   Swepe.
chain-shot.

In the celebrated lampoon upon Richard, king of the
Romans, who was obliged, at the battle of Lewes, to take
refuge in a windmill, the following lines occur:

> " The Kynge of Alemaigne wende to do full wel,
> He saisede the mulne for a castel;
> With hare sharpe swerdes he ground the stel,
> He wende that the sayles were *mangonel !*"[1]

---

[1] *Wende*, thought; *mulne*, mill.

The *caltrap* was a cruel contrivance for galling the feet of
horses.   It was made of iron, and so constructed that, however it might fall, one of its four sharp points should be
erect.   Numbers of them strewed in the enemy's path served
to retard the advance of cavalry, and a retreat was sometimes
secured by dropping them in the flight, and thus cutting off
the pursuit.   Its etymology is uncertain, cheval-trap and
gall-trap have been suggested with nearly equal claims to
probability.

Water-bowgets, or budgets, date from the Crusades, when
water had often to be conveyed across the sandy deserts from
a great distance.   They are represented in various grotesque
forms as—

so that it is a matter of curiosity to know in what manner
they were carried.   Leigh and others call them *gorges;*
but the charge properly known by that name is a whirlpool, as borne in the armes parlantes of the family of
Gorges.

The *mullet*, a star-like figure, has been taken to represent
the rowel of a spur; but a doubt of this derivation of the
charge may be suggested, as the spur of the middle ages had
no rowel, but consisted of one sharp spike.   Some of the old
heralds considered mullets as representations of falling stars
" exhalations inflamed in the aire and stricken back with a
cloud" which, according to Guillim, are sometimes found
"urth like a certain jelly, and assuming the form of

the charge. The substance alluded to bears the name of star-jelly. In the Gentleman's Magazine for 1797, are several communications on this subject, in which there is a great contrariety of opinion, some of the writers contending that it is an animal substance, while others consider it a vegetable. As it is usually found in boggy grounds, Dr. Darwin deemed it a mucilage voided by herons after they have eaten frogs, and Pennant attributed it to gulls. The antient alchemists called it the flower of heaven, and imagined that from it they could procure the universal menstruum; but all their researches ended in discovering that by distillation it yielded some phlegm, volatile salt, and empyreumatic oil.[1]

Personal costume, although mixed up with the very earliest of heraldric devices, furnishes scarcely any regular charges. Excepting shoes, caps, and body-armour, the *maunch* is almost the only one derived from this source. This charge, a familiar example of which occurs in the arms of the noble family of Hastings, represents an antient fashion of sleeve worn soon after the Conquest, but of such an extravagant form that Leigh blazons it a *maunch-maltalé*, a badly-cut sleeve; and certainly the example given by him fully justifies the use of that epithet. The taste for a long pendulous addition to the cuff of the sleeve forms one of the most curious features of the female costume of the twelfth century. According to Brydson, the maunch was a distinguished "favour" bestowed on some knights, being part of the dress of the lady or princess who presented it.

The woodcut (no inappropriate *tail-piece* for the present

---

[1] Modern naturalists place it in the class cryptogamia, and give it the name of *Tremella nostoc*.

chapter) delineates several antient forms of this article. Well may Master Leigh remark, " Of thinges of antiquitee growen out of fashion this is one."

No. 1, Leigh; 3, 4, from Planché's Hist. Brit. Cost.; 2, Arms of Hastings, from the tomb of W. de Valence, Earl of Pembroke, Westminster Abbey.

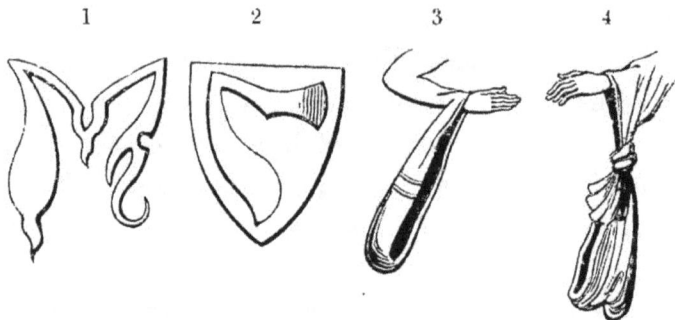

1   2   3   4

𝕸angys be called in armys a sleue.

Boke S. A.

CHAPTER IV.

Chimerical Figures of Heraldry.

" Manye merveylles there ben in that regioun."

Sir John Maundevile.

THE days of the Crusaders were the days of romance. " From climes so fertile in monsters as those through which these adventurers passed," observes Dallaway, " we cannot wonder that any fiction was readily received by superstitious admirers, whose credulity nothing could exhaust." The narrations of those warriors who had the good fortune to revisit their native lands were eagerly seized upon by that new class of literary aspirants, the Romance writers, by means of whose wonder-exciting productions, giants, griffins, dragons, and monsters of every name, became familiarized to all. For ages the existence of these products of a " gothick fancy" was never called in question. The early travellers, such as Marco Polo and our own renowned Sir John Maundevile, pandered to the popular taste, and what those chroniclers of ' grete merveyles' reported in the thirteenth and fourteenth centuries was religiously believed in the sixteenth, and hardly questioned even in the seventeenth. In the early part of this period, indeed, it can scarcely be expected that the multitude at least should have been disabused of the delusion, when the existence of witchcraft was considered an essential part of the common creed,—when a learned herald, like Guillim, could write a tirade against "divellish witches that doe worke the destruction of silly infants, and also of cattel,"—and when the supreme magistrate of these realms could instigate the burning of deformed old women, and write treatises upon " Dæmonology," which, among other matters, taught his loyal and undoubting subjects that these maleficæ were wont to perform their infernal pranks by means of circles, some of which were *square*, and others *triangular!* It was reserved for the advancing light of the eighteenth century to break the spell, and scatter these monsters to the winds. This, however, was not to be done at once; for our grandfathers, and even our fathers, gathered their knowledge of popular *natural* history from a book which contained minute descriptions of the *dragon*, ' adorned with cuts' of that remarkable hexapede, for the edification of its admiring readers !

Under the category of Heraldric Monsters the following deserve especial notice :—

The Allerion	Martlet
Chimera	Opinicus
Cockatrice	Pegasus
Dragon	Sphinx
Griffin	Sagittary
Harpy	Satyr
Lyon-Dragon	Unicorn
Lyon-Poisson	Wyvern
Mermaid	Winged Lyon
Montygre	Winged Bull.[1]

The *allerion* is a fabulous bird without either beak or legs, described by some writers as very small, like a martlet, while others give him the size of an eagle. The name is derived from the circumstance of his being destitute of all his extremities except the wings (ailles). Three such birds, according to the chroniclers of the middle ages, were shot with an arrow from a tower, by Godfrey of Boulogne, duke of Lorraine, at the siege of Jerusalem, during the first crusade; and three allerions upon a bend, in honour of that event, are borne as the arms of the duchy of Lorraine to this day.[2]

The *chimera* is, to use the words of Bossewell, "a beaste or monstre hauing thre heades, one like a Lyon, an other like a Goate, the third like a Dragon."[3]

The *cockatrice*[4] is a cock, with the wings and tail of a

---

[1] In reading this list it will be seen that it contains several monsters not of the 'Gothick' but of the Classical era, as the chimera, harpy, and sagittary; but it is a curious and characteristic fact that the purely classical monsters were never great favourites in heraldry.

[2] Nisbet on Armories, edit. 1718; pp. 12-13.

[3] Workes of Armorie, folio 66.

[4] Cocatryse, basilicus, *cocodrillus!* Prompt. Parv. Camd. Soc.

dragon. The best account of him is given by Leigh : "Thys
though he be but at ye most a foote of length yet is he kyng
of all serpentes[1] of whome they are most afrayde and flee
from. For with his breath and sight he sleath all thynges
that comme within a speare's length of him. He infecteth
the water that he commeth neare. His enemy is the wesell,
who when he goeth to fight with ye cockatrice eateth the
herbe commonlye called Rewe, and so in fight byting him he
dyeth and the wesell therewith dyeth also. And though the
cockatrice be veneme withoute remedye whilest he liueth,
yet when he is dead and burnt to ashes, he loseth all his
malice, and the ashes of him are good for alkumistes, and
namely, in turnyng and chaungeyng of mettall." To this
latter remark he adds, "I have not seene the proofe thereof,
and yet I have been one of Jeber's cokes."

The *dragon* is usually depicted with a serpentine body,
sharp ears, a barbed tongue and tail, strong leathern wings
armed with sharp points, and four eagles' feet, strongly
webbed ; but there are many modifications of this form.
"Of fancy monsters, the winged, scaly, fiery dragon is by
far the most poetical fabrication of antiquity. To no word,
perhaps, are attached ideas more extraordinary, and of greater
antiquity, than to that of dragon. We find it consecrated
by the religion of the earliest people, and become the object
of their mythology. It got mixed up with fable, and poetry,
and history, till it was universally believed, and was to be
found everywhere but in nature.[2] In our days nothing of

---

[1] Hence sometimes called the basilisk, from the Greek βασιλισκος.

[2] Mallet (Northern Antiquities, ch. ix) says, "The thick misshapen walls winding round a rude fortress, on the summit of a rock, were often called by a name
signifying SERPENT or DRAGON. Women of distinction were commonly placed

the kind is to be seen, excepting a harmless animal hunting its insects. The light of these days has driven the fiery dragon to take refuge among nations not yet visited by the light of civilization. The *draco volans* is a small lizard, and the only reptile possessing the capacity of flight. For this purpose it is provided on each side with a membrane between the feet, which unfolds like a fan at the will of the animal, enabling it to spring from one tree to another while pursuing

its food. It is a provision similar to that of the flying squirrel, enabling it to take a longer leap."[1] The annexed cut represents a *dragon volant,* as borne in the arms of

in such castles for security. Thence the romancers invented so many fables, concerning princesses of great beauty guarded by dragons and afterwards delivered by young heroes, who could not achieve their rescue till they had overcome those terrible guards."

[1] Anon. Parag.

Raynon of Kent, and the *draco volans* of the zoologists.   A
fossil flying lizard has been found in the lias of Dorsetshire,
which, to employ the words of Professor Buckland, is "a
monster resembling nothing that has ever been seen or heard
of upon earth, excepting the dragons of romance and
heraldry."

Considering the hideous form and character of the dragon,
it is somewhat surprising to find him pourtrayed upon the
banner and the shield as an honourable distinction; unless
he was employed by way of trophy of a victory gained over
some enemy, who might be symbolically represented in this
manner.   The dragon often occurring at the feet of antient
monumental effigies is understood to typify *sin*, over which
the deceased has now triumphed; and the celebrated monster
of this tribe slain by our patron saint, St. George, was doubtless a figurative allusion to a certain pestilent heresy which
he vehemently resisted and rooted out.   Favine, on the Order
of Hungary, remarks that the French historians speak of
Philip Augustus ' conquering the dragon' when he overcame
Otho IV, who bore a dragon as the standard of his empire.[1]
It has been suggested that the design of commanders in
depicting monsters and wild beasts upon their standards was
to inspire the enemy with terror.[2]

The dragon forms a part of the fictitious arms of King
Arthur; and another early British king bore the surname of
Pen-Dragon, or the ' dragon's head.'   The standard of
the West Saxon monarchs was a golden dragon in a red
banner.   In the Bayeux tapestry a dragon on a pole re-

[1] Brydson's Summary View.

[2] Probably, also, by frightening their horses, to throw their ranks into confusion.

peatedly occurs near the person of King Harold ; and in the
instance which is copied in
the margin, the words ' HIC
HAROLD' are placed over it.[1]
It was an early badge of the
Princes of Wales, and was
also assumed at various pe-
riods by our English monarchs.   Henry III used it at the
battle of Lewes in 1264.

> " Symoun com to the feld,
>   And put up his banere ;
> The Kyng schewed forth his scheld,
>   His *Dragon* fulle austere.
> The Kyng said ' On hie,
>   Symon jeo vous defie!' "
>
> *Robert Brunne.*

"The order for the creation of this 'austere' beast,"
says Mr. Blaauw, " is still extant.   Edward Fitz-Odo, the
king's goldsmith, was commanded, in 1244, to make it ' in
the manner of a standard or ensign, of red samit,' to be
embroidered with gold, and his tongue to appear as though
continually moving, and his eyes of sapphire, or other stones
agreeable to him."[2]

> " Then was ther a Dragon grete and grimme,
>   Full of fyre and also venymme,
> With a wide throte and tuskes grete."[3]

The dragon-standard must have been in high favour with

[1] By an oversight in the drawing some small vestiges of wings have been omitted.
[2] Barons' War, p. 168.
[3] ' Sir Degore.' Warton's Hist. Poet., p. 180, ibid.

commanders, for in the same war we find it unfurled in the opposite cause by the leader of the baronial party:

> " When Sir Simoun wist the dome ageyn them gone,
> His felonie forth thrist, somned his men ilkon,
> Displaied his banere, lift up his Dragoun !"

Robt. Brunne.

"When Sir Simon knew the judgment given against them, his wickedness burst forth, he gathered all his men, displayed his banner, and lifted up his Dragon."[1]　The expression '*his* dragon' must not be understood to imply any peculiar right to the device, for the arms of De Montfort were widely different, viz. 'Gules, a lion rampant, double queué, argent.'　From the indiscriminate use of the monster by different, and even by contending parties, I should consider him merely as the emblem of defiance.　The Dragon must not be confounded with the usual pennon, or standard of an army, as it was employed in addition to it.　Matthew of Westminster, speaking of the early battles of this country, says, "The king's place was *between* the Dragon and the standard."[2]　Among the ensigns borne at Cressy was a burning dragon, to show that the French were to receive little mercy.[3]　This dragon was of red silk, adorned and beaten with very broad and fair lilies of gold, and bordered about with gold and vermilion.'　The French frequently carried a red pennon, embroidered with a dragon of gold. Our Henry VI caused a particular coin to be struck, the reverse of which exhibited a banner charged with a demi-

---

[1] Barons' War, p. 169.

[2] " Regius locus fuit inter *draconem* et standardum."

[3] Barnes's Hist. Edw. III.

dragon, and a black dragon was one of the badges of Edward IV. A red dragon was one of the supporters of Henry VII, Henry VIII, and Elizabeth, whence the title, Rouge-dragon, of one of the existing pursuivants in the College of Arms.

The *griffin*, or griphon, scarcely less famous than the dragon, was a compound animal, having the head, wings, and feet of an eagle, with the hinder part of a lion. He is thus described by Sir John Maundevile in the 26th chapter of his 'ryght merveylous' Travels:

"In that contree [Bacharie] ben many Griffounes, more plentee than in ony other contree. Sum men seyn that thei han the body upward as an egle, and benethe as a lyoun; and treuly thei seyn sothe that thei ben of that schapp. But o Griffoun hathe the body more gret and more strong thane 8 lyouns, of such lyouns as ben o' this half (hemisphere); and more gret and strongere than an 100 egles, suche as we han amonges us. For o Griffoun there wil bere fleynge to his nest a gret hors, or 2 oxen yoked to gidere as thei gon at the plowghe. For he hathe his talouns so longe and so large and grete upon his feet, as thowghe thei weren hornes of grete oxen, or of bugles or of kygn, so that men maken cuppes of hem to drynke of, and of hire ribbes and of the pennes of hire wenges men maken bowes fulle stronge to schote with arwes, and quarell."

Casley says that in the Cottonian Library there was a cup of the description just referred to, four feet in length, and inscribed—

" 𝔊riphi unguis vivo 𝔠uthberto 𝔇unelmensi sacer,"

a dedication which, I must confess, puzzles me sorely. A

7

griffin's claw and the 'saint-bishop' of Durham seem as
absurd a combination of ideas as that presented in the old
proverbial phrase of 'Great A and a Bull's Foot,' or by the
tavern sign of 'The Goat and Compasses.' If wisdom, according to classical authority, lies in a well, so does the wit of
this association.   Another griffin's claw, curiously mounted
on an eagle's leg of silver, which came at the Revolution
from the Treasury at St. Denis, is preserved in the cabinet
of antiquities in the King's Library at Paris.   Three such
talons were formerly kept at Bayeux, and were fastened on
high days to the altar as precious relics!   A 'corne de
griffoun' is mentioned in the Kalend. of Excheq. iii, 176.
Another, about an ell in length, is mentioned by Dr. Grew
in his 'History of the Rarities of the Royal Society,' p. 26.
The Doctor thinks it the horn of a roebuck, or of the *Ibex
mas*.   Leigh says that griffyns " are of a great hugenes, for
I have a clawe of one of their pawes, which should show
them to be as bygge as *two* lyons."   The egg was likewise
preserved as a valuable curiosity, and used as a goblet.
" Item, j œf de griffon, garnis d'argent, od pie et covercle."
The griffin was assumed by the family of Le Dispenser, and
the upper part appears as the crest on the helm of Hugh le
Dispenser, who was buried at Tewkesbury in 1349. Another
strikingly designed representation of this curious animal is
seen at Warwick, at the feet of Richard Beauchamp, who
died in 1439.[1]

The *harpy*, unusual in English armory, has the head and
breasts of a woman, with the body, legs, and wings of a vul-

---

[1] Vide Promptorium Parvulorum, Camd. Soc. voc. *griffoun*.   Leigh's Accedens, &c.

ture. This was a classical monster. Guillim, imitating Virgil,[1] says :

"Of monsters all, most monstrous this ; no greater wrath
God sends 'mongst men ; it comes from depths of pitchy hell;
And virgin's face, but wombe like gulfe insatiate hath ;
Her hands are griping clawes, her colour pale and fell."

The coat 'Azure, a harpy or,' was 'in Huntingdon church' in Guillim's time.

The *lyon-dragon* and the *lyon-poisson* are compound monsters ; the former of a lion and a dragon, and the latter of a lion and a fish. These are of very rare occurrence, as is also the *monk-fish*, or Sea Friar, which Randle Holme tells us 'is a fish in form of a frier.' 'Such a monstrous and wonderful fish,' he adds, 'was taken in Norway.'

The identity of the popular idea of the *mermaid* with the classical notion of the syren is shown in the following passage from Shakspeare :

"Thou rememberest
Since once I sat upon a promontory,
And heard a Mermaid on a dolphin's back
Uttering such dulcet and harmonious breath,
That the rude sea grew civil at her song."

And Brown, in his 'Vulgar Errours,' observes, "few eyes have escaped [that] the picture of a Mermaid, with woman's head above, and fishy extremity below, answers the shape of the antient syrens that attempted upon Ulysses." The heraldric mermaid usually holds a mirror in her right hand and a comb in her left. The existence of mermaids was religiously believed not many ages since, and many accounts

[1] Æn. iii, 212, &c.

of their being captured on the English coast occur in the writings of our old chroniclers, and other retailers of marvels. The specimens exhibited of late years have been pronounced ingenious combinations of the upper half of the ape with the tail of a fish.

The montegre, manticora, or *man-tyger*, had the body of a lion (q. tiger?), the head of an old man, and the horns of an ox. Some heralds, by way of finish, give him dragon's feet.

Butler's well-known line,

"The herald's *martlet* hath no legs,"

has rendered most readers aware of the singular defect of this otherwise beautiful charge. Heraldric authors differ as to the identity of this bird. Its being called in Latin blazon 'merula,' and in French 'merlotte,' the diminutive of 'merle,' has induced some to consider it a blackbird; while others, with greater plausibility, decide in favour of the common house martin, the legs of which are so short and the wings so long that when it alights upon the ground it cannot rise without great difficulty. Hence originated the mistake of pourtraying it without legs, "and for this cause," sagely observes Guillim, "it is also given for a *difference* of younger brethren to put them in minde to trust to their wings of vertue and merit to raise themselves, and not to their legges, having but little land to put their foot on."

The *opinicus* differs slightly from the griffin, having four lion's legs instead of two, and the tail is short like that of a camel. It is used as the crest of the Barber-Chirurgeons Company. The *pegasus* or winged-horse ranks among the chimerical figures of heraldry borrowed from classical fable, and is more frequently employed as a crest or supporter than as a charge. The *sphinx* occurs very rarely. The *satyr* or satyral exhibits a human face attached to the body of a lion, and has the horns and tail of an antelope.

The *sagittary* is the centaur of antiquity—half man, half horse, and is said to have been assumed as the arms of king Stephen on account of the great assistance he had received from the archers, and also because he had entered the kingdom while the sun was in the sign Sagittarius. Sir John Maundevile tells us that in Bacharie " ben many Ipotaynes, that dwellen somtyme in the watre and somtyme on the lond; and thei ben half man and half hors : and thei eten men *when they may take hem*"—an excellent *gloss* upon Mrs. *Glass,* ' First *catch* your hare,' &c.[1]

The *unicorn* is the most elegant of all these fanciful figures, and is too well known as the sinister supporter of the royal arms to need any description. Mr. Dallaway derives the heraldric unicorn from the spike antiently fixed to the head-piece of a war-horse, and resembling a horn; but as this does not account for the cloven hoofs and slender, tufted tail, I should reverse the inference, and derive that appendage from the popular notion of the unicorn.

The unicorn of antiquity was regarded as the emblem of strength; and as the dragon was the guardian of wealth, so was the unicorn of chastity. His horn was a test of poison, and in virtue of this peculiarity the other beasts of the forest invested him with the office of water-' conner,' never daring to taste the contents of any pool or fountain until the unicorn

[1] Vide Vignette at the head of this Chapter for Maundevile's representation of an Ipotayne.

had stirred the waters with his horn to ascertain if any wily serpent or dragon had deposited his venom therein. Upton and Leigh detail the 'wonderful art' by which the unicorn is captured. "A mayde is set where he haunteth, and she openeth her lappe, to whome the Vnicorne, as seeking rescue from the force of the hunter, yeldeth his head and leaueth all his fierceness, and resting himself vnder her protection, sleapeth vntyll he is taken and slayne !"

The Hebrew *reem* being rendered in our version of the Bible unicorn, has confirmed the vulgar notion that the animal intended was the cloven-hoofed and single-horned figure of heraldry; but there is nothing in the word sanctioning the idea that the animal was single-horned; and on referring to the passages in which the term is introduced, the only one which is quite distinct on this point seems clearly to intimate that the animal had *two* horns. That passage is Deut. xxxiii, 17. 'His horns are like the *horns* of the reem;' the word here is singular, not plural, and should have been 'unicorn,' not 'unicorns,' in our version.[1] It has lately been attempted to prove that the reem of Scripture was the animal now known as the nhyl-gau.[2] Reem is translated in the Septuagint by 'μονοκερως,' which is exactly equivalent to our unicorn. If a one-horned animal be contended for, the rhinoceros is the only one now known that is entitled to the attribute of *unicornity*. Leigh declares the unicorn of our science to be a mortal foe to elephants, and such, according to zoologists, is the character of the rhinoceros. These two are, however, the only points of resemblance; for while the

---

[1] Kitto's Pictorial Bible, Job xxxix.
[2] Vide Congregational Mag. 1842 or 43.

unicorn of heraldry is of light and elegant symmetry, the rhinoceros of the African deserts is an animal so clumsy and ponderous that it has been known to require eight men to lift the head of one into a cart.[1]

The *wyvern* is one of the most usual of this description of charges. It is represented as a kind of flying serpent, the upper part resembling a dragon with two fore legs, and the lower part a snake or adder. The name is derived from the Anglo-Saxon 'wivere,' a serpent.

The bull and the lion with the wings of an eagle occasionally occur in continental armory, but I do not recollect an instance of either in English heraldry. The winged lion is the achievement of the city of Venice.

The foregoing enumeration of heraldric monsters includes all that are generally borne, and even some that scarcely ever occur; but Randle Holme, in his 'Academy of Armory,' figures and describes a multitude of others, some of which I strongly suspect to have been the offspring of his own prolific fancy. The triple-headed Cerberus was borne, this writer tells us, by the name of *Goaler*, while another family bore 'the scarlet beast of the bottomless pit:' ensigns of *honour*, truly !

What shall we say of
The *Nependis*, or ape-hog, half ape, half swine;
The *Minocane*, or *Homocane*, half child, half spaniel dog;
The *Lamya*, a compound of a woman, a dragon, a lyon, a
    goat, a dog, and a horse;
The Dragon-tyger, and Dragon-wolf;
The Lyon-wyvern;
The Winged Satyr-fish;

[1] Kitto, ut sup.

The Cat-fish and Devil-fish;

The Ass-bittern (the arms of Mr. Asbitter!)

The Ram-eagle;

The Falcon-fish with a hound's ear;

and

The 'Wonderfull Pig of the Ocean?'

From Holme's Academy of Armory.

Ram-eagle.   Cat-fish.   Ass-bittern.

CHAPTER V.

𝕿𝖍𝖊 𝕷𝖆𝖓𝖌𝖚𝖆𝖌𝖊 𝖔𝖋 𝕬𝖗𝖒𝖘.

"Armes do speak."

Sylvanus Morgan.

THE very earliest of armorial devices are of two classes : the first comprising those which consist of simple lines and tinctures, so disposed as to form an agreeable harmony or contrast; and the second embracing those which convey some sentiment. The first resulted from a study of what was pleasing to the eye; the other expressed the moral attributes of the original bearer, by natural or artificial figures employed as symbols. To illustrate my meaning, let us suppose that two knights, A and B, assume each a coat of arms. A, regarding nothing more than an agreeable effect, embroiders his banner with chequers of red and yellow. B, esteeming himself a valiant soldier, expresses that sentiment by representing upon his silver buckler a lion in the attitude of combat, which, for the purpose of inspiring terror, he paints of a colour resembling that of blood. In the course of a few generations the principles upon which these devices have been framed are reduced to a science, with a regular nomenclature and fixed laws. Then A's banner begins to be spoken of as 'Chequy, gules, and or,' while B's escocheon is described as

' Argent, a lion rampant, gules.'   Again, two followers of A, whom we will call C and D, imitating their chief's example, assume similar devices for their shields and pennons.   C gives the red and yellow chequers of his patron, adding, for distinction's sake, a white bordure, while D surmounts the same device with a diagonal stripe of blue.   In like manner, two -adherents of B, whom we will style E and F, copy the lion from his shield, but give him a different colour, E's lion being black and F's blue.   Carrying the principle a stage further, G, a supporter of D, adopts his blue bend, but omits the chequers of A; and H, a follower of F, retains the colours of his device, but gives three lions instead of one; while I, also retaining those colours, gives his lion or lions walking or passant; and so on to infinity.   This I believe will be found the true theory of the multiplication of armorial bearings.[1]

Thus it will be seen that only a portion of such devices were ever symbolical, and that those which were, in process of time ceased to be so in relation to the successors or dependants of the original assumers.   When surnames were first generally adopted, a personage to whom nature had given a pale visage took the name of White.   His sons might be all ruddy and his grandsons all brown, yet every one of them bore the family name of White.   Again, the original Mr. Wise might have had the misfortune to become the progenitor of a long line of blockheads, and Mr. Smith's descendants have all been tailors; yet, regardless of these circum-

---

[1] "What reason," asks Morgan, "can be given why the three brothers, Warren, Gourney, and Mortimer, should every one bear a severall coat, and derive (hand down) their sirnames to posterity, all of them yet retaining the metal and colour of or and azure, the one *checky*, the other *pally*, and the other *barry ?*" Armilogia, p. 41.

stances, their posterity are all, respectively, Wises and Smiths until this day. So it has necessarily occurred with heraldric devices; and many a gentleman who bears crescents or other celestial insignia, is chiefly intent upon mundane affairs; while many another, whose shield displays the rampant lion possesses the peaceful disposition of a lamb. Strangely at variance with experience is ofttimes found the sentiment of Horace:

> " Fortes creantur fortibus et bonis,
> ——— nec imbellem feroces
> Progenerant aquilæ columbam."

The early treatises on heraldry contain little beyond the technicalities of the science; but in the sixteenth and seventeenth centuries a race of authors arose who bestowed infinite labour upon researches into the origin of heraldric figures and their symbolical meaning. According to these writers, every tincture and bearing adumbrated the natural dispositions of the bearer. The treatises of Leigh and the succeeding heraldrists down to the time of Morgan abound with speculations, often ingenious but still oftener absurd, as to the import of armorial ensigns; and a new system arose sustaining the same relation to heraldry that astrology bears to astronomy. This was called ARMILOGIA, or the Language of Arms; and the length to which it was carried tended perhaps more than any other circumstance to bring the study of legitimate armory into disrepute. In the present Chapter it is my intention to give a few specimens of these theories selected here and there, without any attempt at collation; for their originators are often widely at variance with each other, and, as in most other matters that are purely speculative, we find " quot homines tot sententiæ."

One of the foremost absurdities of this system is the respect paid to the mystic number nine. In whatever point of view we examine the armory of those days, nine prominent features are made to present themselves ; thus there are 9 tinctures, 9 sorts of shields, 9 furs, 9 honourable ordinaries, 9 roundles, 9 differences of brethren, 9 worthy partitions, 9 mesles, 9 abatements of honour, 9 virtues of chivalry, 9 worthies, 9 female ditto, 9 sorts of gentry, 9 duties of heralds, ix artycles of gentilnes, ix vices contrary to gentilmen, ix precious stonys, ix vertues of precious stonys, 9 especial rejoicings, &c. &c. &c.

" Wherefore," asks old Leigh, " have you used the number of nyne in all your demonstracions more than any other?" to which Gerard replies, " Not onely because it is aptest for this science, for that the rules incident thereto chiefly fall out to that number, but that for that of all simple numbers it is most of content. The figure whereof holdeth all other vnder it, as by the Arte of Arithmetique ye may sonest perceve, where ye shall fynde, that all articles and compoundes, be they never so hudge,[1] are made of nyne figures. The golden number also of itselfe, is the last, the whiche ye may equally devyde into three odde partes, which have bin resembled to the blisse of the iii Ierarchies of holines. In the which every one hath a likenes of the Trinitie," with much more equally to the purpose.[2]

Nothing can be more tedious than to follow a zealous *armilogist* through all the windings and turnings into which

---

[1] Huge.   [2] Accedens, fol. 194 et seq.

his fancy leads him. I quote, by way of example, Leigh's remarks on the tincture gules or red :

"The first of these seven coloures is called Geules. And is in colour neither red nor sanguine, but is the verye vermilion itself. For that is right Geule. It is a royal colour, and hath that proper qualitie in it selfe that it may not be gased on any while. For then the eye is wekened therby. The author wherof is profe it selfe. *L.* I thincke you may be to seke for comendacion of this colour, for I have not harde muche either spoken or written in prayse of it. Can ye saye any thyng? *G.* Although it shewe itself to be commendable, yet shall it not wante my prayse. I were nere dryven to the wall, if I had no more to commende this coloure by but that where-with the Frenshe herehaughts[1] did sett forthe their Auriflamb, whiche came frome heaven, as by vaine miracle they fayne. But they that make suche shifte shulde rather have taken occasion to praise the same, for that the red rammes skinnes covered the arke. And that is no fable. Yet for my promise of comendacion, I say to you, it is and longe hath ben used of emperours and kyngs for an apparell of majestie and of judges in their judgement seates. Also God the Father, promysinge redemption to the people, by the passion of Christ, saieth, ' What is he that cometh from Edom, with redd-coloured clothes of Bosra?' which is so costly clothe. Besides this, it is often spoken of in the scripture which I leve of for lengthnynge of time. Nowe wyll I speake of the planett Mars, which is the planett that this colour appertayneth to and is of all other the hotest, and most fyrye. Martianus telleth, he is the armipotent god of battell whose hardy desire is to be avenged with spedy boldenes. Ptolomeus

---

[1] Heralds.

sayeth, this planett maketh a man apte to all firye workes.
L. If this be all the prayse you can gyve him, you will no
more offend me with tediousnes.   *G.* What nedeth more
than enoughe, can ye not understand hereby what the nature
of Mars is?   *L.* Yes, very well.   *G.* Why then I will shewe
you of the precious stone appertainyng to that colour and
planett, which is called a Rubye.   It is a stone of dignitie,
and as Isidore writeth, is of the kynde of carbuncles.   This
precious stone neither fier wasteth or changeth his colour.
This was one of the precious stones that was sett in the brest
lapp of Aron.   Of diuerse authors this is diuersely and won-
derfully commended for hys singuler vertues.   As who list
to rede may finde plentifully inoughe written thereof.   Now
to the colour simple and compounde.   Of itselfe

1, It betokeneth strength, bouldenes with hardenes.

2, with Or, a desire to conquere.

3, with Argent, envie revenged.

4, with Azure, to wynne heaven by good dedes.

5, with Sable, hateth the worlde, with werynes thereof.

6, with Verte, bould of corage in youth.

7, with Purpure, strong in dede, juste in worde, &c."

In like manner our author labours through the remaining
colours, ascribing to each some wonderful virtue.   The irrelevant nature of the observations introduced is occasionally
highly diverting.   Nature, art, metaphysics, religion, history,
are all in turn made to contribute something towards the illustration of the armilogist's theories.   In his disquisition
on Argent or silver, he remarks, " Being fine it is medici-
nable."   His imaginary friend says, " You digresse now, and
meddell with that that apperteineth not to this arte."   At
this Master Gerard waxes wroth and says, " I marvayle what

science arte or misterye it were that an herhaught sholde
have none intelligence thereof? were it never so secret or
profunde.   For, if he have not of all thynges some vnder-
standing, as well as of severall languages he is not worthye
to be an herhaught.   Therefore necessary it is for him to
have an universal knowledge in eche thinge."[1]

I can scarcely hope to interest my reader by a display of
the symbolical meaning of the colours of heraldry, yet as
perchance some one may feel gratified in being able to judge
of his or her own character and dispositions by examining
the family achievement, I will here, as briefly as possible, set
down the result of Master Leigh's philosophy, divested of its
verbiage.

Gold, then, betokens wisdom, justice, riches, and eleva-
tion of mind.   Compounded with silver, it signifies victory
over all infidels, Turks and Saracens; with gules, a disposition to shed one's blood to acquire riches; and with azure, a
disposition to keep what one gets.   Combined with sable it
typifies constancy in all things, particularly in love; with
vert, a joyful possession of riches; and with purpure a friendly
feeling even towards enemies.

Silver alone signifies chastity, charity, and a clear con-
science; but in company with
   gold—the will ' to reuenge Christ's bluddshed.'
   gules—honest boldness.
   azure—courtesy and discretion.
   sable—abstinence.
   vert—virtue (!)
   purpure—the favour of the people.

[1] Accedens. fol. 7.

GULES has already been described.   AZURE, simple, shows a godly disposition, and joined with

    gold—the joyful possession of wealth.

    silver—vigilance in service.

    gules—aptitude to reprove villany.

    sable—sympathy for suffering.

    vert—success in enterprise.

    purpure—wisdom in counsel.

SABLE betokens constancy, divine doctrine, and sorrow for loss of friends.   With

    gold, it means long life.

    silver—fame.

    gules, it excites the fear of enemies.

    azure, it shows a desire to appease strife.

    vert—joy after sorrow.

    purpure—a religious disposition till death.

VERT, *per se*, means joy, love, and gladness.   In poetry it is usually associated with these feelings.   He who bears it with

    gold, is ' all in pleasure and joy.'

    silver—a sure lieutenant.

    gules—a determined fellow.

    azure—has excess of mirth.

    sable—moderation of ditto.

    purpure—bad luck after good fortune.

PURPURE, alone, betokeneth jurisdiction, and combined with

    or—wisdom and riches.

    silver—a peaceable disposition.

    gules—policy in war.

azure—just, but unfortunate, service.
sable—'lamentable as the lapwing.'
vert—'scorpion-like.'
&c.   &c.   &c.

The ordinaries, the lines of partition, &c., according to this system, are all significant : thus the bordure signifies a siege; the fesse, command; the cheveron, great note and estimation; per bend, justice; bendy-undy, some notable enterprise achieved by water; the pile, immortal virtue; nebuly, labour and travail.   Morgan speaks of the " direct line of self-love; the flecked and wavy line of pride; the clouded line of self-conceit; the indented line of envie; the crenelle line of ambition, &c."[1]

Among common charges the rose means mercy and justice; the pomegranate, a true soldier; the billet, justice; the garb, plenty, &c.

The following queer passage occurs in Morgan :[2]

" Some of the ancients were of opinion that the forbidden fruit was an aple of green colour, which we term a pomace : but it might aswel been blew, since we term it a *hurt :* for of that colour is Becanus his Indian fig-tree, which he affirms to be the tree of the forbidden fruit : if it had been red it had been a *tortiaux,* which hath tortered her posterity ever since; if it had been an orange it was the symbole of dissimulation, by which the woman might easily be deceived : if it had been the golden aples of the sun, the pomegranates, it had purple berries within it that left a stain, being a *besant* of a waighty *guilt :* or it might have been silver, for it was fair to the eye, and was a *plate* that served the worst fruit to mankind."

---

[1] Sphere, Nobility Native, p. 101.   [2] Ibid.

Almost every heraldric animal is emblematical of the qualities of the bearer; but as, upon this principle, little honour would redound to the bearers of some species, Guillim tells us that " all sortes of animals borne in armes or ensigns must in blazoning be interpreted in the best sense, that is, according to their most generous and noble qualities, and so to the greatest honour of their bearers. For example, the fox is full of wit, and withall given wholly to filching for his prey. If then this be the charge of an escocheon we must conceive the qualities represented to be his wit and cunning, but not his pilfering and stealing."

The following list of emblematical animals and their parts may amuse some: those whose taste does not lie this way can easily pass it over.

The Ass—patience.
    Bull's head—rage.
    Goat—policy.
    Hart—skill in music.
    Horns of stags, &c.—fortitude.
    Unicorn—strength.
    Lion rampant—courage and generosity.
    Lion passant—majesty, clemency, circumspection.
    Bear—affection for offspring.
    Dog—fidelity, intelligence.
    Hedgehog—provident care.
    Grasshopper—wisdom.
    Serpent—subtlety.
    Snail—much deliberation (!)
    Stork—filial piety, gratitude.
    Eagle—a lofty spirit.
    Wings—celerity, protection.
    Owl—vigilance.

The Pelican—love of offspring.

    Swallow—industry.

    Cock—courage.

    Dolphin—charity.

    Crane—civility.

The *wolf*, according to Upton, signifies a *wrangler in parliament* or assembly!

It does not seem to have occurred to these allegorizing worthies that the tincture of a charge may be diametrically opposed to the signification assigned to the charge itself. For example, the coat, ' Vert, a bull's head or,' by the armilogical rules cited above, would signify, as to the tinctures, pleasure and joy, while as to the charge it would mean rage and fury. Again, ' Purpure, a wolf argent' would mean "a wrangler with a peaceable disposition ! !"

It was my intention to have examined this Language of Arms with more minuteness, but after a little research I find the labour ill-bestowed. He who can relish such far-fetched notions may gratify himself by a perusal of the somewhat rare folio often before quoted, Sylvanus Morgan's ' Sphere of Gentry,' London, 1661; and still further by that of his supplementary ' Armilogia,' a small quarto published in 1666. These works, with many others of this and the preceding centuries, contain much useful scientific information on Heraldry, and generally evince some scholarship, but they are most unnecessarily blended with what Mr. Moule justly designates " a cabalistic jargon,"[1] that renders it a matter of utter impossibility for any person of ordinary patience to read them through. Guillim, whose work is on the whole the most readable of the number, is not altogether free from this laboured absurdity.

---

[1] Bibl. Herald, p. 168.

One feature in many of the early works on Heraldry occasionally renders them exceedingly amusing, and may partly countervail the prosy dulness of armilogy—namely, the fancied attributes of visible objects generally, but of animals in particular. Absurdities in Natural History at which a child would now laugh are gravely advanced, and often supported by quotations from Pliny and other classical authors. A few specimens from Leigh and Guillim are subjoined.

The **Hart**, saith Avicene, " is never troubled with fevers, because he hath no gall. He hath a bone in his hert, as precious as yvery. he feareth muche the voyce of the foxe, and hateth the serpent. He is long lived. For Aristotle writeth, that Diomedes did consecrate a hart to Diana, with a coller of golde about his necke, which had these wordes, DIOMEDES DIANÆ. After whose tyme, almost a thousand yeres, Agathocles the kynge of Sicile did kill the same harte, and offered him up with his coller to Jupiter, in hys temple, which was in Calabria."[1]

" The **Bore** is the ryght Esquier, for he beareth both armor and shielde, and fighteth sternelye. When he determineth to fight, he will frot his left shield the space of halfe a day, against an oke. Because that when he is streking thereon with the tuskes of his enemy, he shal feele no griefe thereof, and when they have fought one day together then they wil depart of themselves, keping good appointment, to meete in the same place, the next day after, yea, and the third day, till one of them be victor."[2]

Of the **Wolf** he says. " It is sayde, if a man be seene of hym first, the man leseth his voyce. But if the wolfe be seene of manne first, then the wolfe leseth his boldenesse

---

[1] Accedens, fol. 90.   [2] Ib. fol. 92.

&nd hardines. Plinie wryteth, he loueth to playe with a
chylde, and that he will not hurt it, tyll he be extreame
houngry, what time he will not spare to devowre it. . . . .
Avicene telleth that he desyreth greatly to eate fishe.   And
Phisiologus writeth that he may not bend his necke backe-
warde, in no moneth of the yere but in May. . . . .   He
enfecteth the wolle of shepe that he byteth, and is adversarye
to them and theyr lambes. . . . .   There is nothynge that
he hateth so much as the knockynge together of two flint
stones, the whiche he feareth more then the hunters.
Aristotle sayeth that all kinde of wolves are contrary to all
kynde of sheepe.   For profe wherof Cornelius Agrippa also
affirmed that if a man make a string of the wolves guts and
put it on the harpe with stringes made of shepes guttes, it
will never bee brought with any consent of harmony to agree
with the other."[1]

Of the 𝕽𝖆𝖇𝖊𝖓 Guillim says : " It hath bene an ancient
received opinion, and the same also grounded upon the warrant of the sacred scriptures (if I mistake not) that such is
the propertie of the Raven, that from the time his young ones
are hatched or disclosed, untill he seeth what colour they will
be of, he never taketh care of them nor ministreth any food
unto them, therefore it is thought that they are in the meane
space nourished with the heavenly dew.   And so much also
doth the kingly prophet, David, affirme, Which giveth fodder
unto the cattell, and feedeth the young Ravens that call upon
him. Psal. 147, 9.   The Raven is of colour blacke, and is
called in Latine, Corvus, or Corax, and (according to Alexander)
hath but one kind of cry or sound which is *Cras, Cras*. When
he perceiveth his young ones to be pennefeathered and black

---

[1] Accedens, fol. 98.

like himself, then doth he labour by all meanes to foster and cherish them from thence forward."[1]

"Some report that those who rob the 𝕿𝖎𝖌𝖊𝖗 of her yong, use a policy to detaine their damme from following them by casting sundry looking-glasses in the way, whereat shee useth long to gaze, whether it be to behold her owne beauty or because when shee seeth her shape in the glasse, she thinketh she seeth one of her yong ones, and so they escape the swiftnesse of her pursuit. And thus," moralizes our author, "are many deceived of the substance, whiles they are much busied about the shadowes."[2]

The following, however, shows that Master Guillim was growing sceptical of some of the 'vulgar errours' of his day :

"Pierius, in his Hieroglyphicks saith, that if a man stricken of a 𝕾𝖈𝖔𝖗𝖕𝖎𝖔𝖓 sit upon an asse, with his face towards the taile of the asse, his paine shall passe out of him into the asse, which shall be tormented for him. In my opinion he that will beleeve this, is the creature that must be ridden in this case !"[3]

<hr/>

[1] Display, p. 230.   [2] Ibid. p. 203.   [3] Ibid. p. 215.

CHAPTER VI.

Allusive Arms—Armes Parlantes.

(Arms of the Family of Debell.)

"Non verbis sed *rebus* loquimur."

A LLUSIVE Arms are of two kinds : first, those which contain charges that relate to the character, office, or history of the original bearer ; and, secondly, those which convey a direct pun upon his name. Of the former description are the covered cups in the arms of Butler, and the bugle-horns in those of Forester.[1]   Several examples of this

---

[1] These seem originally to have been arms of office.   Their "character was strictly emblematical, and their import obvious, consisting, as they generally did, of a representation of the various official implements or ensigns."   "Little doubt can be entertained but that much of our personal heraldry is derived from such a source."   (Woodham's Application of Heraldry to the Illustration of Collegiate Antiquities, p. 79.)

species of bearings are given in the ninth chapter of this
volume under the title of ' Historical Arms.' At present, I
shall confine myself to the second class, which are called, in
Latin blazon, Arma Cantantia, in French, Armes Parlantes,
and in English, **Canting Arms.** Of this kind we have
examples in the arms of Camel, a camel; Colt, 3 colts ;
Blackmore, 3 Moor's heads, &c.

Dallaway, Porny, and other modern writers condemn this
species of bearings, as of recent origin, and unworthy of a
place amongst the classical devices of antient heraldry.
Porny places them in the category of Assumptive Arms—
" such as are taken up by the caprice or fancy of upstarts,
though of never so mean extraction." This notion, with
whomsoever it originated, is decidedly erroneous, for such
charges are found not only in the arms of distinguished
nobles and knights in the very earliest days of hereditary
armory, but occur also in those of several of the sovereign
states of Europe. According to some authors the LIS in the
royal arms of France are a play upon the name of Louis,
antiently spelt *Loys*. The arms of Spain exhibit, quarterly,
a castle and a lion——a pun upon the names of the united provinces of Castile and Leon; and after the conquest of
Granada by Ferdinand and Isabella, a *pomegranate* was
added in the base of the escocheon. As to canting charges
in the arms of subjects, we may observe that, in the earliest
Roll of Arms extant, that of the time of Henry III,[1] at
least nine such occur. To prove this assertion, as well as
to give the reader a sample of antient blazon, I shall quote
them :

---

[1] Between 1240 and 1245. (LXIV in Coll. Arm.)

" Reinold de Moun—de goules ov ung *manche* d'argent.

Nicholas de Moeles—d'argent a deux barres de goules, a trois *molets* en le cheif goules.

Geoffrey de Lucy—de goules a trois *lucies* d'or.

Roger de Merley—barree d'argent et de goulz, a la bordur d'azure, et *merlots* d'or en le bordur.

Hugh de Ferrers—*Vairre*, de argent et d'azur.

Robert Quency—de Goules ung *quintefueil* de hermyne.

Thomas Corbett—d'or deux *corbeaux* noir.

Adam de Swyneburne—de goules a trois testes de *Senglier* d'argent.

Odinel Heron—d'azur a trois *herons* d'argent.

In another Roll, made temp. Edw. II., armes parlantes are still more abundant.

Sire Peres Corbeht—de or, a ij *corbils* de sable.

Sire Robert de Eschales—de goules, a vj e*schalops* de argent.

Suthsex and Suthreye:

Sire Johan Heringaud—de azure, crusule deor a vj *harengs* (herrings) de or.

Kent:

Sire Robert de Sevens, de azure, a iij *vans* de or.

Sire Aumori de Lucy, de azure, crusule de or, a iij *lucys* de or.

Barkschire:

Sire Adam Martel, de sable, a iij *martels* de argent.

Sire William Videlou, de argent, a iij testes de *lou*, de goules.

Bokinghamschire:

Sire Rauf de Cheyndut, de azure, a un *cheyne* de or, a un label de goules.

Sire Johan LE LOU, de argent a ij barres de goules, en le chef iij testes de *lou* de goules.

Estsex :

Sire Johan Passeleu, bende de or e de azure, a un quarter de argent, e un *lu*pard *pass*-aunt de goules.

Sire Johan Heroun, de azure a iij *herouns* de argent.

Suthfolk :

Sire Guy Ferre, de goules, a un *fer*-de-molin de argent, e un bastoun de azure.

Sire Richarde de Cokfeld, de azure, a une croix e iij *coks* de or.

Sire Huge de Morieus, de azure, a iij foiles de *moures* de or.

Northfolk :

Sire ——— Mounpynzon, de argent, a un lion de sable, a un *pinzon*[1] de or en le espandle.

Cauntebrugescire :

Sire Giles de Trompintoun, de azure, crusule de or, a ij *trompes* de or.

Derby et Notingham :

Sire Johan le Fauconer, de argent a iij *faucouns* de goules.

Sire Johan Bordoun, de goules a iij *bordons* de argent.

Huntingdonschire :

Sire Johan de Swyneford, d'argent a iij testes de *cenglers* de goulys.

Norehaunton et Rotelonde :

Sire Geffrey Rossel, de or, a un cheveron azure, e iij roses de goules.

Leycestreschire :

Sire William Bernak, de argent, a une fesse and iij *bernaks* de sable.

[1] Chaffinch.

Herefordeschire :

Sire Peres Corbet, de or a un *corbyn* de sable.

Sire Thomas Corbet, de or a iij *corbyns* de sable.

Schropschire :

Sire Walter Hakelut, de goules, a iij *hackes* daneys de
or, et un daunce de argent.

Northumberland and Comberland :

Sire Odynel Heron, de argent a iij herons de azure.

Sire Johan Malebis, de argent, a iij testes de *bis* de
goules.

In addition to these, I may adduce the following very
antient families, whose arms are not traceable to any grant,
but have been borne immemorially as antient arms.   The
Pelhams bear three *pel*icans, and their crest is a *pea*cock.
The puns in both instances, it must be confessed, are very
poor; still, few will doubt that puns were intended.   The
Arundels bear six swallows, in French *hirondelles*.   The
Barons D'Aquila, temp. Henry III, bore *eagles ;*   the
Bourgchiers, water-*bowgets ;*   the Heringauds, *herrings ;*
Lupus, Earl of Chester, a *wolf's* head; Shouldham, Abbot
of St. Saviour's, *shov*ellers ;   the Bacons, a *boar ;*   the
Wingfelds, *wings;* the Rokewoods, chess-*rooks ;* the Pigots,
pick-axes ; the Boleynes, *bulls'* heads ; the Shelleys, *shells ;*
and an infinity of others.

Dame Julyan Berners was no stranger to such arms, for
she distinctly mentions the coat of Peter de Roches, bishop
of Winchester, who " baar iij rochys (roaches) after his awne
naam."   The cross-*corded*, borne by the *roper* who became
a "nobull man," spoken of by that lady, belongs to the other
class of allusive arms, as conveying a hint at his former
menial occupation.

That this kind of charges became too common in the early part of the seventeenth century, Dallaway is, perhaps, correct in affirming; but those were punning days, and quaint conceits often took the place of true wit.   Camden, the correctness of whose heraldric taste none will presume to question, did not hold *arma cantantia* in so contemptible a light as some of his successors in office have done ; for among the arms granted by him, a list of which is given by Morgan,[1] the following, among others, occur :

> DOBELL of Falmer, co. Sussex, Sable, a *doe* passant between three *bells* argent.[2]
>
> BULLOCK of London.   Bulls' heads.
>
> FOSTER of London.   Bugle-horns.
>
> HAMPSON of Kent.   Hemp-breaks.
>
> FISHER of Staffordshire.   A Kingfisher.
>
> CONIE of Huntingdonshire.   Coneys.
>
> CROWCH.[3]   Crosses formée.
>
> LANGHORN.   Bugle-horns.
>
> CANNON of Pembrokeshire.   Crest. A cannon.
>
> TREHERNE.   Three herns.
>
> CROSS of Lincolnshire.   A cross-crosslet.
>
> KNIGHTLEY.   A lance.[4]

There was a kind of Rebus much in vogue in the fourteenth and following centuries, which, although not regulated by the laws of blazon, possessed somewhat of the heraldric character.

---

[1] Sphere of Gentry.

[2] Vide cut at the head of the present chapter.

[3] Vide English Surnames, p. 72, second edit.

[4] Gibbon, Bluemantle pursuivant, who flourished subsequently to Camden, made a collection of "Allusive Arms" containing some thousands of such coats.   His MS. is in the College of Arms.

Many persons, even those of antient family, who bore regular coats of arms, adopted various figures for the purpose of expressing their names pictorially ; for instance, one John Eagleshead gave as his seal an *eagle's head*, surrounded by the motto,

" HOC AQUILÆ CAPUT EST, SIGNUMQUE FIGURA JOHANNIS."

The Abbot of Ramsay bore, in the same way, *a ram in the sea*, with an appropriate legend. One Harebottle expressed his name by a *hare* upon a *bottle;* while Islip, abbot of Westminster, represented his by a man slipping out of a tree, and supposed to exclaim, " I slip !" These " painted poesies," as Camden styles them, occur chiefly in painted glass windows, in decorated Gothic architecture, and in the title-pages of early printed books.[1]

One of the most singular rebuses I have seen occurs in a window in the chapel at Lullingstone, co. Kent, the seat of Sir P. H. Dyke, Bart. It is that of Sir John Peché. In this instance the arms of the personage are surrounded by a wreath, composed of two branches of a peach tree bearing fruit, every peach being marked with an Old English e ; Peach-é. It is curious that this device proves the true pronunciation of the name, which was formerly supposed to be Peche.

The common rebus, although it did not come into general use until after the introduction of regular heraldry, may boast of a much higher antiquity, for such devices occur as the representatives of names of no less eminence than those

[1] Vide the Chapter of Rebuses, appended to my 'English Surnames,' second edit. p. 261.

of Cicero and Cæsar; not to mention those of celebrated sculptors and mint-masters, who, in the palmiest days of Rome, frequently marked the productions of their genius with a rebus. Taking into consideration the great antiquity of these "name-devices," and their early introduction into the armorial shield, I cannot see any good reason for the strong prejudices which have existed against them in modern times. To me, indeed, they appear not only 'allowable' but 'commendable' armory; for arms, like names, are signs of personality, and therefore those which 'speak to the eye' most intelligibly are preferable to those charges which have in themselves no meaning.[1]

There can be no doubt but that, from the mutations our language has experienced within the last six centuries, many of the allusions contained in coats of arms are greatly obscured, while others are totally lost. The arms of the family of Eschales, now written Scales, exhibit eschalops (escallops), and those of Sykes, fountains—a *syke*, in the northern dialects, signifying a spring, or rather that kind of well, which was formerly sunk within the precincts of a camp.

In order to show how numerous allusive arms are in English armory, I will here give a list of those occurring in the Baronetage as it stood in 1836,[2] omitting, for the sake of brevity, the details of the blazon.

Bacon. (Crest.) A boar.
Shelley. Three whelk-*shells*.

---

[1] It is a fact not unworthy of notice that Nicholas Breakspeare (Pope Adrian IV) and William Shakspeare both bore canting-arms; the former, 'Gu, a broken spear, or;' and the dramatist, 'Argent, on a bend sable, a spear of the first.'

[2] Debrett, edited by Wm. Courthope, Esq. [now Rouge-Croix.]

BURDETT of Bramcote. Six birds (martlets).

FOULIS. Three leaves (feuilles, Fr.)

PALMER. (Crest.) A demi panther, holding a palm-branch. Motto: " Palma virtuti."

RIVERS. Two bars dancetté. Query: if these were not originally *wavy*, to represent *rivers?*

MANSELL. Three maunches.

HAZLERIGG. Three hazel-leaves.

GORING. Three annulets (rings!)

WOLSELEY. (Crest.) A wolf's head.

BURGOYNE. Three *birds* (martlets), and three talbots (*canes*).

HAMPSON. Three hemp-breaks.

SWINBURNE. (Crest.) A demi boar.

ASHBURNHAM. (Crest.) An ash tree.

BROOKE. (Crest.) A *Brock* (O. E. for badger).

BURDETT of Burthwaite. Three birds (martlets).

HEAD. Three unicorns' heads.

OXENDEN. Three oxen.

PARKER of London. A stag's head.

RAMSDEN. Three ram's heads.

COLT. Three colts.

WARRENDER. (Crest.) A rabbit.

FEATHERSTONHAUGH. Three feathers.

SHEFFIELD. Three garbs (sheaves).

CUNLIFFE. Three conies.

WOLFF. (Crest.) A wolf.

BERNARD-MORLAND. Quarters a bear.

COOTE. Three cootes.

HERON. Three herons.

SYKES. Three fountains (sykes, vide p. 126).

FLETCHER. Four arrow-heads.

BEEVOR. (Crest.) A beaver.

HUNTER-BLAIR. Three hunting horns.

MILLER. A cross moline.

CALL. Three trumpets.

GOULD. *Or,* a griffin segreant.

BARING. A bear's head.

LAMB. Three lambs.

BOUGHEY-FLETCHER. Four arrows.

TROWBRIDGE. An antient bridge.

MILNES. Three windmill-sails.

BALL. A hand-grenade.

BAYNES. Cross bones.

METCALFE. Three calves.

KAY. (Crest.) A griffin's head holding a key.

LETHBRIDGE. A bridge.

HARTWELL. A hart.

SHELLEY. Three whelk shells, as before.

LOCKHART. A heart within a fetter-lock.

FRASER. Three cinquefoils, or rather strawberry-leaves
     (Fr. *fraises*).

CORBET. A corby or raven.

WOOD of Gatton. A tree.

BAIRD. A boar.

COCKERELL. Two cocks.

FLETCHER of Carrow. Four arrow-heads.

SHEAFFE. Three garbs (sheaves).

ANDERSON. A saltier or St. Andrew's cross.

BROKE. (Crest.) A brock or badger.

WYLIE. A [*wily*] fox.

GRIFFIES-WILLIAMS. Four griffins.

WALLER. Three walnut leaves. (Crest.) A walnut tree.

OAKES. Three oak branches.

TROTTER. (Crest.) A horse!

BROOKE of Colebrook. A brock again.

DALRYMPLE-HORN (Elphinstone). Three bugle-horns.

KEY. Three keys.

FOSTER (Antiently written Forester). Three bugle-horns.

HOLYOAKE-GOODRICKE. (Crest.) An oak tree with a scroll
   containing the words " Sacra Quercus."

PAULETT. Three swords. The sword was the distinctive
   mark of St. Paul.

ROE. (Crest.) A roebuck.

A more thorough acquaintance with English archaisms and
provincialisms would probably enable one to detect numerous
other bearings corresponding with the surnames of the
bearers ; but these seventy examples, cited from one branch
of our lesser nobility only, are fully sufficient to prove that
there is nothing mean or disgraceful in canting or allusive
arms.

It would be a matter of little difficulty to fill fifty pages
with arms of this description, but a few more, and those of
the most remarkable, may be given. The family of *Still* bear
guttée d'eau, drops of water ; STILLA, Lat. a drop ; *Drope*,
Lord Mayor of London, also bore guttée; and *Harbottle*
bore three drops or. *Vere*, Earl of Oxford, gave a boar, in
Latin VERRES.

Clear, Bright, Day, and *St. Clere* bear a ' sun in splendour ;' the same luminary is also given by D*yson* and
Pear*son;* while Dela*luna* bears a crescent, and *Ster*ling
stars.

The crest of *Holden-Rose,* as given in Baker's Northamptonshire, may be briefly described as a hand HOLDING A
ROSE !

Harrison bears a hedgehog, in French *herisson ;* Pascall,
a paschal-lamb ; and Keats three cats !

And bears gules a Roman **&** argent !

Brand, Lord Dacre, bears two *brands,* or antient swords,

9

in saltire; Hose, three *legs* couped at the thigh; and Pickering, a *pike* between three *annulets*.

"Le même usage (says Salverte) a été alternativement cause et effet." We have already seen that multitudes of armorial ensigns have been borrowed from the bearers' names—it is asserted by several authors that, in many cases, *surnames were borrowed from arms.* Salverte[1] thinks that many of the chiefs who were engaged in the Crusades assumed and handed down to their posterity names allusive to the charges of their banners. He also notices, from the history of Poland, the fact that there were in that country, in the twelfth century, two families called respectively *Rose* and *Griffon,* and he thinks "we may with probability suppose, that both took from their arms those names, which no longer subsist, because hereditary surnames were not yet established in Poland." In Sweden, again, according to this learned writer, there is *proof* that the nobles followed such a practice. "One who bore in his arms the head of an ox assumed the name of OXENSTIERN (front de bœuf;) and another took the name of SPARR, on account of the cheveron which formed the principal feature of his coat."

"A particular instance of the armorial ensign being metonymically put for the bearer of it, occurs in the history of the Troubadours, the first of whom was called the Dauphin, or knight of the Dolphin, because he bore this figure on his shield. In the person of one of his successors, the name Dauphin became a title of sovereign dignity. Many other surnames were in this manner taken from arms, as may be inferred from the ordinary phraseology of romance,

[1] Essai sur les Noms, &c., I, 240.

where many of the warriors are styled knights of the lion, of the eagle, of the rose, &c., according to the armorial figures they bore on their shields."[1] At tournaments the combatants usually bore the title of Knights of the Swan, Dragon, Star, or whatever charge was most conspicuous in their arms.[2]

The arms of Trusbut are three water-bowgets, ' Très boutz.' Mr. Montagu thinks the name was taken from the bearings.[3]

The royal line of Plantagenet derived their appellation from the *Planta genesta,* their very antient badge.

There is certainly some probability that a few of our English surnames, particularly those derived from the animal kingdom, come immediately from an heraldrical source; though it would be a matter of great difficulty positively to ascertain whether the names or the arms were adopted first.

Without attempting to decide, therefore, which had the earliest existence, I shall annex certain surnames of an heraldrical character, which have found their way into our family nomenclature, and give the more prominent features of the blazon borne with those names, leaving it to the reader to form his own conclusions:

1. CROSS. Many families of this name bear crosses and crosslets.
2. SALTIRE bears billets and a bordure, but not the ordinary so called.
3. CHEVERON bears two cheverons.
4. CANTON. Several families are so designated, but not one of them bears the canton of heraldry.

[1] Brydson's Summary View of Heraldry, pp. 98-9.
[2] Menestrier.
[3] Study of Heraldry, p. 70.

5. Billet. The same remark applies.

6. Gore. In various coats, crosslets, lions and bars, but not one
    gore, the only hint at the name being *bulls' heads* in two or
    three coats.

7. Pile. A cross and four nails.

8. Mascle. Some families of *Mascall* bear barry of eight, others
    fleur-de-lis and a bordure, and the family of *Mascule*, a fesse.

9. Roundle. *Roundell* does not bear this charge.

10. Barry. Of the many families of this name some bear barry,
    bars and barulets; and Barr bears (int. al.) a *bar*.

11. Paly. Two families bear bends; but not one *paly*.

12. Delves. The family of Delves bear these in several arrangements.

Pale, Fesse, Chief, Bend, Quarter, and an infinity of
the names of charges, do not occur as English surnames.

Of the etymology of the somewhat common name
Crown-in-shield, I am entirely ignorant; nor do I find any
arms assigned to it.

(Rebus of De Aquila.)

CHAPTER VII.

Crests, Supporters, Badges, etc.

(Gilderedge. Bourchier Exmew.)

HITHERTO our attention has been principally directed to the escocheon and its charges. It now remains to treat of those heraldric ornaments which surround the shield, as crests, helmets, wreaths, mantlings, supporters, scrolls, mottoes, and badges: and first, of crests, and their accompaniments.

Every one must have remarked that when the heraldric insignia of a family are represented in full, the shield or escocheon is surmounted with a helmet, the antient covering for the warrior's head. These helmets are drawn according to certain fixed rules. Although their general shapes are as various and fanciful as those of shields, their positions, &c. are regulated by the rank of the bearers: for instance, the sovereign's helmet is of gold, full faced, and open, with six bars; that of dukes is of steel, placed a little in profile, and defended with five gold bars; that of baronets and knights is of steel, full-faced, the visor up, and without bars; and that of esquires and gentlemen is also of steel with the visor down, ornamented with gold, and placed in profile. According to some authors, the helmets of bastards should be turned to the sinister or left side, to denote their illegitimacy.[1]

Upon the top of the helmet is the *wreath*, which was originally a kind of chaplet surrounding the warrior's head. It was composed of two bands, or skeins of silk twisted together and tinctured of the principal metal and colour of the arms. The wreath is used in the majority of bearings, but occasionally a ducal coronet or a chapeau occurs instead.[2] From this ornament, whether wreath, chapeau, or coronet, rises the CREST.

The word crest appears to be derived from the Latin *crista*, the comb or tuft which grows upon the heads of many species of birds. The idea, as well as the name, was doubtless borrowed from this source. The crest was sometimes called a COGNIZANCE from cognosco, because by its means the wearer was *known* or distinguished on the field of battle.

Crests were originally worn by military commanders upon the apices of their helmets as the proud distinction of their rank; and, by adding to their apparent stature, served to give them a formidable aspect. They also enabled their soldiers to rally round their persons, and to follow their

---

[1] Berry, Encycl. Herald.

[2] The ducal coronet antiently denoted command, and the chapeau, dignity; but in their modern application they have no such meaning.

movements in the confusion of the battle. The tall plumes of birds, human heads, and figures of animals in a rampant posture, seem to have been among the earliest devices made use of.

The antiquity of crests for the uses above referred to, is far greater than that of the introduction of heraldry. The helmets of the divinities and heroes of the classical era are thus decorated. The owl on that of Minerva may be cited as an example. Jupiter Ammon is represented as having borne, as a crest, a ram's head, which Alexander the Great adopted in token of his pretended descent from that deity. The use of crests by antient warriors is alluded to by Phædrus in his fable of the battle of the mice and weasels, where the generals of the former party are represented as wearing horns fastened to their heads :

> " Ut conspicuum in prælio
> Haberent signum quod sequerentur milites."
>
> *Fab. LIII.*

In heraldry, the adoption of crests is modern compared with that of coat-armour,[1] and many families at the present time have no crests. This is easily accounted for. We have seen that they were at first used exclusively by commanders. In time, however, the spirit of imitation led persons of inferior rank to assume those of their feudal superiors ; and hence far less regularity is found in the heraldry of crests

---

[1] Edward III is the first monarch who introduced a crest (the lion statant-guardant) into his great seal. But this cannot be regarded as the first instance of the use of crests, for they appear nearly half a century earlier upon the seals of Edmund Crouchback, Earl of Lancaster. That they were in common use in Chaucer's time is obvious from the poet's description of the one borne by Sire Thopas, the tower and lily. Vide page 81.

than in that of coat-armour. In many cases crests have been borrowed from one or other of the charges of the shield : hence if the coat contain a lion rampant, the crest is frequently a demi, or half lion, or a lion's head ; and should three or six eagles occupy the shield, another eagle often serves as a crest.

With respect to the material of which the actual crests were composed, some assert that it was leather, or pasteboard stiffened and varnished, to preserve it from the wet ; but the few that I have had an opportunity of inspecting are composed of more substantial materials. Thus the crest of one of the Echingham family, ' a demi-lion rampant,' on a helmet preserved in Echingham church, co. Sussex, is of wood, and that of a knight of the Pelham family in Laughton church, in the same county, ' a peacock in his pride,' is of iron.

The crests engraved at the head of this chapter have been selected on account of their singularity.[1]

The flourished ornament behind the crest, and which is often made to encompass the entire armorial insignia, was originally either a mantle of estate, worn when the warrior was not actually engaged in battle, and tinctured of the metal and colour of his arms,[2] or from the *lambrequin*, a small piece of cloth or silk employed to protect the helmet from rain, as well as to prevent the polished steel from dazzling the eyes of the spectator. The jags and flourishes are con-

---

[1] The crest of Exmew is generally blazoned as ' a dove supporting a text r by a branch of laurel.' As to the letter, it is certainly an X, not an R ; and the bird is quite as much like a sea-gull, or MEW, as a dove. Hence a rebus upon the name was doubtless intended ꭓ-MEW ! The crest of Bourchier shows the manner in which the crest was affixed to the helmet.

[2] Herald-painters of the present day neglect this rule, and generally paint the mantlings red, doubled or lined with white or ermine.

jectured to represent the cuts which a valiant knight would
receive in battle; and hence the extravagant fashion of painting these mantlings was probably intended as a compliment to
the prowess of the bearer.

SUPPORTERS are those figures which stand on each side of
the escocheon, and appear to support, or hold it up. In
Latin blazon they are termed Talamones and Atlantes, and
in French *supports* or *tenans*. As crests are more recent
than coat-armour, so supporters are of later date than
crests.

Menestrier, the great classic of French heraldric literature,
deduces the origin of supporters from the antient tournaments, at which it was customary for the knights who
engaged in those chivalrous exercises to have shields of their
arms adorned with helmets, mantlings, wreaths, crests, and
other ornamental appendages suspended near the lists. These
were guarded by pages and armour-bearers fantastically
attired as Saracens, Moors, Giants, and Mermaids, or dis-
guised with skins to resemble lions, bears, and other animals.
The figures adopted in this kind of masquerade became afterwards the supporters of the family achievement.

As I have not had the good fortune to read Menestrier's
work, and only know it through quotations, I am unable to
ascertain by what arguments and proofs his hypothesis is
strengthened; but I may be allowed to express my doubts as
to this picturesque origin of supporters. The account of it
given by Anstis, in his Aspilogia, appears to me to be far
more probable:

" As to supporters, they were (I take it) *the invention of
the graver*, who, in cutting, on seals, shields of arms, which
were in a triangular form and placed on a circle, finding a
vacant place at each side and also at the top of the shield,

thought it an ornament to fill up the spaces with vine branches, garbs, trees, flowers, plants, ears of corn, feathers, fretwork, lions, wiverns, or some other animals, according to their fancy.[1]

" If supporters had been esteemed formerly (as at this time) the marks and ensigns of nobility, there could be no doubt but there would have been then, as now, particular supporters appropriated to each nobleman, exclusive of all others; whereas, in the seals of noblemen affixed to a paper wrote to the Pope, in the year 1300, the shields of arms of twenty-seven of them are in the same manner supported (if that term may be used) on each side by a wivern, and seven of the others by lions; that of John de Hastings hath the same wivern on each side of his shield of arms, and also on the space over it; in the manner as is the lion in the seals of Hache, Beauchamp, and De Malolacu. The seals of Despencer, Basset, and Baddlesmere, pendent to the same instrument, have each two wiverns, or dragons, for supporters; and that of Gilbert de Clare, three lions, placed in the form above mentioned. The promiscuous usage of wiverns to fill the blank in the seals is obvious to all who are concerned in these matters.

" But what is a stronger argument is, that the same sort of supporters as those here mentioned is placed in the seals of divers persons whose families were never advanced to the peerage, and who, not styling themselves knights, doubtless were not bannerets; persons of which degree (if I mistake not) now claim supporters during their lives, as well as knights of the Garter, and some great officers of state.

---

[1] In the seal of Ela, Countess of Salisbury, who was born in 1196, two lions rampant, or rather *crawling*, are introduced to fill up the spaces *on each side of the lady's effigies*. It is engraved in Sandford's Geneal. Hist.

Instances of this kind are often met with; nay, the engraver hath frequently indulged his fancy so far as to insert figures which do not seem proper, according to the present notion of supporters to arms; as two swords on each side the arms of Sir John de Harcla; and St. George fighting with the Dragon on one side, and the Virgin with Our Saviour in her arms on the other side, of a seal affixed to a deed executed by Lord Ferrers, whose arms, on the impress of a seal pendent to a deed, dated 17th May, 9° Henry VI, have not any supporters. This, as well as many other omissions of supporters, by many noblemen, in their old seals, seems likely to imply that they were not the right of the nobility exclusive of others.

"When supporters were first assumed, if there were two on one seal, they were generally the same; but sometimes there was only one, and sometimes three, as may be seen on various seals.

"The manner of placing these supporters was also very different; as sometimes, when the shield lay on the side, the supporters have been placed so as to seem to be supporting the crest, as appears in the seal of the Earl of Arundel, in which seal there is not any coronet. Some were placed all standing one way; and, if but one, it was placed sometimes on one side of the shield of arms, and sometimes on the other: sometimes, again, it was placed at the bottom, and the arms set on it; and sometimes behind, with the arms against it, and the head above the shield, and in a helmet, as in the seal of William, Lord Fitz-Hugh, 12th Henry VI."

From a MS. of Wingfeld, York Herald, deposited in the College of Arms, it appears that many families below the rank of nobility antiently used supporters, and it is asserted that the descendants of persons who used them have a right to perpetuate them, however they were acquired. Many examples are cited of commoners having used supporters from an early period : some in virtue of high offices, as those of Lords Warden of the Cinque Ports ; Comptrollers of the Household, &c. ; others without any such qualification, as, for instance, the Coverts of Sussex, the St. Legers of Kent, the Carews of Surrey, the Savages of Cheshire, the Pastons of Norfolk, &c. In the hall at Firle Place, co. Sussex, are the arms of Sir John Gage, Comptroller of the Household to Queen Mary, supported by two greyhounds. The descendants of that gentleman, long afterwards elevated to the peerage by the title of Viscount Gage, continue to use the same supporters. A few other instances of such resumption occur.

By a singular anomaly the Baronets of Nova Scotia are allowed by their patents of creation to carry supporters, while the English Baronets, their superiors both in dignity and antiquity, have not that privilege. Some of these, however, as well as distinguished naval and military commanders, have, at various times, received the royal license to use them.

I have attempted, in vain, to collect an authentic list of the supporters of the royal arms of England from the time of Edward III, when, according to some authors, they were first assumed. There are discrepances in the authorities which are not easily accounted for. They are seldom agreed upon those of any early sovereign. For example, Berry gives Richard II a lion and a hart ; Fosbroke says, *two angels*, and makes him the first king who adopted supporters. Henry IV, according to Nisbet, had two angels ; Dallaway says, a lion and an antelope ; and Sandford, a swan and an antelope ! To Henry V, Nisbet assigns two antelopes, while Willement, out of Broke, gives him the lion and antelope. The probability is that all parties are right, each having reference to a particular instance in which the respective supporters are employed. One thing is certain, that while the colours and charges of the shield have remained unchanged from a very early date, the supporters have experienced many vicissitudes. Edward IV changed his supporters at least three times; and until the reign of James I, when the lion and unicorn became stationary, the royal supporters do not seem to have been regarded as part of the *hereditary* ensigns of the kingdom.[1]

I shall only add on this subject some extraordinary fashions in the use of supporters. I am inclined to think that these adjuncts to arms originated, partly, in the corbels of Gothic architecture, on which shields are frequently supported in the hands of angels.[2] Numerous instances of this kind occur in antient churches and halls built in the decorated style. Sometimes these angels are vested in terrene habiliments, as in the annexed cut, from a drawing of a sculptured stone among the ruins of Robertsbridge Abbey.

Shields of arms are sometimes supported by a single animal, as in the case of the arms of Prussia, where an eagle with two heads performs that duty. Several instances of arms borne upon the breast of an eagle are found in English heraldry: the following occur to my recollection, namely, those of

---

[1] The following are the royal supporters, as given in Sandford's Genealogical History: Richard II, two angels; Henry IV, swan and antelope; Henry V, lion and antelope; Henry VI, two antelopes; Edward IV, lion and bull; Edward V, lion and hind; Richard III, two boars; Henry VII, dragon and greyhound; Henry VIII, lion and dragon; Edward VI, lion-guardant crowned and dragon; Mary, eagle and lion; Elizabeth, as Edward VI; James I, &c. lion and unicorn, as at present.

[2] According to Nisbet, the earliest royal supporters of England were two angels. The transition from one angel to two, and from two angels to two quadrupeds is very natural.

Richard Earl of Cornwall, brother of Henry III,[1] those
of the Lathams of Latham, in the fourteenth century,[2]
and those of John le Bray, on his seal attached to a
deed dated 1327.[3] A curious instance of this kind of
supporter occurs in the arms of the lord of the manor of
Stoke-Lyne, co. Oxon. The figure employed in this case
is neither angel nor eagle, but a hawk. When Charles I
held his parliament at Oxford, the then lord of Stoke-Lyne
having rendered him an important service, the king offered
him the honour of knighthood, which he gratefully declined,
and merely requested the royal permission to place the arms
of his family upon the breast of a hawk. This being granted,
the lords of the manor have ever since employed a hawk
displayed as their supporter.[4]

There is another species of supporter, the use of which seems to
have been almost restricted to the
fifteenth and sixteenth centuries, and
which is seldom noticed in our books
of heraldry. The arms are represented upon a banner, the staff of
which is supported by an animal in
a rampant, or, more usually, in a
sejant, posture. The arms of Sir
Roger Fynes, Treasurer of the Household to Henry VI, are thus represented over the great gate of Hurst-
monceux castle, built by him. The
supporter is the *alaunt,* or wolf-dog,[5]

[1] C. S. Gilbert's Cornwall, pl. 3.   [2] Ormerod's Cheshire.
[3] Archæologia, vol. xxx.   [4] Hone's Table Book.
[5] In the above sketch I have ventured to supply the head which in the original
is wanting.

and the scroll round the pole seems to have contained a motto, which is now illegible.

Some very singular supporters occur in French heraldry. Under the *ancien régime* the arms of most of the great officers of state were supported by ensigns emblematical of their various duties; for example—

Officers.	*Supporters.*
The Admiral of France bore	Two anchors.
Vice-Admiral,	One anchor in pale behind the shield.
Great Huntsman,	Two bugles at the dext. and sin. bases of the shield.
Grand Master of Artillery,	Two mounted cannons at ditto.
Grand Marshal,	At the base of the shield a cloud, from the dexter side of which proceeds a hand holding a sword in pale, and from the sinister, another hand holding a baton of office.
Grand Louvetier, (Wolf-hunter,)	Two wolves' heads at the base corners of the shield.
Grand Esquire,	Two swords in pale with sashes.
Grand Butler,	Two bottles ornamented with the royal arms.

The most singular supporters, perhaps, in the whole circle of heraldry are those of the noble French family of Albret. Two lions couchant, wearing helmets, support the lower part of the shield, and, above, are two eagles, each standing with one foot upon the head of the lion, while with the other he holds the upper part of the escocheon. The French armorists make a distinction between *supports* and *tenans:* in this instance the lions are known by the former term, and the eagles by the latter.

Mottoes will form the subject of a short separate chapter: it therefore only remains, in this brief view of extra-scutal insignia, to notice BADGES.

Some families, as has already been observed, have no crests; a still greater number have no mottoes; and supporters belong to an exclusive few. Badges are still more unusual, and in modern times it would perhaps be a matter of difficulty to enumerate twenty families who use them.

Badge, in its ordinary acceptation, signifies the mark or token of any thing; thus we are accustomed to call fetters the *badge* of slavery, and a plain gold ring the *badge* of matrimony; and thus in a figurative, or moral sense, Shakspeare says,

"Sweet mercy is nobility's true *badge.*"

The word is of uncertain etymology. Junius derives it from 'bode,' or 'bade,' a messenger, and supposes it to be a *contractio per crasin* from 'badage,' the credential of a messenger. Skinner and Minsheu, again, deduce it from 'bagghe,' Dutch, a jewel, or from 'bague,' French, a ring.

But Johnson, with more reason, considers it a derivative of the Latin ' *bajulo,*' to carry.

> " But on his breast a bloody cross he bore,
>   The dear resemblance of his dying lord ;
>   For whose sweet sake that glorious *badge* he wore."
>
> *Spenser.*

In heraldry, *badges* are a kind of subsidiary arms used to commemorate family alliances, or some territorial rights or pretensions.[1] Sometimes, also, and perhaps more generally, they serve as trophies of some remarkable exploit achieved by an ancestor of the bearer. In the feudal ages most baronial families had their peculiar badges, and their dependents were recognized by having them embroidered upon their sleeves or breasts. They were generally placed upon a ground tinctured of the livery colours of the family.[2] Something analogous to this fashion is retained in the crest which adorns the buttons of our domestic servants, and still more so in the badges by which the firemen and watermen of London are distinguished. Badges were also employed in various other ways, as, for example, on the furniture of houses, on robes of state, on the caparisons of horses, on seals, and in the details of gothic edifices. An instance of the various applications of the badge of one noble family has been familiar to me from childhood—the Buckle, the badge assumed by Sir John de Pelham in commemoration of his having been

---

[1] Montagu, Guide, p. 48.

[2] The coat-armour of a great family was of too sacred a character to be used as the personal ornament or distinction of their retainers, the private herald only excepted ; and it was long ere this functionary was allowed to invest himself in his master's armorials.

principally concerned in the capture of John, king of France, at the battle of Poictiers.[1] This trophy occurs, as an appendage to the family *arms*, into which it is also introduced as a quartering; on the *ecclesiastical buildings* of which the family were founders, or to which they were benefactors;[2] on the architectural ornaments of their *mansions* at Laughton, Halland, &c.; on antient *seals;* as the *sign of an inn* near their estate at Bishopstone, &c.; and among the humbler uses to which the BUCKLE has been applied may be mentioned the decoration of the cast-iron chimney-backs in the farmhouses on the estate, the embellishment of milestones, and even the marking of sheep. Throughout the whole of that part of eastern Sussex over which the Pelham influence extends there is no 'household word' more familiar than the 𝔓𝔢𝔩𝔥𝔞𝔪 𝔅𝔲𝔠𝔨𝔩𝔢.[3]

The following are the badges of a few other antient families :

The Lords Hungerford used a golden garb, which seems to have been taken from the arms of the Peverells, whose co-heiress married William Lord Hungerford, temp. Henry V. They were ' Azure, three garbs or.'

Edward Lord Hastings, who married the grand-daughter and heiress of the peer just named, bore on his standard the

---

[1] Vide Chapter IX.

[2] Viz. Warbleton Priory, Robertsbridge Abbey, and the churches of Thundridge, (co. Herts.), Crowhurst, Burwash, Laughton, Chiddingly, Ripe, East Hothly, Wartling, and Dallington. As a proof of the value of heraldric insignia in ascertaining the founders of antient buildings, it may be remarked that, so far as I am aware, the Buckles which adorn the whole of the *churches* here enumerated, furnish the only evidence (and most irrefragable evidence it must certainly be admitted to be) that the family of Pelham were concerned in their erection or enlargement. There are *histories* as well as ' sermons' ' in stones!'

[3] From a Paper on the ' Pelham Buckle' read before the first meeting of the Archæological Association at Canterbury, 11th September, 1844.

garb with a sickle—another badge of the Hungerfords—united by a golden cord.

John de Willoughby de Eresby, temp. Edward III, used two buckles, which he probably borrowed from the arms of his wife, the heiress of Roceline: 'Gules, crusily and three buckles argent.'

One of the Nevilles, Lords Bergavenny, bore two badges: first, two staples interlaced, one gold, the other silver; and second, a fret gold: these occur on a tomb at Mereworth, co. Kent.[1]

The badge of the Lords Dacre was an escallop united to a ragged staff, as in the margin.

The family of Parr used a tuft of daisies; and the Percies a silver crescent:

> "The minstrels of thy noble house,
>   All clad in robes of blue,
>   With silver crescents on their arms,
>   Attend in order due."
>
> *Hermit of Warkworth.*

In the 'Rising of the North Countrie' this badge and the *dun bull* of the Nevilles are mentioned. Of the latter we are told:

> "Lord Westmoreland his ancyent raysde,
>   The *dun bull* he rays'd on hye,
> And three dogs with golden collars,
>   Were there set out most royallye."[2]

Mowbray, Duke of Norfolk, used the punning device of

---

[1] Montagu.

[2] The dogs here alluded to were greyhounds, a Yorkist badge.

lions and *mulberry*-trees; and Vere, Earl of Oxford, a long-necked silver bottle, with a blue cord, allusive to his hereditary post of lord high chamberlain.

Sometimes these insignia answered the double purpose of the crest and the badge. Some badges, however, as Mr. M. remarks, are not at all suitable for crests. This applies particularly to *Knots*, which were composed either of silk, or of gold and silver lace, and were antiently a favourite species of badge. The families of Harrington, Wake, Bouchier, Stafford, Heneage, and others, each bore a peculiar knot.

The regal heraldry of this country is peculiarly rich in badges. Mr. Montagu has, with great research, compiled a nearly perfect list of them from William Rufus to James I, to which the reader who desires further information on this subject is referred.[1] Meantime I shall notice a few of the most celebrated.

The broom-plant, or *planta-genesta*, was introduced by Henry II. From this badge the illustrious line of Plantagenet derived their surname. The story of its origin, be it true or false, is well known.

The first monarch who assumed the rose was Edward I, who bore the flower or, the stalk green. From this, in some way as yet unexplained, probably originated the white and red roses of his descendants, the rival houses of York and Lancaster. Richard II adopted the white hart and white falcon, both of which afterwards became the titles of pursuivants. The white swan of Henry IV is said to have been derived from the Bohuns, Earls of Hereford, the family of his first wife. The double S,[2] concerning which so much con-

[1] Guide, p. 59.

[2] Still retained in the collar of SS.

jecture has been wasted, was another badge of this monarch.

"The device of Margaret of Anjou, Queen of Henry VI, was a daisy, in allusion to her name :

> ' The daise a floure white and rede,
> In French called la belle Margarete.'
>
> Chaucer."

The extensive use of badges by the retainers of princes is shown by the order of Richard III for the making of thirteen thousand *boars* "wrought upon fustian," to be used at his coronation.

The rose and portcullis are amongst the most familiar of royal badges. These were used by the Tudors. The Tudor rose was a blending of the white and red roses of the two factions, united in this line of sovereigns. The portcullis came originally from the family of Beaufort. James I combined the dexter half of the Tudor rose with the sinister moiety of the Scottish thistle, ensigned with a crown. At present, when the badges of the three kingdoms are represented with the royal arms, little attention is paid to heraldric propriety. The rose, shamrock, and thistle are figured, not *secundum artem*, but according to the fancy of the painter.

Henry VIIIth's regard to heraldric matters is shown by his giving to pieces of ordnance names corresponding with the titles borne by the officers of arms.[1] This is further exemplified by the names he gave the ships composing his fleet, as Hart, Antelope, Tegar, and Dragon. The smaller vessels were mostly distinguished by the names of the royal

[1] Vide Chapter XI.

badges, such as the Fawcon and Fetterlock, Portquilice, Hynde, Double-Rose, Hawthorn,[1] &c.[2] Some of these badges are still retained as signs of inns, particularly the Swan and White-Hart, both of which should be ducally gorged and chained, though these appendages, from the ignorance of sign-painters, are frequently omitted.

[1] The 'Hawthorn' is probably the 'crown in a bush,' used in conjunction with the letters 🝔.🝔. as the badge of Henry VII. This badge originated in the finding of the crown of Richard III in a bush after the battle of Bosworth-Field. (Vide Fosbroke's Encycl. of Antiq. p. 757.)

[2] Montagu, p. 75, from a MS. in the Pepys. Lib. Cambridge.

(Abbot Islip's Rebus, vide p. 125)

CHAPTER VIII.

Heraldric Mottoes.

"We ought to be meek-spirited till we are assured of the honesty of our ancestors; for covetousness and circumvention make no good *motto* for a coat."

Collier.

A MOTTO is a word, or short sentence, inserted in a scroll placed generally under a coat of arms, and occasionally over the crest. The word is Italian, and equivalent to *verbum*. As usual with things of long standing, a variety of opinions exists as to the origin of these pithy and interesting appendages to family ensigns. It would be erroneous to suppose that mottes belong exclusively to Heraldry, for they are of much more antient date than the first outline of that system.   Both sacred and profane history furnish us with proofs of their very early use.   The declaration of the Almighty to Moses,[1] " I am that I am," may be regarded as a motto expressive of the immutability of the Divine perfections.   Among mankind, mottoes must have been chosen to express the predominant feelings of piety, love, moral virtue, military courage, and family pride, as soon as those feelings manifested themselves, that is to say, in the earliest stages of social existence.   Without tarrying to enter into the philosophy of this subject, it will be sufficient for us here to inquire in what way these brief expressions of sentiment became the almost indispensable adjunct to the armorial honours of individuals and of families.

The origin of heraldric mottoes might probably be traced to two sources, in themselves diametrically opposed to each other; I mean Religion and War.   " Extremes," we are told, " sometimes meet," and certainly these two feelings did coalesce in the institutions of chivalry, if we may be allowed to prostitute the holy name of religion by identifying it with the frenzy which possessed the human mind in such enterprises as the Crusades.   It is uncertain whether we ought to deduce the origin of mottoes from those devout ejaculations, such as ' 𝔇𝔯𝔢𝔡𝔢 𝔊𝔬𝔡!'—'𝔍𝔢𝔰𝔲 𝔪𝔢𝔯𝔠𝔶—𝔏𝔞𝔡𝔶 𝔥𝔢𝔩𝔭𝔢,' which occur on antient tombs, or from the *word of onset*, employed by generals on the battle-field to stimulate their soldiers to great feats of prowess.   The preponderance in point of number of religious mottoes would incline us to the former supposition; but the general opinion of our best

---

[1] Vide Exodus, iii, 14.

authors favours a military origin. The war-cry, known in
Latin as the *Clamor militaris*, in French as the *Cri de guerre*,
and in the Scottish language as the *Slughorn*, or *Slogan*, is
of very remote antiquity. In early scripture history we have
an example in " The sword of the Lord and of Gideon," the
word of onset employed by the Hebrews against the Midianites
in the valley of Jezreel.[1] Among barbarous nations at the
present day it has its representative in the war-whoop, or
yell, employed as well to animate the courage of their own
party as to inspire terror in the hearts of their enemies.
From an early period the phrase ' a boo !' was employed by
the Irish for these purposes. This expression, in course of
time, became the motto of many of the great families of that
island, with the adjunct of their surname or the name of their
chief fortress. Hence the ' *Crom a boo*' of the Earls of
Leinster; the ' *Shanet a boo*' of the Earls of Desmond; the
'*Butler a boo*' of the Butlers; the ' *Galriagh a boo*' of the
Bourkes, Lords Clanricarde, &c. &c. In England, France,
and other countries, an invocation of the patron saints,
St. George, St. Denis, &c. constituted the war-cry of the
common cause; but in intestine wars each party had their
separate cry, and every commander urged on his forces by
the well-recognized shout of his own house. That this practice prevailed in England so recently as the close of the
fifteenth century appears from an Act of Parliament, passed
in the tenth year of Henry VII, to abolish these cries as
productive of rancour among the nobles, who, with their retainers, were thenceforth enjoined to call only upon St. George
and the king.

The following are some of the antient *cris-de-guerre* :

---

[1] Vide Judges, vii, 18.

The kings of France, 'Montjoye[1] St. Denis!'

The kings of England, 'Montjoye Notre Dame, St. George!'

Edward III (in a skirmish near Calais) 'Ha! St. Edward! Ha! St. George!'

The dukes of Burgundy, 'Montjoye St. Andrew!'

The kings of Scotland, 'St. Andrew!'

The dukes of Normandy, 'Dieu aye!' (aide.)

The emperors of Germany, 'A dextre et a sinistre!'

The counts of Milan, 'Milan the Valiant!'

The counts of Hainault, 'Hainault the Noble!'

The use of mottoes became very fashionable in England from the example of Edward III. The motto of the Garter, '𝕳𝖔𝖓𝖎 𝖘𝖔𝖎𝖙 𝖖𝖚𝖎 𝖒𝖆𝖑 𝖞 𝖕𝖊𝖓𝖘𝖊,' with the order itself, dates from this reign.[2] Edward made use of various mottoes suited to different occasions and circumstances. Many of these are now obscure, and appear destitute of point, such as 'It is as it is,' embroidered upon a white linen doublet made for this king. Others are more easily understood, as the daring and profane couplet wrought upon his surcoat and shield, provided to be used at a tournament:

> " 𝕳𝖆𝖕, 𝖍𝖆𝖕, 𝖙𝖍𝖊 𝖂𝖞𝖙𝖍𝖊 𝕾𝖂𝖆𝖓;
> 𝕭𝖞 𝕲𝖔𝖉𝖊'𝖘 soul 𝕴 am 𝖙𝖍𝖞 𝖒𝖆𝖓!"

Mottoes upon antient seals are extremely rare. Mr. Montagu says, "I have examined many hundred early seals

---

[1] By *Montjoye* is supposed to be intended the national banner, on which the figure of some saint was embroidered.

[2] The motto of the royal arms, 'Dieu et mon droit,' is older, and is ascribed to Richard I.

and engravings and drawings of seals preserved in the British Museum, and I know but of about half a dozen . . . . One is of the year 1418, inscribed 'SIGILLUM JEAN DE JUCH,' and contains the motto 𝕭𝖎𝖊𝖓 𝕾𝖚𝖗. Perhaps the very earliest instance of a motto anywhere is afforded by the seal of Sir John de Byron, appended to a deed dated 21ᵒ Edward I."[1] The motto here is CREDE BERONTI, surrounding the arms.[2]

Many mottoes retain their original orthography, and stand in Old English or Old French. The greater number are Latin or French, though we occasionally see mottoes in Welsh, Irish, Cornish, Scottish, and Italian; and I have even met with two or three in Greek.

Mottoes have been divided into three sorts: the enigmatical, the sentimental, and the emblematical. A better classification might probably suggest itself; but, in the absence of one, I shall make use of this in the examples which follow.

The ENIGMATICAL are those whose origin is involved in mystery, as that of the Duke of Bedford, "Che sara, sara," *What will be, will be;* and that of the Duke of Bridgewater, "Sic donec," *Thus until——!* A late barrister used "Non Bos in Lingua," *I have no Bull upon my Tongue!* alluding to the Grecian didrachm, a coin impressed with that animal, and expressive, probably, of the bearer's determination not to accept a bribe.[3] The motto of the Lords Gray was *"Anchor, fast anchor,"* and that of the Dakynses, of Derbyshire, " 𝖘𝖙𝖗𝖎𝖐𝖊 𝕯𝖆𝖐𝖞𝖓𝖘; 𝖙𝖍𝖊 𝕯𝖊𝖛𝖎𝖑'𝖘 𝖎𝖓 𝖙𝖍𝖊 𝕳𝖊𝖒𝖕𝖊"— enigmatical enough, certainly!

[1] Guide, p. 56.
[2] The modern motto of the family is ' Crede Biron.'
[3] ' Per linguam bos inambulat.' Ant. proverb.

SENTIMENTAL mottoes are very numerous. A multitude of them are of a religious character, as "Spes mea in Deo," My hope is in God; "In Deo salutem," In God I have salvation; "Sola virtus invicta," Virtue alone is invincible; "Non mihi, sed Christo," Not to myself, but to Christ; "Sub Cruce," Under the Cross. Many are loyal and patriotic, as "Vincit amor patriæ," Love of country conquers; "Non sibi sed patriæ," Not for himself, but for his country; "Patria cara, carior Libertas," My country is dear, but my liberty is dearer. Others are philanthropic, as "Homo sum," I am a man; "Non sibi solum," Not for himself alone. Treffry of Cornwall used ' 𝔚𝔥𝔶𝔩𝔢 𝔊𝔬𝔡 𝔴𝔶𝔩𝔩𝔢,' and Cornwall of the same county, ' 𝔚𝔥𝔶𝔩𝔢 𝔩𝔶𝔣𝔣 𝔩𝔞𝔰𝔱𝔢𝔱𝔥.'

But the most curious class of mottoes are the EMBLEMATICAL, some of which allude to the charges in the arms, and others to the surname, involving a pun. Of those allusive to the arms or crest, the following are examples: That of the Earl of Cholmondeley is "Cassis tutissima virtus," Virtue the safest helmet; alluding to the helmets in his arms: and that of the Egertons, "Leoni, non sagittis fido," I trust to the lion, not to my arrows; the arms being a lion between three pheons or arrow-heads. The crest of the Martins of Dorsetshire was an ape, and their motto, HE . WHO . LOOKS . AT . MARTIN'S . APE, MARTIN'S . APE . SHALL . LOOK . AT . HIM !

Much wit, and, occasionally, much absurdity are found in punning mottoes. That the soundness of a sentiment is not necessarily injured, however, by the introduction of a pun, is proved by such mottoes as these :—

ADDERLEY of Staffordshire. *Addere Le*-gi Justitiam Decus. 'Tis a support to the Law to add Justice to it.

FORTESCUE (E.) *Forte Scu*-tum salus ducum. A strong shield is the safety of commanders.

PETYT. Qui s'estime *petyt* deviendra grand. He who esteems himself little shall become great.

JEFFERAY of Sussex. *Je feray* ce que je diray. I shall keep my word.

Some mottoes are intentionally ambiguous, as—

HONE of Ireland. *Honesta* Libertate, OR, *Hone*, sta Libertate. With a just Liberty, OR, Hone, support liberty!

VERNON. *Vernon* semper viret, OR, *Ver non* semper viret; Vernon ever flourishes, OR, Spring does not always bloom.

By far the greater number, however, exhibit punning for its own sake; for example—

BELLASISE. Bonne et *belle assez.* Good and handsome enough.

CAVE of Northamptonshire. *Cave!* Beware!

D'OYLEY of Norfolk. '𝕯𝖔' 𝖓𝖔 '𝖕𝖑𝖑,' 𝖖𝖚𝖔𝖙𝖍 𝕯𝖔𝖞𝖑𝖊!

DIXIE of Leicestershire. Quod *dixi dixi.* What I've said I have said.

ESTWICK. *Est hic.* Here he is.

FAIRFAX. Fare, fac! Speak, do! (A word and a blow!)

HART of Berks. Un cœur fidelle. A faithful *heart.*

ONSLOW. Festina lentè. *On slow!* OR, Hasten cautiously.

PIEREPONTE. *Pie repone te.* Repose piously.

SCUDAMORE. *Scutum amor*is divini. The shield of Divine Love.

COURTHOPE. *Court hope!*

Here is a *truism:*

VERE Earl of Oxford. *Vero* nil *verius.* Nothing truer than truth.

And here a *Cockneyism :*

WRAY of Lincolnshire. Et juste et *vray.*   Both just
and true.

" *Set on !"* says SETON, Earl of Wintoun ; " *Boutez en
avant !"* Lead forward ! says Viscount Buttevant ;

> ' 𝔉𝔦𝔤𝔥𝔱 𝔬𝔫,' 𝔮𝔲𝔬𝔱𝔥 𝔉𝔦𝔱𝔱𝔬𝔫!
> ' 𝔖𝔪𝔦𝔱𝔢,' 𝔮𝔲𝔬𝔱𝔥 𝔖𝔪𝔦𝔱𝔥!

Pugnacious fellows !

Many a gibe has found vent in a motto.   A London
tobacconist who had set up his carriage, requiring a motto
for his arms, was furnished with " QUID *rides ?"* Why do
you laugh ? and a great hop-planter found the following
chalked beneath the arms upon his chariot :

> " Who'd 'a thought it,
>   *Hops* had bought it ?"

Dr. *Cox Macro,* the learned Cambridge divine, consulting
a friend on the choice of a motto, was pithily answered with
" *Cocks may crow !"*

There are some 'lippes,' as Camden says, which like ' this
kind of lettuce.'   For the behoof of such the following list
is set down, without regard to any classification :

CAVENDISH.   *Cavendo* tutus.   Safe by caution.

CHARTERIS, Earl. (Crest, an arm brandishing a sword ;
over it) This *is* our *Charter !*

FANE, Earl of Westmoreland.   *Ne vile* FANO. Dishonour
not the temple.   The first and second words allude
to his descent from the family of *Neville.*

GRAVES of Gloucestershire.   *Graves* disce mores. Learn
serious manners.

COLE. Deum *cole*, Regem serva. Fear God, serve the King.

JAMES. *J'aime jamais.* I love ever.

COLLINS. *Colens* Deum et Regem. Reverencing God and the King.

MAJOR of Suffolk. (Arms, three Corinthian columns.) Deus *major* columnâ. God is a greater support than pillars.

WAKE of Somersetshire. *Vigila* et ora. *Watch* and pray.

PUREFOY of Leicestershire. *Pure foy* ma joye. Sincerity is my delight.

RIVERS of Kent. Secus rivos aquarum. By the rivers of waters.

POLE of Devon. *Pollet* virtus. Virtue bears sway.

TEY of Essex. *Tais* en temps. Be silent in time.

WISEMAN of Essex. Sapit qui Deum sapit. He is *wise* who is wise towards God.

PAGITT of Surrey. *Pagit* Deo. He covenants with God.

MAYNARD, Viscount. *Manus* justa *nardus*. A just hand is a precious ointment.

MOSLEY of Northumberland. *Mos legem* Regis. Agreeable to the King's law.

ROCHE, Viscount de Rupe, &c. Mon Dieu est ma *Roche*. My God is my Rock.

VINCENT. *Vincenti* dabitur. It shall be given to the conqueror.

VYVYAN. Dum *vivimus vivamus*. While we live, let us live.

TEMPLE, Viscount Cobham. *Templa* quam dilecta. How beloved are thy *Temples!*

ALGOOD. Age omne bonum. Do *all good.*

Having *drawn* thus largely upon the humour of motto-coiners, and, perchance, upon the patience of those readers who can *draw* no amusement from such conceits, I now *draw* this chapter to a close, by quoting the motto of the antient company of the *wire-drawers* of the city of London, which is, Latinè, "Amicitiam *trahit* amor," and Anglicè, Love *draws* friendship!

(Conjectural origin of the Pile, p 63)

CHAPTER IX.

Historical Arms—Augmentations.

(Badge of Pelham.)

"In perpetuum per gloriam vivere intelliguntur."

Justinian.

BY Historical Arms I mean those coats which, upon the
testimony either of record or tradition, have been acquired by an act of the original bearer, and which exhibit
some trophy or circumstance connected therewith to the eye
of the spectator. AUGMENTATIONS are marks of honour,
granted by the sovereign, and *superadded* to the paternal

11

arms; and borne, for the most part, upon a canton or inescocheon, sometimes upon a chief, fesse, or quarter. This
class of arms, the most interesting in the whole range of
heraldry, has been subdivided into eight kinds; viz. 1, Those
derived from acts of valour; 2, From acts of loyalty; 3, From
royal and other advantageous alliances; 4, From favour and
services; 5, From situation; 6, From profession, &c.; 7, From
tenure and office; and 8, From memorable circumstances
and events.[1]

It may be almost unnecessary to observe, that many of
the anecdotes about to be related are of a very apocryphal
description, referring to periods antecedent to the introduction of armorial bearings. Some of these, however, may be
correct in the incidents though incorrect in point of time;
and doubtless, in many cases, the arms have been assumed
in rather modern times, to commemorate the exploits of ancestors of a much earlier period; the highly-prized family
tradition having been confided to the safer custody of the
emblazoned shield. At all events, I deliver them to the
reader as I find them set down in 'myne authoures,' and leave
the *onus probandi* to the families whose honour is concerned
in their perpetuation.

First among these pictorial mementoes should be noticed
the well-known cognizance of the Prince of Wales, the Ostrich
Feathers, the popular origin of which is known to every school-

---

[1] Vide 'The Principal Historical and Allusive Arms borne by Families of the
United Kingdom; collected by an Antiquary,' quarto, Lond. 1803. Moule says,
" But few copies of the work were sold, and the remaining impressions were
destroyed in the fire at the printing-office, which has rendered it *a particularly
scarce book.*" (Bibl. Herald., p. 497.) On this account I am induced to make
extensive use of the volume, and to carry this chapter much beyond my original
intention.

boy. Whether the King of Bohemia fell by the trenchant blade of the Black Prince himself, or by that of some knight or ' squier of lowe degree,' it would now be useless to inquire; and whether the feathers and the mottoes, **Jch Dien** and **Houmout,** signifying respectively in old German, ' I serve,' and 'A haughty spirit,' had any relation to that event is altogether a matter of dubiety. It has been shown by Mr. J. G. Nichols[1] that the King of Bohemia used (not ostrich feathers, but) a pair of vulture's wings as a crest. It further appears that the *badge* of the Black Prince was *a single feather*, while, on his tomb at Canterbury, the *three* feathers are represented singly upon a shield, the quill of each being attached to a scroll, with the motto ICH . DIENE. The popular version of the story, however, is somewhat supported by the fact that an ostrich, collared and chained, with a nail in his beak, was a badge of the Bohemian monarchs; and Mr. Nichols suggests that the feathers may probably have been adopted by Edward as a trophy of his victory. Randle Holme deduces the three ostrich feathers from a totally different source, and asserts that they were the ensign of the princes of Wales during the independence of that country, prior to the invasion of the English. After this event, (he adds) the eldest sons of the kings of England, as princes of Wales, continued the badge ensigned with a coronet, with the motto, 'Ich Dien,' I serve; to express the sentiment that, although of paramount dignity in that country, they still owed allegiance to the crown of England.[2] It is asserted by other authorities that a single ostrich feather was borne as a badge by Edward III, by all the brothers and descendants of the Black Prince, and by Thomas Mowbray, duke of Norfolk, who was descended

[1] Archæologia, xxix.
[2] Harl. MS. 2035.

by the female line from Thomas de Brotherton, fifth son of
Edward I.   In the Harl. MS. 304, we are told that,

"𝕿𝖍𝖊 ostrich fether, sylber, and pen gold, is the King's.
𝕿𝖍𝖊 ostrich fether, pen and all sylber, is the Prince's.
𝕿𝖍𝖊 ostrich fether, gold, y𝖊 pen ermyne, is the Duk of Lancaster's.
𝕿𝖍𝖊 ostrich fether, sylber, and pen gobone, is the Duk of
        Somersett's."

Who has not heard of the '𝕭𝖊𝖆𝖗 𝖆𝖓𝖉 𝖗𝖆𝖌𝖌𝖊𝖉 𝖘𝖙𝖆𝖋𝖋'
of the earls of Warwick?   This is a combination of two
badges of that antient line, which sprang, according to the
family tradition, from Arthgal, one of the knights of King
Arthur's 'Round Table.'   *Arth* or *Narth*, in the British
language, is said to signify a bear; hence this ensign was
adopted as a rebus or play upon his name.   Morvidus, another
earl of the same family, a man of wonderful valour, slew a
giant with a young tree torn up by the roots and hastily
trimmed of its boughs.   In memory of this exploit his successors bore as their cognizance a silver staff in a shield of
sable.[1]

The supporters of the Scottish family of Hay, earls of
Errol, are two husbandmen, each carrying an ox-yoke.   In
the year 980, when the Danes invaded this island, an engagement took place at Longcarty, near Perth, in which
Kenneth III was routed.   An honest yeoman, yclept John
de Luz, and his two sons, were ploughing in a field hard by
the scene of action.   Seeing their countrymen fly before the
victorious enemy, these stalwart ploughmen stopped them in
a narrow pass with the gear of their ploughs, and upbraiding

---

[1] " Arthgal, the first Earl of Warwick, in the days of King Arture, and was one
of the Round Table; this Arthgal took a *bere* in his arms, for that, in Britisch,
soundeth a bere in English."   (Leland's Collect.)

them with cowardice induced them to stand the brunt of a new attack. The Danes, astonished at this unexpected turn of affairs, which they attributed to the arrival of fresh succours, wheeled about and made a hasty retreat, and the Scots obtained a signal victory. Kenneth, to reward the valour of his faithful subject, gave him as much land in the district of Gowrie, as a falcon, flying from his fist, should measure out before he perched. Hence the supporters and the crest (a falcon rising) of this family. The earls of Kinnoul, a younger branch of the family, further allude to the circumstance first mentioned in their motto, RENOVATE ANIMOS, ' Rouse your courage,' or ' Rally.'

There are still existing indubitable evidences of a great conflict on the spot referred to in this legend; and it may be admitted that the ancestors of the family were concerned in it; but the above heraldic ensigns must be considered to have been adopted as remembrances of long past events, albeit their assumption may have taken place at a very early period.

The family of Keith, earls Marischal, bear *Argent, on a chief or, three pallets gules,* OR *gules, three pallets or.* These ensigns likewise originated in an engagement between the Scots and the Danes. An ancestor of the Keiths having greatly distinguished himself in a battle near Dundee, in which Camus, the Danish general, was killed, the Scottish monarch, Kenneth III, charmed with his valour, dipped his royal fingers in the blood of the Dane and drew three stripes or pallets on the top of his chieftain's shield. Hence the arms of Keith. As in the former instance,

this anecdote assumes the existence of armorial bearings, at too remote a date, though, as in that case, there are evident vestigia of a great battle at the place referred to. A stone called ' Camus's Cross' was standing a few years since; and in the last century a large tomb, inclosed with four huge stones, containing bones, conjectured to have been those of the Northman, was discovered near the spot.[1]

Bulstrode, of Bulstrode, co. Bucks, bore, as a crest, *A bull's head, erased gules, attired argent, between two wings of the same.* When William the Conqueror subdued this kingdom he gave the estate of this family to one of his own followers, and lent him a thousand men for the purpose of taking possession, *vi et armis.* The rightful owner calling in the aid of some neighbouring gentlemen, (among others, the ancestors of the Penns and the Hampdens,) gallantly resisted the invader, intrenching himself with an earthwork, which is still pointed out as evidence of the truth of the story. It seems that the besieged party, wanting horses, mounted themselves upon *bulls,* and, sallying out of their camp, so affrighted the Normans that many of the latter were slain and the rest put to flight. The king hearing of this strange affair, and not wishing to push matters to an imprudent extent, sent for the valiant Saxon, with a promise of safe conduct to and from his court. The Saxon paid the Conqueror a visit, riding upon a *bull,* accompanied by his seven sons similarly mounted. The result of the interview was that he was allowed to retain his estate. In commemoration of these events, he assumed the crest above described, together with the name of *Bull-strode!!* The whole narration exhibits strong characteristics

---

[1] A very similar coat of arms, borne by the Lloyds of Denbighshire, Barts., is said to have originated under similar circumstances in 1256.

of that peculiar genus of history, known as ' Cock and *Bull* stories,' although it is probably quite as true as a distich preserved in the family, that

" 𝔚𝔥𝔢𝔫 𝔚𝔦𝔩𝔩𝔦𝔞𝔪 𝔠𝔬𝔫𝔮𝔲𝔢𝔯𝔢𝔡 𝔈𝔫𝔤𝔩𝔦𝔰𝔥 𝔤𝔯𝔬𝔲𝔫𝔡,
𝔅𝔲𝔩𝔰𝔱𝔯𝔬𝔡𝔢 𝔥𝔞𝔡 𝔭𝔢𝔯 𝔞𝔫𝔫𝔲𝔪, 𝔗𝔥𝔯𝔢𝔢 𝔥𝔲𝔫𝔡𝔯𝔢𝔡 𝔓𝔬𝔲𝔫𝔡.[1]

Among those Welsh chieftains who gallantly defended their country from the aggressions of the English, in the reign of Henry II, was Kadivor ap Dynawal, who recaptured the castle of Cardigan, by scalade, from the Earl of Clare. For this action he was enriched by Rhys, prince of South Wales, with several estates, and permitted to bear, as coat armour, a castle, three scaling-ladders, and a bloody spear. These arms were borne by Kadivor's descendants, the Lloyds of Milfield, co. Cardigan, baronets, till the extinction of the family in the last century.

Williams, of Penrhyn, co. Caernarvon, Bart., bore, among other charges, *three human heads*, in commemoration of the exploit of Edwyfed Vychan, the great ancestor of his house, who in an engagement with the followers of Ranulph, earl of Chester, came off victorious, having killed three of their chief commanders. This happened in the thirteenth century.[2]

The Vescis, Chetwodes, Knowleses, Tyntes, Villierses, and various other families, bear crosses in their arms, traditionally derived from the period of the Crusades.

Sir Ancel Gornay attended Richard I on his crusade, and was present at the capture of Ascalon, where he took a Moorish king prisoner. From this circumstance he adopted as his crest, ' A king of the Moors habited in a robe, and crowned, kneeling, and surrendering with his dexter hand,

---

[1] Hist. and Allusive Arms.   [2] Ibid.

his sword, all proper.' This crest was continued by the
Newtons, of Barr's Court, co. Gloucester, one of whom married the heiress of the Gornays. Among several other armorial ensigns dated from this same battle of Ascalon is the
crest of Darrell, which may be briefly described as, 'Out of a
ducal coronet a Saracen's head appropriately vested,' and
which was assumed by Sir Marmaduke Darrell, in commemoration of his having killed the infidel King of Cyprus;
also the arms and crest of Minshull, of Cheshire, 'Azure, an
estoile issuant out of a crescent, in base argent.' *Crest,* 'An
Eastern warrior, kneeling on one knee, habited gules, legs
and arms in mail proper; at his side a scymitar sable, hilted
or; on his head a turban with a crescent and feather argent,
presenting, with his sinister hand, a crescent of the last.'
These bearings were assigned to Michael de Minshull for
his valour on that occasion, but the particular nature of his
exploits is not recorded.

The Bouchiers, earls of Essex, bore ' Argent, a cross engrailed gules, between four water-bowgets sable. *Crest.*
The bust of a Saracen king, with a long cap and coronet, all
proper.' All these bearings are emblematical of the crusades;
and the water-bowgets are a play upon the name. "In the
hall of the manor-house of Newton, in the parish of Little
Dunmowe, in Essex," says Weever,[1] "remaineth, in old
painting, two postures (figures;) the one for an ancestor of
the Bouchiers, combatant with another, being a Pagan king,
for the truth of Christ, whom the said Englishman overcame;
and in memory thereof his descendants have ever since borne
the head of the said infidel, as also used the *surname of
Bouchier,*" in conformity with an antient practice, by which,

[1] Fun. Mon., p. 629.

as Saintfoix informs us, great heroes were honoured with the *" glorious surname"* of BUTCHER !¹

The arms of Willoughby, Lords Willoughby of Eresby, were 'Sable, a cross engrailed or,' and their *Crest*, 'A Saracen's head crowned frontè, all proper.' The only account I have seen of the origin of these ensigns is contained in the following lines, occurring in Dugdale's Baronage. A Willoughby *loquitur*.

"Of myne old ancestors, by help of Goddes might,
(By reason of marriage and lineal descent,)
A Sarasyn king discomfit was in fighte,
Whose head my creste, shall ever be presénte."

Sir Christopher Seton, ancestor of the Earls of Wintoun, at the battle of Methven, in 1306, rescued King Robert Bruce from the English. For this service Robert gave him his sister, the lady Christian, in marriage, and the following augmentation to his paternal arms: 'Surtout, an inescocheon per pale gules and azure; the first charged with a sword in pale proper, hilted and pommelled, and *supporting a falling crown* within a double tressure all or; the second azure a star of twelve points argent, for Wintoun.'

Robert Bruce desired that his heart might be carried to Jerusalem, and there interred in holy ground. The office of conveying it thither devolved upon his faithful and now sorrowing knight, Sir James Douglas, who was unfortunately slain on his return by the infidels, in the year 1331. To commemorate this service his descendants have ever since borne 'Argent, a human heart royally crowned proper; on a chief azure, three mullets of the first.' This stalwart soldier

¹ Vide ' English Surnames,' 2d edit. p. 100.

is said to have been engaged in fifty-seven battles and ren-
contres with the English, and thirteen with the Saracens, all
in the space of twenty-four years.   Certes, he must have
been one of the noblest ' butchers' of his time !

The family of Pelham (now represented by the Earl of
Chichester) bear, as a quartering, ' Gules, two demi-belts,
paleways, the *buckles* in chief argent.'   This augmentation
was allowed to the family in the early part of the seventeenth
century; but they had previously, for many generations,
borne the Buckle as a badge.   They also occasionally gave
it as a crest, together with a cage—both in commemoration
of the capture of John, king of France, at Poictiers, by Sir
John de Pelham.   The story is thus briefly told by Collins :[1]

"Froysart gives an account, that with the king were
taken beside his son Philip, the Earl of Tankerville, Sir
Jaques of Bourbon, the Earls of Ponthieu and Eue, with
divers other noblemen, who being chased to Poictiers, the
town shut their gates against them, not suffering any to
enter; so that divers were slain, and every Englishman had
four, five, or six prisoners; and the press being great to take
the King, such as knew him, cry'd, *Sir, yield, or you are
dead:* Whereupon, as the chronicle relates, he yielded himself to Sir Dennis Morbeck, a Knight of Artois, in the
English service, and being afterwards forc'd from him, more
than ten Knights and Esquires challeng'd the taking of the
King.   Among these Sir Roger la Warr, and the before-
mentioned John de Pelham, were most concerned ; and in
memory of so signal an action, and the King surrendering
his sword to them, Sir Roger la Warr, Lord la Warr, had
the crampet, or chape of his sword, for a badge of that

[1] Vol. ii, p. 87, edit. 1768.

honour; and John de Pelham (afterwards knighted) had the buckle of a belt as a mark of the same honour, which was sometimes used by his descendants as a seal-manual, and at others, the said buckles on each side a cage; being an emblem of the captivity of the said King of France, and was therefore borne for a crest, as in those times was customary. The buckles, &c. were likewise used by his descendants, in their great seals, as is evident from several of them appendant to old deeds."

It is somewhat remarkable that Froissart, Walsingham, Knyghton, and the other early chroniclers, are silent as to the names of the King's captors; and were the story unsupported by strong indirect evidence, their silence would be almost fatal to its authenticity; but the occurrence of the Buckle upon the stonework of many ecclesiastical buildings founded by Sir John de Pelham himself and his immediate successors,[1] sufficiently corroborates the undisputed family tradition.[2]

The chape or crampet of a sword (the ornament at the end of the scabbard which prevents the point from protruding) is still borne as a badge by the Earl de la Warr, a lineal descendant of the Sir Roger la Warr referred to in the above extract.

The crest of the antient family of De la Bere is ' a ducal coronet or, therefrom issuant a plume of five ostrich feathers per pale argent and azure.' This was conferred upon Sir Richard de la Bere, knight-banneret, by Edward the Black Prince, in reward for his having rescued him from imminent

---

[1] Enumerated at p. 146.

[2] The vignette at the head of the present chapter was copied from a brick at Laughton Place. The inscription, which is in relievo, is W. P. (William Pelham) LAN DE GRACE 1534 FVT CEST MAYSON FAICTE.

danger on the memorable field of Cressy. The ducal coronet is emblematical of military command, and the feathers are an evident derivation from the Prince's own badge. There is (or was at the beginning of the present century) in an old house at Cheltenham, the property of his lineal descendants, a painting supposed to be nearly contemporary with the occurrence, which represents the Prince in the act of conferring this mark of honour upon his faithful follower.[1]

The crest of Dudley of Northamptonshire, Bart. was 'Out of a ducal coronet or, a woman's bust : her hair dishevelled, bosom bare, a helmet on her head with the stay or throat-latch down proper.' From a MS. in the possession of this family, written by a monk about the close of the fourteenth century, it appeared that the father of Agnes Hotot (who, in the year 1395, married an ancestor of the Dudleys,) having a quarrel with one Ringsdale concerning the proprietorship of some land, they agreed to meet on the 'debateable ground,' and decide their right by combat. Unfortunately for Hotot, on the day appointed he was seriously ill; "but his daughter Agnes, unwilling that he should lose his claim, or suffer in his honour, armed herself cap-a-pie, and, mounting her father's steed, repaired to the place of decision, where, after a stubborn encounter, she dismounted Ringsdale, and when he was on the ground, she loosened the stay of her helmet, let down her hair about her shoulders, and, disclosing her bosom, discovered to him that he had been conquered by a

---

[1] The painting is upon panel. An engraving of it is given in Bigland's Gloucester, vol. i, p. 312. Hist. and Allus. Arms, p. 52.

woman." This valiant lady became the heiress of her family, and married a Dudley, whence the latter family derived their right to this crest.

Sir Richard Waller was at the battle of Agincourt, where he took prisoner Charles, duke of Orleans, father of Charles XII (afterwards King of France). This personage was brought to England by his captor, who held him in 'honourable restraint' at his own mansion, at Groombridge, co. Kent, during the long period of twenty-four years, at the termination of which he paid 400,000 crowns for his ransom. In accordance with the chivalrous spirit of that age, the captor and captive lived together on terms of the strictest friendship. This appears from the fact that the Duke, at his own expense, rebuilt for Sir Richard the family house at Groombridge. He was also a benefactor "to his parish church of Speldhurst, where his arms remain in stonework over the porch."[1] Previously to this event the family arms had been the punning device of 'Sable, on a bend voided argent, three *walnut* leaves or,' and the crest, ' A *walnut* tree fructed proper.' To one of the lower boughs of this tree was now appended a shield, charged with the arms of France—'Azure, three fleurs-de-lis or, differenced with a label of three points;' an augmentation which continues to be borne by the descendants of Sir Richard Waller to this day.

Burton of Salop, and Rivers of Kent, bear [2] white roses, commemorative of the services rendered by their ancestors to the faction distinguished by this badge, while the Lutterells of Somerset, bear, as a crest, the white boar of

---

[1] Hist. and Allus. Arms, p. 60.

[2] I use the present tense *bear*, although in many cases the families may have become extinct.

Richard III, ensigned on the shoulder with the Lancastrian red rose! The white and red roses in the arms of families, as partisans of the two rival houses, would furnish matter for a whole chapter; but I must pass on.

Augmentations have sometimes been made to the arms of English families by foreign monarchs. Thus Sir Henry Guldeforde, knight, having rendered assistance to Ferdinand and Isabella of Spain, in the reduction of Granada, received from them the honour of knighthood, with permission to add to his ancestral arms, 'On a canton Argent, the arms of Granada, viz. a pomegranate, the shell open, grained gules, stalked and leaved proper.' John Callard, esq. a retainer of the said Sir Henry, for his valour on the same occasion, acquired the following coat: 'Gyronny of six pieces, or and sable; on each division or, a Moor's head couped sable.' William Browne, esq. called by Holinshed "a young and lusty gentleman," another follower of Guldeforde, was honoured with an augmentation, viz. 'On a chief argent, an eagle displayed sable,'—the arms of Sicily, which was then an adjunct to the Spanish crown.

The Duke of Norfolk bears on his 'bend argent' 'an escocheon or, charged with a demi-lion rampant within a double tressure, flory and counter-flory; an arrow pierced through the lion's mouth all gules.' This is an augmentation nearly resembling the arms of Scotland, and was granted to the Earl of Surrey, afterwards Duke of Norfolk, for his services against the Scots at Flodden Field, in 1513. It will be recollected that when the body of James IV was found after the battle, it was pierced with several arrows, the cause of his death.

As a further memorial of this victory the Earl gave, as the badge of his retainers, a white lion, one of the supporters of his house, trampling upon the red lion of Scotland, and tearing it with his claws.

Several English families bear their arms upon the breast of an eagle with two heads. This is the standard of the German empire, and it has been granted to such families for military and other services. The Lord Arundel of Wardour, in the reign of Elizabeth, received this distinguished mark of honour by patent from the Emperor Rodolph II, for valorous conduct against the Turks, whom, as the avowed enemies of Christianity, he opposed with all the enthusiasm of a crusader of more antient times. He was at the same time created a Count of the Empire, and, on returning to England, was desirous of taking precedence according to his German title. But this step was violently opposed by the peers, and the Queen, being asked her opinion of his claim, answered, "that faithful subjects should keep their eyes at home, and not gaze upon foreign crowns, and that she, for her part, did not care her sheep should wear a stranger's mark, nor dance after the whistle of every foreigner!"[1]

The Bowleses of Wiltshire, and the Smiths of Lincolnshire, received appropriate arms about the same time for their services against the Turks, under the same Emperor.[2]

The assumption of the arms of an enemy slain or captured in war, though permitted by the heraldric canon of early times, seems not to have been very usual in this country; yet instances are not wanting of arms so acquired. In 1628, Sir David Kirke, knight, reduced Canada, then in the power of the French, and took the admiral De la Roche prisoner.

[1] Gough's Camden, vol. i, p. 89.

[2] *Bowles*—' Azure, a crescent argent, in chief the sun or.' *Smith*—' Vert a cheveron gules between three Turks' heads couped in profile proper, their turbans or.' This was an augmentation borne quarterly with the antient arms of Smith.

For this service he received as an augmentation, 'A canton azure charged with a talbot sejant, collared and leash reflexed argent, sustaining a faulchion proper,' this being the coat of his captive.

Charles I rewarded many of his adherents with augmentations of arms—the only recompense some of them ever received. The favourite marks of honour were the crown, rose, and lion of England.

Sir Palmes Fairborne, knighted by Charles II for his defence of Tangier against the Moors, had permission to bear as his crest, 'An arm in armour couped at the elbow, lying on a wreath sustaining a sword; on the point thereof a Turk's head, turbaned all proper.' The epitaph on this commander, on his tomb in Westminster Abbey, was written by Dryden; and had nothing more sublime proceeded from his pen, his name would be as little known to posterity as that of the hero he celebrates.

> "Alive and dead *these* walls he will defend,
>   Great actions great examples must attend ;
>   The Candian siege his early valour knew,
>   Where Turkish blood did his young hands imbrew ;
>   From thence returning with deserved applause,
>   Against the Moors his *well-fleshed* sword he draws," &c. &c.

Sir Cloudesley Shovel, the celebrated admiral, received, by the express command of William III, a grant of arms blazoned thus: 'Gules a cheveron ermine between two crescents in chief argent, and a fleur-de-lis in base or,' to commemorate two great victories over the Turks and one over the French. This is one of the most appropriate coats I remember to have seen.

It would be impossible (even were it desirable) within the

limits I have assigned myself, to notice all the arms and augmentations which have been granted to heroes, naval and military, for services performed during the last, and at the commencement of the present, century. A superabundance of them will be found in the plates attached to the ordinary peerages, &c. Suffice it to say, that in general they exhibit a most wretched taste in the heralds who designed them, or rather, perhaps I should say, in the personages who dictated to the heralds what ensigns would be most agreeable to themselves. Figures never dreamed of in classical armory have found their way into these bearings : landscapes and *words* in great staring letters across the shield, bombshells and bayonets, East Indians and American Indians, sailors and soldiers, medals and outlandish banners, *figures of Peace, and grenadiers of the 79th regiment !*[1] Could absurdity go farther ?

But, lest I should be thought unnecessarily severe upon the armorists of the past age, I annex the arms of Sir Sidney Smith, a veteran who certainly deserved *better things*

---

[1] Supporters of Sir William Draper, K. B. (Hist. and Allus. Arms, p. 227.)

of his country. I shall not attempt to blazon them, as I am
sure my reader would not thank me for occupying a page
and a half of a chapter—already perhaps too long—with
what would in this case be *jargon* indeed.   Shades of
Brooke, and Camden, and Guillim, and Dugdale! what
think ye of this?

II. The second class of Historical Arms is composed of
those derived from ACTS OF LOYALTY. The earliest coat of
this kind mentioned by the author of the volume before
quoted, is that of Sir John Philpot, viz. 'Sable a bend
ermine,'—his paternal arms—impaling, 'Gules a cross between four swords argent, hilts or'—an augmentation
granted to Philpot for killing Wat Tyler with his sword
after Walworth, the mayor, had knocked him down with his
mace, in the presence of Richard II, in 1378.

Ramsay, earl of Holderness, temp. James VI, bore as an
augmentation impaling his paternal arms, 'Azure, a dexter
hand holding a sword in pale, argent, hilted or, piercing a
human heart proper, and supporting on the point an imperial
crown of the last.'   This was granted to Sir John Ramsay,
who was also rewarded with the title just mentioned, for
having saved the young monarch's life from assassination by
Ruthven, earl of Gowrie, by piercing the assassin to the
heart. The story of this attempt upon the 'British Solomon'
is too well known to the reader of Scottish history to need
copying in these pages. The whole narration, enshrouded
in mystery, is now almost universally discredited, and the
affair regarded as a pretended plot, to answer a political
purpose.   It is sufficient to say that Gowrie and his father,
Alexander Ruthven, fell victims to it, while Ramsay was
rewarded for his share in the transaction as above stated.[1]

[1] Vide Robertson, Smollet, Stewart, &c. *in loco;* Grose's Antiq. of Scotland, &c.

Erskine, earl of Kelly, and Sir Hugh Harris, two other individuals concerned in this plot, also received augmentations.[1]

The notorious Colonel Titus, temp. Charles II, was rewarded for his services in the restoration of the king, with an augmentation, viz. ' quarterly with his paternal arms, Or, on a chief gules, a lion of England.' ' Lions of England' were likewise assigned to the following families for their loyalty to the Stuarts : Robinson of Cranford, Moore, Lord Mayor of London, Lane of Staffordshire, &c. The crest of the last-mentioned family is ' A demi-horse salient argent, spotted dark grey, bridled proper, sustaining with his fore feet a regal crown or ;' in allusion to the circumstance of Charles's having been assisted in his escape, after his defeat at Worcester, by a lady of this family, whose servant the king personated by riding before her on horseback. In this guise Charles arrived safely at Bristol, and at length, after many hair-breadth escapes and a circuitous tour of the southern counties, reached Brighthelmstone, whence he set sail for the continent.

The arms granted to the family of Penderell for concealing Charles II in the oak at Boscobel, and otherwise assisting his escape, and those assigned on the same occasion to Colonel Careless (or CARLOS, as it was the king's humour afterwards to name him) were exactly *alike* in charges, though different in tincture.

CARLOS. ' Or, on a mount an oak-tree proper ; over all a fesse gules, charged with three regal crowns proper.

PENDERELL. ' Argent, on a mount an oak-tree proper; over all a fesse sable, charged with three regal crowns proper.'[2]

[1] Hist. and Allus. Arms, pp. 316-18.

[2] The name of Carlos is presumed to have become extinct ; that of Penderell is

III. The third class of Historical Arms are those of
ALLIANCE. I shall content myself with an example or two.
The arms[1] and dexter supporter[2] of the Lyons, earls of Strath-
more, evidently allude to a connexion with the royal line of
Scotland, and the crest of the family is, 'On a wreath vert and
or, a *lady* couped below the girdle, inclosed within an arch
of laurel, and holding in her right hand the royal thistle, all
proper.' Sir John Lyon, an ancestor of this house, having
gained the favour of King Robert II, that monarch gave him
in marriage his daughter, the lady Jane. To perpetuate so
splendid and beneficial an alliance, his descendants have ever
since continued to represent this princess as their crest.

The Seymours, dukes of Somerset, bore quarterly with
their paternal arms, the following: ' Or, on a pile gules,
between six fleurs-de-lis azure, three lions of England,' an
augmentation originally granted by Henry VIII to Jane
Seymour, his third wife. These ensigns, it will be seen, are
a composition from the royal arms.

IV. The fourth are derived from FAVOUR and SERVICES.
The antient arms of Compton, subsequently created earls
of Northampton, were ' Sable, three helmets argent.' For
services rendered to Henry VIII, William Compton, esq.
received permission to place ' a lion of England' between the
helmets.

Thomas Villiers, first Earl of Clarendon, bore, ' Argent,

by no means so. The representative of the family still continues to receive the
pension of 100 marks originally granted to Richard Penderell. Several members
of the family, in various conditions in life, have been connected for some generations with the county of Sussex. One of them, a few years since, kept an inn at
Lewes, bearing the sign of the *Royal Oak.*

[1] A lion rampant within a double tressure, &c.

[2] A unicorn.

on a cross gules, five escallops or [originally derived from the
Crusade under Edward I] a crescent for difference; and on
an inescocheon argent, the eagle of Prussia, viz. displayed
sable, &c. &c., charged on the breast with F. B. R. for
Fredericus, Borussorum Rex.' This was an augmentation
granted to that nobleman by Frederick, king of Prussia, as
a mark of the high value he set upon certain diplomatic
services in which he had been engaged. The augmentation
was ratified at the Heralds' office by the command of
George III.

The Earl of Liverpool, in addition to his paternal arms,
bears ' on a chief wavy argent, a cormorant sable, holding in
his beak a branch of laver or sea-weed vert.' This augmentation (being the arms of the town of Liverpool) was made to
the arms of Charles Jenkinson, first Earl of Liverpool, at the
unanimous request of the mayor and municipality of that
town, signified by their recorder.

V. A very interesting class of Allusive Arms is composed
of those derived from the SITUATION of the original residences
of the respective families. The following are instances:

Wallop, earl of Portsmouth, 'Argent, a bend wavy sable.'
The name of Wallop is local, and it was antiently written
Welhop. Wallop, or Welhope, is the name of two parishes
in Hampshire, so denominated from a fountain or *well*,
springing from a *hope* or hill in the vicinity, and giving
birth to a small river, which becomes tributary to the Tese.
Here, in very antient times, this family resided, and from
the little river referred to the surname was adopted, while
the bend wavy in the arms alludes both to the river and the
name.

Stourton, Lord Stourton, ' Sable, a bend or, between six
fountains proper.' The river Stour rises at Stourton, co.

Wilts, from six fountains or springs. The family name is derived from the place, and the arms from this circumstance. The bend may be regarded as the pale of Stourton park, as three of the sources of the river are within that inclosure and three beyond it.

Shuckburgh, a parish in Warwickshire, is remarkable for that kind of fossil termed *astroit*, which resembles the mullet of heraldry. The family who, in very antient times, derived their surname from the locality, bear three mullets in their arms.[1]

The Swales of Swale-hall, co. York, bear 'Azure, a bend undé argent.' Some consider this a representation of the river Swale, though Peter Le Neve thinks it a rebus for the name of *Nunda*, whose heiress married a Swale.[2]

Highmore of High-moor, co. Cumberland: 'Argent, a crossbow erect between *four* moor-cocks sable; their legs, beaks, and combs, gules.' This family originated in the moors of that county, *unde nomen et arma*. The author of ' Historical and Allusive Arms ' says that they branched out into three lines, called from the situation of their respective places of abode, HIGHMORE, MIDDLEMORE, and LOWMORE. It is curious that the Middlemore branch gave as arms the crossbow and *three* moor-cocks; while the Lowmores bore the crossbow and *two* moor-cocks only. Had the family ramified still further into ' *Lowermore*,' it is probable that branch must have rested content with a *single* moor-cock, while the ' *Lowestmores*,' carrying out the same principle of gradation, could not have claimed even a solitary bird, but must have made shift with their untrophied crossbow.

---

[1] Sable, a cheveron between three astroits, or mullets, argent. (Historical and Allusive Arms.)

[2] Ibid.

On the other hand, ' *Highermore* ' would have been entitled to *five*, and ' *Highestmore* ' to *six*, head of game, in addition to the family weapon!

Hume, of Nine Wells, the family of the great historian, bore 'Vert, a lion rampant argent within a bordure or, charged with *nine wells* or springs barry-wavy azure and argent.' " The estate of Nine Wells is so named from a cluster of springs of that number. Their situation is picturesque; they burst forth from a gentle declivity in front of the mansion, which has on each side a semicircular rising bank, covered with fine timber, and fall, after a short course, into the bed of the river Whitewater, which forms a boundary in the front. These springs, as descriptive of their property, were assigned to the Humes of this place as a difference in arms from the chief of their house."[1]

VI. Of arms alluding to the PROFESSION or pursuits of the original bearer, I shall adduce but few instances, as they generally exhibit bad taste, and a departure from heraldric purity; *e. g.* Hooper, Bishop of Gloucester and Worcester, the champion and martyr of the Protestant cause, bore '. . . . a lamb in a burning bush; the rays of the sun descending thereon proper.'

Michael Drayton bore 'Azure gutté d'eau [the drops of Helicon!] a Pegasus current in bend argent.' *Crest,* ' Mercury's winged cap amidst sunbeams proper.' These classical emblems appear foreign to the spirit of heraldry, which originated in an unclassical age. Still it might have been difficult to assign to this stately and majestic poet more appropriate armorials.

The supporters chosen by Sir George Gordon, first Lord

---

[1] Hist. and Allus. Arms, p. 400.

Aberdeen, a celebrated jurist, were *two lawyers;* while (every man to his taste) Sir William Morgan, K.B., a keen sportsman, adopted *two huntsmen* equipped for the chase, and the motto ' Saltando cave,' *Look before you leap.* Could anything be more pitiful ?

VII. Arms derived from TENURE and OFFICE are a much more interesting, though less numerous, class than the preceding.

" The tenure of the lands of Pennycuik, in Midlothian, obliges the possessor to attend once a year in the forest of Drumsleich (near Edinburgh) . . . to give a blast of a horn at the king's hunting; and therefore Clerk of Pennycuik, baronet, the proprietor of these lands, uses the following crest :"[1] ' A demi-forester, habited vert, sounding a hunting-horn proper;' and motto, ' FREE FOR A BLAST.' Most of the English families of Forester, Forster, and Foster have bugle-horns in their arms, supporting the idea that the founders of those families derived their surnames from the office of Forester, held by them in times when the country abounded in woody districts. This office was one of considerable honour and emolument.

The crest of Grosvenor is ' a hound or talbot statant or;' and the supporters 'two talbots reguardant or,' &c. Both these ensigns and the name allude to the antient office of the chiefs of this family, which was that of **le Gros Veneur,** great huntsman, to the Dukes of Normandy.

Rawdon, earl of Moira, ancestor of the Marquis of Hastings; ' Argent, a fesse between three pheons or arrowheads sable.' *Crest,* in a mural coronet argent, a pheon sable, with a sprig of laurel issuing therefrom proper. *Sup-*

[1] Hist. and Allus. Arms, (1803.)

porters, two huntsmen with bows, quivers, &c. &c. This family were denominated from their estate, Rawdon, near Leeds, co. York, which they originally held under William the Conqueror. A rhyming title-deed, purporting to have been granted by him, but evidently of much later date, was formerly in the possession of the family:

"**I William King,** the thurd yere of my reigne,
Give to thee, Paulyn Roydon, Hope and Hopetowne,
Wyth all the bounds, both up and downe,
From Heaven to yerthe, from yerthe to hel;
For the and thyn ther to dwell,
As truly as this Kyng-right is myn;
For a cross-bowe and an arrow,
When I sal come to hunt on Yarrow;
And in token that this thing is sooth,
I bit the whyt wax with my tooth."

The family of Pitt, earl of Chatham, bore 'Sable, a fesse *chequy* argent and azure, between three bezants or pieces of *money*,' in allusion to the office the original grantee held in the EXCHEQUER. The Fanshawes also bore chequy, &c., for the same reason.

The Woods of Largo, co. Fife, bear ships, in allusion to the office of Admiral of Scotland, antiently hereditary in that family.

The antient Earls of Warren and Surrey bore 'chequy, or and azure.' There is a tradition that the heads of this family were invested with the exclusive prerogative of granting licenses for the sale of malt liquors, and that it was enjoined on all alehouse-keepers to paint the Warren arms on their door-posts. Hence the chequers, still seen at the entrances of many taverns, were supposed to have originated, until the discovery of that ornament on an inn-door among the ruins of Pompeii proved the fashion to have existed in classical times.   Its origin is involved in obscurity; it may have been placed upon houses of entertainment to show that some game analogous to the modern chess and backgammon might be played within.

Here we may be allowed to digress, to say a few words on the origin of *inn signs,* which are generally of an heraldric character.   In early times the town residences of the nobility and great ecclesiastics were called Inns; and in front of them the family arms were displayed.   In many cases these Inns were afterwards appropriated to the purposes of the modern hotel, affording temporary accommodation to all comers.[1] The armorial decorations were retained, and under the name of signs directed the public to these places of rest and refreshment.   On calling to mind the signs by which the inns of any particular town are designated, a very great majority of them will be recognized as regular heraldric charges.   In addition to the full armorials of great families, as the Gordon Arms, the Pelham Arms, the Dorset Arms, we find such signs as the Golden Lion, Red Lion, White Lion, Black Lion, White Hart, Blue Boar, Golden Cross, Dragon, Swan, Spread Eagle, Dolphin, Rose and Crown, Catherine-Wheel, Cross-Keys, *cum multis aliis,* abundant

---

[1] " Over against the parish church [of St. Olave, Southwark] on the south side of the streete was sometime one great house builded of stone, with arched gates, which pertained to the Prior of Lewes in Sussex, and was his lodging when he came to London : it is now a common hostelry for travellers, and hath to sign the Walnut-Tree." (*Stowe*, p. 340.) The last remains of this inn were destroyed in making the approach to the new London Bridge. For an account of them, see ' Archæologia,' vol. xxv, p. 604.

everywhere. These were originally, in most cases, the properly emblazoned armories of families possessing influence in the locality; and frequently the inns themselves were established by old domestics of such families. But owing to the negligence of mine host, or the unskilfulness of the common painter, who from time to time renovated his sign, the latter often lost much of its heraldric character; the shield and its tinctures were dropped, and the charges only remained; while by a still further departure from the original intention, three black lions, or five spread eagles, were reduced to one. A house in the town of Lewes was formerly known as the "Three Pelicans," the fact of those charges constituting the arms of Pelham having been lost sight of. Another is still called "The Cats," and few are aware that the arms of the Dorset family are intended.[1] In villages, innumerable instances occur of signs taken from the arms or crests of existing families, and very commonly the sign is changed as some neighbouring domain passes into other hands. There is a kind of patron and client feeling about this—feudality some may be disposed to call it—which a lover of Old England is pleased to contemplate.

VIII. The last species of Historical Arms are those which relate to Memorable Circumstances and Events which have occurred to the Ancestors of the families who bear them.

Stanley, earl of Derby. *Crest.* 'On a chapeau gules, turned up ermine, an Eagle with wings expanded or, feeding an Infant in a kind of cradle; at its head a sprig of oak all proper.' This is the blazon given in "Historical and Allusive Arms;"[2] but Collins[3] blazons the Eagle as '*preying*

---

[1] The supporters of this family are 'two leopards argent, spotted sable.'
[2] Page 437.   [3] Peerage, II, 486.

upon' the Infant.   This crest belonged originally to the family of Lathom or Latham, whose heiress, Isabella, married Sir John Stanley, afterwards Lieutenant of Ireland, Lord of the Isle of Man, and K. G. in the fourteenth century. According to tradition it originated in the following manner : One of the Lathams of Latham, co. Lancaster, having abandoned and exposed an illegitimate son in the nest of an eagle in a wood called Terlestowe Wood, near his castle, afterwards discovered, to his great astonishment, that the 'king of birds,' instead of devouring the helpless infant, had conceived a great liking for him, supplying him with food, and thus preserving his life.   Upon witnessing this miraculous circumstance the cruel parent relented, and, taking home the infant, made him his heir.   A 'various reading' of the tale states that Sir Thomas Latham, being destitute of legal issue, and wishing to adopt an illegitimate son, a proceeding to which his wife would not be likely to become a party, resorted to the *ruse* of having the infant placed in the cyrie of an eagle, and then, taking his lady into the park, coming, as if by accident, to the place, at the moment when the eagle was hovering over the nest.   Help—of course *accidental*—being at hand, the little fellow was rescued from his perilous couch, and presented to the lady, who pressed him to her bosom, and, ignorant of his consanguinity to her lord, joyfully acquiesced in his proposal to make the foundling heir to their estate.

According to Bishop Stanley's 'Historicall Poem touching ye Family of Stanley,' and Vincent's MS. Collection in the College of Arms, the Lord of Latham was "fowerscore" at the time he adopted this infant,

> " Swaddled and clad
> In a mantle of redd ;"

—a statement which discredits both versions of the story as given above. These authorities further inform us that the foundling received the baptismal name of Oskell, and became father of the Isabella Latham who married Sir John Stanley.

In Seacome's 'History of the House of Stanley' there is an account, derived from another branch of the family, which coincides with the second-mentioned, with the important addition that the adopted child was discarded before the death of Sir Thomas Latham. It is further said, that on the adoption Sir Thomas had assumed for his crest "an Eagle upon wing, turning her head back and looking in a sprightly manner as for something she had lost," and that on the disowning, the Stanleys (one of whom had married the legal heiress to the estate) "either to distinguish or aggrandize themselves, or in contempt and derision, took upon them the Eagle and Child," thus manifesting the variation and the reason of it.

It is scarcely necessary to state, that the Sir Oskell of the legend has no existence in the veritable records of history; and Mr. Ormerod, the learned historian of Cheshire, who is connected by marriage with the family of Latham, thinks the whole story may be "more safely referred to ancestral Northmen, with its scene in the pine-forests of Scandinavia." [1]

[1] In the History of Birds, by the Rev. Edward Stanley (now Bishop of Norwich), vol. i, 119, are some interesting anecdotes of the asportation of infants by eagles, illustrative of the family crest, and the corresponding story of King Alfred's peer, "Nestingum," who received that name from his having been found, in infancy, in the nest of an eagle. For further remarks, vide Mr. Ormerod's interesting paper on the "Stanley Legend," in the Collect. Topog. et Geneal. vol. vii, which has been reprinted in the form of a private tract.

The subjoined engraving relates to this legend.   It is copied from a cast [1] taken from an oak carving attached to the stall of James Stanley, bishop of Ely, in the collegiate church now cathedral of Manchester, of which he was warden.   The figures below the trees are a REBUS [2] of masons or stone-cutters, termed, in mediæval Latin, *Lathomi;* and the castellated gateway they are approaching is that of Latham Hall, the scene of the tradition.

Trevelyan of Somersetshire, Bart. ' Gules, a horse argent armed or, issuant from the sea in base, party per fesse wavy,

---

[1] Penes Rev. Henry Latham, M. A., Rector of Selmeston, &c. &c., to whose kindness I am much indebted.

[2] Vide notice of *Rebuses,* at p. 125.

azure and of the second.' This family primarily bore a very
different coat: their present armorials were assumed "on
occasion of one of their ancestors swimming on horseback
from the rocks called Seven Stones to the Land's End in
Cornwall, at the time of an inundation, which is said to have
overwhelmed a large tract of land, and severed thereby those
rocks from the continent of Cornwall."[1] This story may
appear rather improbable, but it should be remembered that
some similar disruptions of land from the coast, such as the
Goodwin Sands, Selsey Rocks, &c. are authentic matters of
history. Whether the most powerful of the equine race,
which are, even under far more favourable circumstances,
"vain things for safety," would be able to outbrave the
violence of the sea necessary to produce such a phenomenon,
I leave to better horsemen than myself to decide.

The arms of Aubrey de Vere, the great ancestor of the
earls of Oxford,[2] in the 12th century, were 'Quarterly, gules
and or; in the first quarter a star or mullet of five points or.'
"In the year of our Lord 1098," saith Leland,[3] "Corborant,
Admiral to Soudan of Perce [so our antiquary was pleased
to spell Persia,] was fought with at Antioche, and discomfited
by the Christians. The night cumming on yn the chace of
this bataile, and waxing dark, the Christianes being four
miles from Antioche, God, willing the saufté [safety] of the
Christianes, shewed a white star or molette of five pointes on
the Christen host; which to every mannes sighte did lighte
and arrest upon the standard of Albry de Vere, there shyn-
ing excessively!" The mullet was subsequently used as a

[1] C. S. Gilbert's Cornwall, vol. i.
[2] The earldom of Oxford continued in this family during the unprecedented
period of five centuries and a half.
[3] Itin. vol. vi, p. 37.

badge by his descendants. "The Erle of Oxford's men had a starre with streames booth before and behind on their lyverys."[1]

Thomas Fitz-Gerald, father of John, first earl of Kildare, bore the sobriquet of Nappagh, Simiacus, or the Ape, from the following ludicrous circumstance. When he was an infant of nine months old, his grandfather and father were both killed in the war waged by them against M'Carthy, an opposing chief. He was then being nursed at Tralee, and his attendants, in the first consternation caused by the news of the disaster, ran out of the house, leaving the child alone in his cradle. A large ape or baboon, kept on the premises, with the natural love of mischief inherent in that mimic tribe, taking advantage of the circumstance, took him from his resting-place and clambered with him to the roof of the neighbouring abbey, and thence to the top of the steeple. After having carried his noble charge round the battlements, exhibiting the while various monkey tricks heretofore unknown to nursery-maids, to the no small consternation and amazement of the spectators, he descended with careful foot, *ad terram firmam*, and replaced the child in the cradle. In consequence of this event the earls of Kildare and other noble branches of this antient line assumed as a crest, 'An ape proper, girt about the middle and chained or,' and for supporters, two apes. The addition of the *chain* is singular.

Stuart, of Hartley-Mauduit, co. Hants. 'Argent, a lion rampant gules, debruised by a bend raguly [popularly termed a *ragged staff*] or.' Sir Alexander Stuart, or Steward, knight, an ancestor of this family, in the presence of Charles VI of France, encountered a lion with a sword, which breaking

---

[1] Leland, Collect. vol. ii, p. 504.

he seized a part of a tree, and with it killed the animal. This so much pleased the king, that he gave him the above as an augmentation to his paternal arms.[1]

Maclellan Lord Kirkcudbright bore as a crest, 'A dexter arm erect, the hand grasping a dagger, with a human head on the point thereof, couped proper.' In the reign of James II, of Scotland, a predatory horde of foreigners, who entered that kingdom from Ireland, committed great ravages in the shire of Galloway; whereupon a royal proclamation was issued ordering their dispersion, and offering, as a reward to the captor or killer of their chieftain, the barony of Bombie. Now it happened that one Maclellan, whose father had been laird of Bombie, (and had been dispossessed of it for some aggressions on a neighbouring nobleman,) was the fortunate person who killed the chieftain; thus singularly regaining his ancestral property. The crest originated in the circumstance of his having presented to the king the marauder's head fixed upon the point of a sword.

The head is variously blazoned as that of a *Saracen, Moor,* or *Gipsey,* and the question might here be started, 'Who were the lawless band that made the inroad referred to?' The terms Moor and Saracen were in early times applied indiscriminately to Mahometans of every nation, but it cannot be supposed that these intruders were followers of the False Prophet, for we have no record of any such having found their way into regions so remote. Neither is it probable that they were the wild or uncivilized Irish, whose manners and language would have been recognized in the south-western angle of Scotland, which is only separated from Ireland by a narrow channel that could be crossed in a few

---

[1] Or, a fesse chequy argent and azure.

hours. The most probable opinion is that they belonged to that singular race, the *Gipseys*, who first made their appearance in Germany, Italy, Switzerland, and France, between the years 1409 and 1427. Admitting that a tribe of them found their way soon after from the continent into Ireland, it seems exceedingly likely that a detachment of that tribe should have crossed over to Scotland in the reign of James, between 1438 and 1460. As the Gipseys on their first settlement were black, and could be traced to an oriental source, and as they disavowed Christianity, they were very naturally considered as Saracens, by a rule analogous to that which makes all the inhabitants of Christendom Franks in the eyes of a Turk. I have made this little digression because this instance of a Gipsey's head is probably unique in British Heraldry, and because the tradition perfectly coincides in point of time with the actual ingress of the Gipseys into this part of Europe.

The crest of the Davenports of Cheshire, a family as numerous, according to the proverb, as 'dogs' tails,' is 'a man's head couped below the shoulders in profile, hair brown, a halter about his neck proper.' According to the tradition of the family, it originated after a battle between the Yorkists and Lancastrians, in which one of the Davenports, being of the vanquished party, was spared execution by the commander on the opposite side, on the humiliating condition that he and all his posterity should bear this crest.

When Queen Elizabeth made Sir John Hawkins paymaster of the navy in 1590, she gave him a coat of arms appropriate to his profession, and as a crest, in allusion to his *laudable* concern in the slave trade, 'A demi-negro proper, manacled with a rope,' the very symbol which, more than two hundred years afterwards, was used to stamp infamy on those concerned in it, as well as abhorrence and detestation of the slave trade itself.[1]

It would be a matter of little difficulty to produce a great number of additional instances of armorials allusive to the personal history or office of the original grantee; but let it be mine rather than that of the fatigued reader to cry

'𝔒𝔥𝔢, 𝔧𝔞𝔪 𝔰𝔞𝔱𝔦𝔰!'

Anonymous Paragraph.

CHAPTER X.

Distinctions of Rank and Honour.

ANY treatise on Heraldry, whatever its scope or its design, would certainly be deemed defective if it did not embrace this subject. Heraldry consists of two distinct parts, namely, *first*, the knowledge of titles and dignities, the proper sphere of each, and the ceremonials connected with them; and, *secondly*, the science of blazon, or the rules by which armorial insignia are composed and borne. One treats of honours; the other of the symbols of those honours. The first, though some will refuse to concede it that distinction, is a science; the second partakes the nature of both a science and an *art*. The immediate object of this humble volume is armory or blazon, its history and its philosophy; yet I should scarcely feel justified in passing over, in silence, the other branch of heraldry, abounding as it does with 'Curiosities.' It is not, however, my intention to write a dissertation on the orders of nobility, their origin, their privileges, or their dignity; for the general reader, who happens to be uninformed on these points, can readily consult numerous authorities respecting them, while more profound students, should any such deign to read my lucubrations, would scarcely deem what could be said in the course

of a short chapter sufficient. I must therefore refer the
former class to their peerages, or books of elementary
heraldry, while the latter will not require that I should point
out the learned tomes of Segar, Selden, Markham, and the
various other 'workes of honour,' of which our literature has
been so remarkably prolific. To relieve the tedium occasioned by the constant reference to or, and gules, and ermine;
and bend, and fesse, and cheveron; and lions rampant and
eagles displayed, which must necessarily occur in a book of
heraldry, even in one which professes to treat of its
'Curiosities,' I intend here, *currente calamo*, to lay before
the reader a few jottings which have occurred to me in the
course of my heraldric and antiquarian researches.

It has been observed that " among barbarous nations
there are no family names. Men are known by *titles* of
honour, by *titles* of disgrace, or by *titles* given to them on
account of some individual quality. A brave man will be
called the lion, a ferocious one the tiger. Others are named
after a signal act of their lives, or from some peculiarity of
personal appearance; such as the slayer-of-three-bears, the
taker-of-so-many-scalps, or straight-limbs, long-nose, and so
on. Some of these, especially such as express approbation
or esteem, are worn as proudly by their savage owners as
that of duke or marquis is by European nobles.[1] They confer a distinction which begets respect and deference amongst

[1] It is not unworthy of remark that among the North American Indians, symbols
are employed for the purpose of distinguishing their tribes. The Shawanese nation,
for example, was originally divided into twelve tribes, which were subdivided into
septs or clans, recognized by the appellations of the Bear, the Turtle, the Eagle,
&c. In some cases individuals, particularly the more eminent warriors, formerly
assumed similar devices, commemorative of their prowess. "And this," says Mr.
R. C. Taylor, an American antiquary, " is *Indian Heraldry*, as useful, as commemo-

the tribes, and individuals so distinguished obtain the places of honour at feasts, and they are the leaders in battle. It is nearly the same in modern civilized life; titled personages are much sought after and fêted by the tribes of untitled; and are, moreover, the leaders of fashion. The only difference between the savage and civilized titles of honour is, that in the former case they can only be obtained by deeds; they must be earned; which is not always the case with modern distinctions."

All titles of honour indubitably originated in official employments, though, in the lapse of ages, they have become, as to the majority, entirely honorary. This will appear on an etymological inquiry into the meaning of the titles still enjoyed in our social system. Thus, DUKE is equivalent with *dux*, a leader or commander, and such, in a military sense, were those personages who primarily bore this distinction. MARQUIS, according to the best authorities, signifies a military officer to whom the sovereign intrusted the guardianship of the marches or borders of a territory. An EARL or count was the lieutenant or viceroy of a county, and the geographical term owes its origin to the office. A vice-comes, or VISCOUNT, again, was the deputy of a count. The derivation of BARON is more obscure; still there was a period when official duties were required of the holders of the title. To descend to the lesser nobility, KNIGHT is synonymous with servant, a servant in a threefold sense, first to religion, next to his sovereign, and thirdly to his ' ladye;' while an ESQUIRE was in antient times *ecuyer* or *scutifer*, the knight's shield-bearer. Among the Orientals official duties are still attached

rative, as inspiriting to the red warrior and his race, as that when, in the days of the Crusades, the banner and the pennon, the device and the motto, the crest and the war-cry exercised their potent influence on European chivalry."

to every title of honour; and it is worthy of remark that the highest of all titles, that of king, has never, in any country, been merely honorary; the responsible duties of government having always been connected with it.

In sovereigns, whom our old writers quaintly term 'fountains of honour,' is vested the right of conferring dignities, and it is by a judicious use of this prerogative that the balance of a limited monarchy is properly preserved. Were there no difference of grade amongst the subjects of a state, the monarch would be too far removed from his people, and mutual disgust or indifference would be the consequence. A well-constituted peerage serves as a connecting link between the sovereign and the great body of his subjects, and may therefore be regarded, next to the loyal affections of the people, the firmest prop of the throne.

I know that, in these utilitarian days, this position is frequently and fiercely controverted, and that probably by many who have never read the following eloquent passage of Burke —a passage which though *decies repetita placebit*, and which I therefore introduce without apology:

" To be honoured and even privileged by the laws, opinions, and inveterate usages of our country, growing out of the prejudice of ages, has nothing to provoke horror and indignation in any man. Even to be too tenacious of those privileges is not absolutely a crime. The strong struggle in every individual to preserve possession of what he has found to belong to him, and to distinguish him, is one of the securities against injustice and despotism implanted in our nature. It operates as an instinct to secure property, and to preserve communities in a settled state. What is there to shock in this? Nobility is a graceful ornament to the civil order. It is the Corinthian capital of polished society.

Omnes boni nobilitati semper favemus was the saying of a wise and good man. It is, indeed, one sign of a liberal and benevolent mind to incline to it with some sort of partial propensity. He feels no ennobling principle in his own heart who wishes to level all the artificial institutions which have been adopted for giving a body to opinion and permanence to fugitive esteem. *It is a sour, malignant, and envious disposition, without taste for the reality, or for any image or representation of virtue, that sees with joy the unmerited fall of what had long flourished in splendour and in honour.* I do not like to see anything destroyed, any void produced in society, any ruin on the face of the land."[1]

It is a fact not perhaps generally known that poverty formerly disqualified a peer from holding his dignity. In the reign of Edward IV, George Neville, duke of Bedford, was degraded on this account by Act of Parliament. The reason for this measure is given in the preamble of the Act: "Because it [poverty] causeth great extortion, &c. to the great trouble of all such countries where the estate [of the impoverished lord] happens to be."[2]

Happily for some of its members, no such prerogative is now exercised by Parliament.

Dignities and titles, like other things, are of course estimated by their rarity. "If all men were noble, where would be the noblesse of nobility?" In no country has so much prudence been displayed in regard to the multiplication of titles as in England. On the continent, as every one is aware, there is such a profusion of titled persons that, excepting those of the highest orders, they are very little respected on the

---

[1] Reflections on the Revolution in France.
[2] Blackstone, Rights of Persons, ch. xii.

score of honour. Titles are so cheap that persons of very indifferent reputation not unfrequently obtain them; and hence the Spanish proverb : " Formerly rogues were hung on crosses, but now crosses are hung upon rogues !" A German potentate once requested to be informed what station an English esquire occupied in the ladder of precedence, and was answered, that he stood somewhat higher than a French count, and somewhat lower than a German prince ! There was certainly more truth than courtesy in the reply.

Much has been written on the orders of precedence. I am neither disposed nor qualified to handle so delicate a subject; but the following table, showing how the various grades were formerly recognized by their *hawks,* is so curious that I do not hesitate to introduce it :

" An *eagle,* a *bawter* (vulture), a *melown;* these belong unto an *emperor.*

A *gerfalcon,* a *tercell* of gerfalcon are due to a *king.*

There is a *falcon* gentle and a *tercell* gentle ; and these be for a *prince.*

There is a *falcon* of the *rock;* and that is for a *duke.*

There is a *falcon* peregrine ; and that is for an *earl.*

Also there is a *bastard;* and that hawk is for a *baron.*

There is a *sacre* and a *sacret;* and these ben for a *knight.*

There is a *lanare* and a *laurell;* and these belong to a *squire.*

There is a *merlyon;* and that hawk is for a *lady.*

There is an *hoby;* and that is for a *young man.*

There is a *goshawk;* and that hawk is for a *yeoman.*

There is a *tercell;* and that is for a *poor man.*

There is a *spave-hawk;* she is an hawk for a *priest.*

There is a *muskyte*; and he is for an *holy-water clerk.*"
To this list the 'Jewel for Gentre' adds,
" A *kesterel* for a *knave* or *servant.*"[1]

Occupying a kind of intermediate rank between the
peerage and the commons stands the order of Baronets.
These, though really commoners, participate with peers the
honour of transmitting their title to their male descendants.
James I, the founder of this order, pledged himself to limit
its number to two hundred, but successive sovereigns, possessing the same right to enlarge as he had to establish it,
have more than quadrupled the holders of this dignity.

Baronets are in reality nothing more than hereditary
knights, and some families who have been invested with the
honour have gained little by it, seeing that their ancestors
regularly, in earlier times, acquired that of knighthood. It
is no unusual thing in tracing the annals of an antient
house, to find six or seven knights in the direct line, besides
those in the collateral branches. In the family of Calverley,
there was, if I mistake not, a *succession* of SIXTEEN knights.
This was a 'knightly race' indeed.

Of knighthood Nares remarks, " Since it was superseded
by the order of Baronets, it has incurred a kind of contumely
that is certainly injurious to its proper character. It has
been held cheaper by the public at large, and I fear also by
the sovereign himself. How often do we hear the remark
when a *Sir* or *Lady* is mentioned, 'He is *only* a Knight,'
or 'She is *only* a Knight's lady.' "

We have seen that knight is synonymous with servant.
So also is theign or thane, one of the oldest titles of

---

[1] Cited in Nares's Herald. Anom.

Northern nobility.   Bede translates it by Minister Regis.
Sometimes these thanes were servientes regis more literally
than would suit the ambition of modern courtiers, for in
Doomsday Book we find them holding such offices as
Latinarius, Aurifaber, Coquus, interpreter, goldsmith, cook.
Lord Ponsonby bears three combs in his arms, to commemo-
rate his descent from the Conqueror's barber !

Sir John Ferne traces the origin of knighthood to
Olybion, the grandson of Noah; and Lydgate and Chaucer
speak of the knights of Troy and Thebes.   But the honour
is not older than the introduction of the feudal system.
When the whole country was parcelled out under that
system, the possessor of each *feu* or *fee* (a certain value in
land) held it by knight's service, that is, by attending the
summons of the king, whenever he engaged in war, properly
equipped for the campaign, and leading on his vassals.
Knighthood was obligatory, as the possessor of every fee
was bound to receive the honour at the will of his sovereign
or other feudal superior.   Such knights were, in reference
to their dependants, styled lords.   Greater estates, consisting
of several knights' fees, were denominated Baronies, and
the possessor of such an estate was called a Baron, or
Banneret, on account of his right to display a square
banner in the field—an honour to which no one of inferior
rank could pretend.

Military aid was commonly all the rent which was required of a vassal.   Sometimes, however, sums of money
which now appear ludicrously small, or provisions for the
lord's household, were also demanded; and not unusually
these payments were commuted for a broad arrow, a falcon,
or a red rose.   From such rents numerous coats of arms
doubtless originated.

Knights are addressed as *Sir*, derived from the French Sire or Sieur, which was primarily applied to lords of a certain territory, as Le Sieur de Bollebec. This title was not limited to knighthood, for the great barons also used it. So also did ecclesiastics, even those holding very small benefices. I have found no instances of priests being called Sir, since the Reformation, except Shakspeare's Sir Hugh Evans, in the Merry Wives of Windsor, and there the dramatist evidently alludes to the practice of earlier times than his own. Two other applications of the expression may be noticed—*Sire* is a very respectful mode of address to a king; but what shall we say of the Scots, who apply it in the plural to women, and even to an individual of that sex—*Eh Sirs?*

To distinguish this, the most antient order of knights, from those of the Garter, Bath, and others, they are called Knights-Bachelors. ("What," asks Nares, "are the wives and children of a *bachelor?*") The etymology of this word in all its senses, is extremely obscure; so much so that scarcely any two authorities are agreed upon it. Menage, according to Johnson, derives it from *bas chevalier;* an unfortunate hypothesis, certainly, for it would make the compound word mean 'knight low-knight.'

Knighthood at the present day, so far from being restricted to the profession of war, is often given, says Clark,[1] "to gownsmen, physicians, burghers, and artists." Nares adds, "brewers, silversmiths, attorneys, apothecaries, upholsterers, hosiers, and tailors;" and continues, "I do by no means wish to see such persons placed out of the reach of honours, or deprived of the smiles and favours even of

---

[1] History of Knighthood, quoted by Nares.

royalty. King Alfred undoubtedly showed his wisdom in honouring merchants." He regards knighthood *inappropriate*, however, to the avocations named; but surely he could not have reflected that the successive changes which have come over the face of society have altered the import of nearly every title amongst us. The title of duke (*dux, general*) is as inappropriate when bestowed upon a civilian as that of knight—nay, more so; for in knighthood the erroneous application dies with the person honoured, while the dukedom (generalship) is hereditary.

The lowest titles borne in England are those of *Esquire* and *Gentleman*—titles which Coke (as Blackstone observes) has confounded together. Nor is it easy to discriminate between them, as every esquire is a gentleman, although every gentleman may not be an esquire. In the reign of Henry VI this difference is observable, namely, that the heads of families were commonly accounted esquires, while younger sons were styled gentlemen.

Esquireship, like knighthood, is a military dignity; and its origin is perfectly clear. In the earliest times, possibly in the days of Olybion himself, every warrior of distinction was attended by his armour-bearer. Hence in the romances of the middle ages we find the knight almost invariably attended by a subordinate personage, half-friend, half-servant, who carried his shield and other armour, and who thence acquired the designation of ecuyer, esquire, or (Anglicè) shield-bearer. In later periods, knights selected one, or more frequently, several, of their principal or most valiant retainers, to officiate as esquires during a campaign. These, in the event of a successful issue of the war, they often enriched with lands and goods, giving them, at the same time, the privilege of bearing armorial ensigns, copied in part from their own, or otherwise, according to circumstances.[1] After such a grant the person honoured became an esquire in another sense, as the bearer of *his own shield;* and in this sense all persons at the present day whose claim to bear arms would be admitted by the proper functionaries, are virtually, *scutifers, armigers,* or *esquiers.* But there is a more restricted use of the term, bearing relation to the honour in a civil rather than a military aspect, as we shall shortly see.

By the courtesies of common life, now-a-days, every person a little removed from the *ignobile vulgus* claims to be an esquire; and comparatively few, even among the better informed classes, know in what esquireship really consists. For the behoof of such as are confessedly ignorant of this branch of heraldry, and are not too proud to learn, I subjoin the following particulars, gathered from various respectable authorities. REAL esquires, then, are of seven sorts :

1. Esquires of the king's body, whose number is limited to four.

2. The eldest sons of knights, and *their* eldest sons born during their lifetime. It would seem that, in the days of antient warfare, the knight often took his eldest son into the wars for the purpose of giving him a practical military education, employing him meanwhile as his esquire. Such certainly was Chaucer's *squier.* With the knight

> " ther was his son, a young SQUIER,
> A lover, and a lusty bachelor . . . . .
> And he hadde be somtime in chevachie,[2]
> In Flaunders, in Artois, and Picardie."

---

[1] Vide pp. 34, 35.

[2] A military expedition.

3. The eldest sons of the younger sons of peers of the realm.

4. Such as the king invests with the collar of SS, including the kings of arms, heralds, &c. The dignity of esquire was conferred by Henry IV and his successors, by the investiture of the collar and the gift of a pair of silver spurs. Gower the poet was such an esquire by creation. In the ballad of the King (Edward IV) and the Tanner of Tamworth we find the frolicsome monarch creating a dealer in cowhides a squire in this manner :

> " A coller, a coller here, sayd the king,
>   A coller he loud gan crye ;
>   Then would he[1] lever than twentye pound,
>   He had not beene so nighe.
>
>   A coller, a coller, the tanner he sayd,
>   I trowe it will breed sorrowe ;
>   After a *coller* commeth a *halter*,
>   I trow I shall he hang'd to-morrowe."

5. Esquires to the knights of the Bath, *for life*, and their eldest sons.

6. Sheriffs of counties *for life*, coroners and justices of the peace, and gentlemen of the royal household, while they continue in their respective offices.

7. Barristers-at-law, doctors of divinity, law, and medicine, mayors of towns, and some others, are said to be of scutarial dignity, but not actual esquires.

Supposing this enumeration to comprise all who are entitled to esquireship, it will be evident that thousands of

---

[1] The Tanner.

persons styled esquires are not so in reality. It is a prevailing error that persons possessed of £300 a year in land are esquires, but an estate of £50,000 would not confer the dignity. Nothing but one or other of the conditions above mentioned is sufficient; yet there are some who contend that the representatives of families whose gentry is antient and unimpeachable, and who possess large territorial estates, are genuine esquires. This, however, does not seem to have been the opinion of such persons themselves two or three centuries ago, for we find many gentlemen possessing both these qualifications who, in documents of importance, such as wills and transfers of property, content themselves with the modest and simple style of *Yeoman*.

The mention of the word yeoman reminds us of the misappropriation of this expression in modern times. The true definition of it, according to Blackstone, is, one "that hath free land of forty shillings by the year; who is thereby qualified to serve on juries, vote for knights of the shire, and do any other act where the law requires one that is *probus et legalis homo*." Now, however, it is applied almost exclusively to farmers of the richer sort,[1] even though they do not possess a single foot of land. The yeomen of the feudal ages were as much renowned for their valorous deeds on the

[1] There are two other expressions applied to this respectable class which are extremely incorrect, namely, *gentlemen-farmers* and *tenant-farmers*. A person who by birth, education, and wealth, is entitled to the distinction of gentleman, and who chooses to devote his capital to agriculture may be properly designated a *farming-gentleman*, though the occupation of a large estate without those qualifications can never constitute a *gentleman*-farmer. *Tenant-farmer*, a phrase which has lately been in the mouth of every politician, is as fine a piece of tautology as 'coat-making tailor' or 'shoe-mending cobbler' would be.

"It maketh me laugh to see," says Sir John Ferne's *Columel*, "a jolly peece of worke it were, to see plow-men made Gentle-men!"

14

battle-field, as those of a later period were for their wealth. In the sixteenth century it was said—

> " 𝕬 𝕶𝖓𝖎𝖌𝖍𝖙 𝖔𝖋 𝕮𝖆𝖑𝖊𝖘, 𝖆 𝖘𝖖𝖚𝖎𝖗𝖊 𝖔𝖋 𝖂𝖆𝖑𝖊𝖘,
> 𝕬𝖓𝖉 𝖆 𝖑𝖆𝖎𝖗𝖉 𝖔𝖋 𝖙𝖍𝖊 𝕹𝖔𝖗𝖙𝖍 𝕮𝖔𝖚𝖓𝖙𝖗𝖊𝖊,
> ## 𝕬 𝖄𝖊𝖔𝖒𝖆𝖓 𝖔𝖋 𝕶𝖊𝖓𝖙, 𝖜𝖎𝖙𝖍 𝖍𝖎𝖘 𝖕𝖊𝖆𝖗𝖑𝖞 𝖗𝖊𝖓𝖙,
> 𝖂𝖔𝖚𝖑𝖉 𝖇𝖚𝖞 𝖙𝖍𝖊𝖒 𝖔𝖚𝖙 𝖆𝖑𝖑 𝖙𝖍𝖗𝖊𝖊."

It is much to be regretted that this substantial class of men is almost extinct. To how few are the words of Horace now applicable—

> " Beatus ille, qui procul negotiis,
> Ut prisca gens mortalium,
> *Paterna rura* bobus exercet suis."

> " Happy the man whose wish and care
> A few paternal acres bound;
> Content to breathe his native air
> *On his own ground.*"

But I am violating the laws of precedence in noticing yeomen before gentlemen.   The term *gentleman* is, perhaps, one of the most indefinite in the English language. George IV prided himself in being the finest gentleman in Europe; every peer of the realm is a *gentleman;* every judge, member of parliament, and magistrate is a *gentleman;* every clergy-man, lawyer, and doctor is a *gentleman;* every merchant and tradesman is a *gentleman;* every farmer and mechanic is a *gentleman;* every draper's errand-boy and tailor's apprentice is a *gentleman;* and every ostler who, " in the worst inn's worst room," treats the stable-boy with a pot of ale is there-upon declared to be a *gentleman.* So say the courtesies of society; but there is the legal and heraldric, as well as the social, gentleman.

"As for GENTLEMEN (says Sir Thomas Smith[1]) they be made good cheape in this kingdom: for whosoever studieth the laws of the realm, who studieth in the universities, who professeth liberal sciences, and (to be short) who can live idly and without manual labour, and will bear the port, charge, and countenance of a gentleman, he shall be called master, and taken for a gentleman." This is the legal definition; but the heralds of former days recognized several different classes of gentlemen; Sir John Ferne, in his 'Blazon of Gentry,'[2] enumerates the following:

1. Gentlemen of ancestry, with blood and coat-armour perfect; namely, those whose ancestors, on both sides, have, for five generations at least, borne coat-armour.

2. Gentlemen of blood and coat-armour perfect, but not of ancestry; being those descended in the fifth degree from him 'that slewe a Saracen or Heathen Gentle-man;' from him that won the standard, guidon, or coat-armour of a Christian gentleman, and so bare his arms; from him that obtained arms by gift from his sovereign; or from him that purchased an estate to which arms appertained. To this order likewise belong a yeoman who has worthily obtained arms and knighthood; and a yeoman who has been made a doctor of laws and has obtained a coat of arms.

3. Gentlemen of blood perfect, and coat armour imperfect; the 'yonger blouds' of a house, of which the elder line has failed after a lineal succession of five generations.

4. Gentlemen of blood and coat-armour imperfect; the *third* in lineal descent from him who slew a Saracen gentle-

---

[1] Quoted by Blackstone.   [2] Page 89 et seq.

man, &c. &c. &c., as under the third description; also the
natural son of a gentleman of blood and coat-armour perfect,
and the legitimate son of a yeoman, by a gentlewoman of
blood, &c., being an inheritrix.

5. Gentlemen of coat-armour imperfect : those who have
slain an infidel gentleman, &c., *ut supra;* also gentlemen of
paper and wax.

6. Gentlemen, neither of blood nor coat-armour, are of
three orders; namely, 1, *Apocrafat*—Students of common
law and grooms of the sovereign's palace, having no coat-
armour; 2, *Spiritual*—A churl's son made a priest, canon,
&c.; and 3, *Untriall*—He who being brought up in the service of a bishop, abbot, or baron, enjoys the bare title of
gentleman; and he that having received any degree of the
schools, or borne any office in a city so as to be saluted
Master.

As Saracen-killing has long ceased to be a favourite amusement,—as the winning of standards is an undertaking as rare
as it is perilous,—as few in protestant England have the good
fortune to serve abbots and bishops,—and, as a grant of arms
by the heralds is a somewhat expensive affair,—how very few
have now the chance of becoming *gentlemen* in the heraldrical sense of the term.   Widely at variance with the
courtesies of every-day life are these antiquated laws of
chivalry !

We have seen that nearly every man, from the throne to
the stable, each in his own sphere, is recognized as a gentleman; yet how few, notwithstanding, like to be so described
in a legal, formal manner.   Formerly, it was customary to
add GENT., as an honourable distinction to one's name, in the
address of his letters, in his will, or upon his tombstone; but
in these days nothing short of ESQ. is deemed respectful.

This foible, however, is not a thing of yesterday; for so long ago as 1709, Mr. Isaac Bickerstaff, of the Tatler, says : "I have myself a couple of clerks; one directs to Degory Goosequill, *Esquire*, to which the other replies by a note to Nehemiah Dashwell, *Esquire*, with respect."

What courtesy at first concedes, the party honoured soon learns to exact. The tenacity with which many persons of some pretensions to family, but with very few of the other qualifications which are supposed to belong to the character of a gentleman, adhere to the courtesy title of *Esq.* must have been observed by every one. I have heard of persons of this description, who, from the pressure of circumstances, have entered into trade, being mortified by its omission; though their own good sense must have suggested to them the absurdity of such an address as "Nicholas Smith, Esq. Tailor," or "Geoffry Brownman, Esq. Butcher." Not long since a *squireen* of this order (in a southern county), who eked out the little residuum of his patrimony by the occupation of a farm comprising a few acres of hops, on receiving a letter from the local excise-officer respecting the hop-duty with which he was charged, felt his dignity much insulted at being styled in the address plain *Mr.* Full of rage at the insolence of the official, he appealed to the collector, expecting, probably, that he would reprimand the offender with great severity. The collector, however, treated the matter as a joke, but ordered his clerk to strike out *Mr.* from the beginning of the name, and to add Esq. at the end. This was not satisfactory to the insulted party, who determined to appeal to a higher court. He accordingly paid a visit to the magistrates in petty sessions assembled at H——, and a dialogue somewhat like the following took place.

Chairman. What is your application?

Squireen (with a low salaam). Sir, I come here to have my title confirmed.

Chairman (in surprise). To what title do you allude, Sir?

Sq. I have the honour to be an Esquire; and I have here a document to show that I have not been treated with the respect due to my rank. I demand a summons for the writer of this letter.

The letter was handed to the bench, and the chairman, looking doubtfully at his colleagues, requested our squireen to withdraw while his application was considered. He withdrew accordingly, and the magistrates were not a little amused with the case. Fortunately, a gentleman who had witnessed the scene before the collector happened to be present, and he having related the particulars, the bench ordered the applicant to be recalled. The cry of " N. M. *Esquire!* N. M. *Esquire!*" resounded along the room and down the staircase. That gentleman responded to the call with great alacrity, and approached the bench with another profound obeisance; while the chairman, assuming all the gravity he could command, said—

Sir; the magistrates have considered your application, and although they would not feel justified in issuing a summons against the offending party, yet they have come to an unanimous decision that your claim to be considered an Esquire is well founded. Sir, I have the satisfaction to inform you that YOUR TITLE IS CONFIRMED!

A third inclination followed this highly satisfactory sentence, and our Esquire left the court with as much dignity as if he had just been created an earl, or rather with as much as Don Quixote exhibited in the stable-yard, after the innkeeper had conferred upon him the honour of knighthood.

The *Country Squires* may be regarded as an extinct race; and though in the present advanced state of society we can scarcely wish to see that rude and stalwart order revived, yet there are many parts of their character which certainly deserve the imitation of their more polished descendants. The subjoined description of an antient worthy of this class, Mr. Hastings, of Dorsetshire,[1] though familiar to many readers, I venture to introduce.

"Mr. Hastings was low of stature, but strong and active, of a ruddy complexion, with flaxen hair. His clothes were always of green cloth, his house was of the old fashion, in the midst of a large park, well stocked with deer, rabbits, and fishponds. He had a long narrow bowling-green in it, and used to play with round sand bowls. Here, too, he had a banquetting room built, like a stand, in a large tree! He kept all sorts of hounds, that ran buck, fox, hare, otter, and badger; and had hawks of all kinds, both long and short winged. His great hall was commonly strewed with marrow-bones, and full of hawk-perches, hounds, spaniels, and terriers. The upper end of it was hung with fox-skins of this and the last year's killing. Here and there a pole-cat was intermixed, and hunters' poles in great abundance. The parlour was a large room, completely furnished in the same style. On a broad hearth, paved with brick, lay some of the choicest terriers, hounds, and spaniels. One or two of the great chairs had litters of cats in them, which were not to be disturbed. Of these, three or four always attended

---

[1] He was living in 1638, and was son, brother, and uncle to three successive earls of Huntingdon. An account of him coinciding in many particulars with the one here given is painted in gold letters beneath an original portrait in the possession of his descendants: it is said to have been written by the celebrated earl of Shaftesbury. (Vide Bell's Huntingdon Peerage.)

him at dinner, and a little white wand lay by his trencher
to defend it, if they were too troublesome. In the windows,
which were very large, lay his arrows, crossbows, and other
accoutrements. The corners of the room were filled with his
best hunting and hawking poles. His oyster table stood at
the lower end of the room, which was in constant use twice a
day, all the year round, for he never failed to eat oysters
both at dinner and supper, with which the neighbouring
town of Pool supplied him. At the upper end of the room
stood a small table with a double desk, one side of which
held a Church Bible, the other the Book of Martyrs. On
different tables in the room lay hawks-hoods, bells, old hats,
with their crowns thrust in, full of pheasants' eggs; tables,
dice, cards, and store of tobacco-pipes. At one end of this
room was a door, which opened into a closet, where stood
bottles of strong beer, and wine, which never came out but
in single glasses, which was the rule of the house; for he
never exceeded himself, nor permitted others to exceed.
Answering to this closet, was a door into an old chapel,
which had been long disused for devotion; but in the pulpit,
as the safest place, was always to be found a cold chine of
beef, a venison pasty, a gammon of bacon, or a great apple-
pie, with thick crust, well baked. His table cost him not
much, though it was good to eat at. His sports supplied
all, but beef and mutton, except on Fridays, when he had
the best of fish. He never wanted a London pudding, and
he always sang it in with " My part lies therein-a." He
drank a glass or two of wine at meals; put syrup of gilly-
flowers into his sack; and had always a tun glass of small
beer standing by him, which he often stirred about with
rosemary. He lived to be an hundred, and never lost
his eyesight, nor used spectacles. He got on horseback

without help, and rode to the death of the stag at four-score."[1]

In consequence of the cheapness of titles in foreign countries, our esquires and gentry are frequently under-valued by strangers, who can form no idea of an untitled aristocracy. We are accustomed to consider no families noble except those possessing the degree of baron, or some superior title; and the branches, even of a ducal house, after a certain number of removes from the titled repre-sentative cease to be noble. On the continent it is other-wise: all the descendants of a peer are noble. Our antient gentry, possessed of the broad lands which have descended to them through a long line of ancestors, are virtually more noble, in the heraldric sense of the term, than dukes and marquises who are but of yesterday. New nobility cannot compensate for the want of antient gentry.

The caviller will perhaps ask, concerning some of the rambling observations contained in this chapter, and the subject which has called them forth, *Cui bono?* He may also mutter something about the nobility of virtue, as the only one worth possessing. Well, well, let him enjoy his opinion, and maintain it if he can; but until he has con-vinced me that true integrity and exalted benevolence cannot reside beneath a coronet, and that the nobility of station obliterates or neutralizes that of virtue, I shall beg leave also to enjoy mine; admitting, meanwhile, the correctness of a sentiment quaintly, though wisely, advanced by Sir John

---

[1] " The hall of the Squire," says Aubrey, " was usually hung round with the insignia of the squire's amusements, such as hunting, shooting, fishing, &c.; but in case he were Justice of Peace it was *dreadful to behold.* The skreen was garnished with corslets and helmets, gaping with open mouths, with coats of mail, launces, pikes, halberts, brown bills, bucklers, &c."

Ferne: "That kind of gentry which is but a bare noblenes of bloud, not clothed with vertues (the right colours of a gentleman's coat-armour) is the *meanest*, yea, and the *most base* of all the rest: for it respecteth but onely the body, being derived from the loynes of the auncestors, not from the minde, which is the habitation of vertue, the inne of reason, and the resemblaunce of God; and, in true speach, this gentry of stock *only* shal be said but a shadow, or rather a painture of nobility."[1]

> " **Manners makyth man,**
> **Quoth William of Wykeham.**"

[1] Glory of Generositie, p. 15.

CHAPTER XI.

Historical Notices of the College of Arms.

(Arms of the College.) [1]

" Their consequence was great in the court, in the camp, and, still more than either, in the council; as negociators they had great influence; they were conspicuous for judgment, experience, learning, and elegance; they gained honour whenever they were employed."—*Noble.*

WE have seen, in a former chapter, that at an early period the sovereign and his greater nobles retained in their respective establishments certain officers called heralds, whose duties have been slightly alluded to. In the

[1] The vignette is copied from the common seal of the College, which has the following legend in Roman characters:

+ SIGILLVM · COMMVNE · CORPORACIONIS · OFFICII · ARMORVM.

present chapter the reader will find a hasty sketch of the history of these functionaries in their incorporated capacity as a **College of Arms.**

The College of Arms, or, as it is often called, the " Heralds' College," owes its origin as a corporation to a monarch who has the misfortune to occupy a very unenviable place in the scroll of fame; to a man whose abilities and judgment would have received all due honour from posterity had they been coupled with the attributes of justice and benevolence, and attended with a better claim to the sceptre of these realms. But, whatever may be said of Richard III as an usurper, a murderer, and a tyrant, impartial justice awards to him the credit of a wise and masterly execution of the duties of the regal office.   Many of the regulations in the state adopted by him and continued by his successors bear the impress of a mind of no despicable order.   One of his earliest acts was the foundation of this college.   " Personally brave, and nurtured from his infancy in the use of the sword, he was more especially ambitious of preserving the hereditary dignity and superior claims of the **White Rose.**   He supported, at his own charge, Richard Champneys, Falcon herald, whom upon his accession he created Gloucester king of arms, and at whose instance he was further induced to grant to the body of heralds immunities of great importance."[1]   His letters patent for this purpose bear date March 2d, 1483, the first year of his reign.   The heraldic body, as originally constituted, consisted of twelve of the most approved heralds, for whose habitation he assigned a messuage in the parish of All Saints in London, called Pulteney's Inn, or Cold Harbore.[2]   As

[1] Dallaway.

[2] The former appellation was given to this mansion because it was originally the inn or town residence of Sir John Poulteney, who flourished under Edward III,

usual with every fraternity of those times, the newly-constituted college had a chaplain, whose stipend was fixed at £20 per annum. The 'right fair and stately house,' as it is termed by Stowe, was first presided over by Sir John Wriothesley, or Wrythe, whose arms were assumed by the body, and are still perpetuated on their corporate seal. For the better performance of the duties of the heralds, the kingdom was divided into two provinces, over each of which presided a king of arms. The title of the officer who regulated all heraldric affairs south of the river Trent was *Clarenceux*, and that of him who exercised jurisdiction northward of it, *Norroy*. From this statement it must not be inferred that kings of arms had not previously existed, for there were a *Norroy* and a *Surroy*[1] (q. d. 'northern king' and 'southern king,') as early as the reign of Edward III; although their duties were not so well defined nor their authority so great as both became after the incorporation of the college. Over both these, as principal of the establishment, was appointed *Garter*, king of arms, an office instituted by King Henry V, and so called from his official connexion with the order of knighthood bearing that designation. Next in point of dignity to the provincial kings, stood several *heralds* bearing peculiar

and was four times lord mayor. Stowe calls it Cole-Herbert, but by other authors it is generally spelt as in the text. The name Cold-Harbour is common to many *farms* in the southern counties of England. There are several in Sussex which are by no means remarkable for the bleakness of their situation, and a house in Surrey bearing this singular designation is placed in a remarkably sheltered spot, at the foot of a range of hills. Harbour means not only a sea-port or haven, but any place of shelter or retreat : the epithet 'cold' is doubtless a corruption of some other word.

[1] The title of Surroy was changed to Clarenceux by Henry V, in compliment to his brother Thomas, duke of Clarence ; the first king of this name having been the private herald attached to the duke's establishment.

titles, and the third rank was composed of pursuivants, or students, who could not be admitted into the superior offices until they had passed some years of probationary study and practice in the duties of their vocation. These three degrees, it is scarcely necessary to state, still exist in the corporation. From a very early period Garter exercised, and still continues to exercise, a concurrent jurisdiction with the two Provincial Kings of Arms in the grant of Armorial Ensigns, but he had many exclusive privileges; as the right of ordering all funerals of peers of the realm, the two archbishops, the bishop of Winchester, and knights of the Garter; he only could grant arms to these individuals; he was consequently a person of no inconsiderable importance.

The duties of the officers of arms at this period consisted in attending all ceremonials incident to the king and the nobility, such as coronations, creations, the displaying of banners on the field of battle or in the lists, public festivities and processions, the solemnization of baptisms, marriages, and funerals, the enthronization of prelates, proclamations, and royal journeys or progresses. The importance of the presence of heralds at royal funerals of a somewhat later date, is shown in the two following extracts :[1]

" And incontinent all the heraudes did off their cote-armour, and did hange them upon the rayles of the herse, *cryinge lamentably* in French, ' The noble king Henry the seaveneth is dead ;' and as soon as they had so done, everie heraude putt on his cote-armure againe, and cried with a loude voyce, ' Vive le noble Henry le viijth.' "

At the interment of Prince Arthur, 1502 :

" At every Kurie elyeson an officer of arms with a high voyce said for Prince Arthure's soule and all Christian soules,

---

[1] Quoted by Dall. p. 141.

Pater-noster . . . . . . His officer of arms, *sore weeping*, toke off his coate of armes, and cast it along over the cheaste right lamentablie." [1]

The fees demanded on the occasions before recited were considerable, but the officers of arms had another source of revenue, namely, the largesses or rewards for proclaiming the styles and titles of the nobility. These were optional, and generally corresponded to the rank and opulence of the donors. " On Newe-yeares-day," [1486], says Leland, " the king, being in a riche gowne, dynede in his chamber, and gave to his officers of armes vi*l*. of his Largesse, wher he was cryed in his style accustomede. Also the quene gave to the same officers x*ls*. and she was cried in her style. At the same time my lady the kyngs moder gave xx*s*. and she was cried Largesse iij tymes. De hault, puissaunt, et excellent Princesse, la mer du Roy notre souveraigne, countesse de Richemonde et de Derbye, Largesse. Item, the Duc of Bedeforde gave x*ls*. and he was cried, Largesse de hault et puissaunt prince, frere et uncle des Roys, duc de Bedeforde, et counte de Penbroke, Largesse. Item, my lady his wiff gave xiij*s*. iiij*d*. and she was cried, Largesse de hault et puissaunt princesse, duchesse de Bedeforde et de Bokingham, countesse de Penbrok, Stafford, Harford, et de Northampton, et dame de Breknok, Largesse. Item, the Reverende Fader in God the Lorde John Fox, Bishop of Excester, privy seale, gave xx*s*. Item, th' Erle of Aroundell gave x*s*, and he was cried, Largesse de noble et puissaunt seigneur le counte d'Aroundell, et seigneur de Maltravers. Item, th' Erle of Oxinforde gave xx*s*. and he was cryede, Largesse de noble et puissaunt le Counte d'Oxinforde,

---

[1] At modern funerals it is no part of the heralds' duty to render their 'coats' *guttée des larmes!*

Marquis de Develyn, Vicount de Bulbik, et Seigneur de
Scales, Graunde Chamberlayn, et Admirall d'Angleter,
Largesse.   Item, my lady his wiff xx*s.* and she was cried,
Largesse de noble et puissaunt Dame la Countesse d'Oxinford,
Marquise de Develyn, Vicountesse de Bulbik, et Dame de
Scales, &c. &c."

Another perquisite of the heraldic corps were great
quantities of the rich stuffs, such as velvet, tissue, and cloth
of gold, used as the furniture of great public ceremonials.
The following are some of the fees claimed by the officers
on state occasions, as recorded in one of the Ashmolean
MSS.

> " At the coronacion of the Kinge of England c*l.* [1], appareled in
> scarlet.
>
> " At the displaying of the King's banner in any campe . . . . . .
> c markes.
>
> " At the displaying of a Duke's banner, £20.
>
> " At a Marquis's, 20 markes.
>
> " At an Earle's, x*l.*, &c. &c.
>
> " The Kinge marrying a wife £50, *with the giftes of the King's
> and Queen's uppermost garments !*
>
> " At the birth of the King's eldest son, 100 markes; at the
> birth of other younger children, £20.
>
> " The King being at any syge (siege) with the crowne on his
> head, £5.

" The wages due to the officers of armes when they go owt of
the land:

> " Garter 8*s.* a day: every of the other kings 7*s.*: every
> herald 4*s.*: every pursuivant 2*s.*: and theyr ordinary
> expences."

---

[1] Equal, probably, to £1200 or £1500, at the present value of money.

To return to the thread of our history : at the death of Richard III,[1] all his public acts were declared null and void, as those of an usurper, and the heraldic body, in common with others, fell under the censure of Henry. Driven from their stately mansion of Cold-Harbour, they betook themselves to the conventual house of Rounceval, near Charing Cross, which had been a cell to the priory of Rouncevaulx, in Navarre, and suppressed with the rest of the alien priories by the jealous policy of Henry V. Here they remained for many years, though only by sufferance, for Edward VI granted the site to Sir Thomas Cawarden.

It must not be imagined that the heralds were created merely for the purpose of acting as puppets in the pageantry of the court and the camp : they had other and more useful functions to perform. The genealogies of noble and gentle families were intrusted to their keeping, and thus titular honours and territorial possessions were safely conveyed to lawful heirs, when, in the absence of proper officers, and a recognized depository for documents, much confusion might have been produced by disputed claims. The ecclesiastics had formerly been the chief conservators of genealogical facts, but at the dissolution of the monasteries by Henry VIII, the documents containing them were scattered to the winds. Hence it became necessary to adopt some more general and better regulated means of collecting and transmitting to posterity the materials of genealogy, and out of this necessity sprang those ' progresses' of the kings of arms and heralds through the various counties, called VISITATIONS. Some

---

[1] After the death of Richard upon the field of Bosworth, a pursuivant (perhaps one of his own creation) was employed to carry his remains to Leicester. ;" His body naked to the skinne, not so much as one clout about him," says Stowe, " was trussed behinde a *Pursuivant of Armes*, like a hogge or calfe."

15

faint traces of these visitations occur, it is true, before the
Reformation, and even before the incorporation of the
heralds, namely, as early as 1412; but it was not until 1528
that they were systematically attended to.[1]   After the latter
date they were continued about once in every generation,
or at intervals varying between twenty-five and forty years.
The officers, under the warrant of the earl-marshal, were
bound to make inquisitions respecting the pedigree of every
family claiming the honour of gentry, and to enter the
names, titles, places of abode, &c. in a book.   Many such
books, between the date just referred to and the year 1687,
are now existing in the College of Arms, while many copies
of them, and a few of the originals, are in the British
Museum and in private collections.   To most of the pedigrees thus entered were attached the family arms, which
received the confirmation of the 'kings' when satisfactory
evidence of the bearer's right to them could be adduced.[2]

[1] Among the Dugdale MSS. are the following memoranda of Tong, Norroy,
made during a visitation of Lancashire, temp. Henry VIII: "John Talbot of
Salebury, a verry gentyll Esqwyr, and well worthye to be takyne payne for."
"Sir John Townley of Townley. I sought hym all day rydynge in the wyld
contrey, and his reward was ij", whyche the gwyde had the most part, and I had as
evill a jorney as ever I had." "Sir R. H. Knyght. The said Sir R. H. has put
awaye the lady his wyffe, and kepys a concobyne in his howse, by whom he has
dyvers children. And by the lady aforsayd he has Leyhall, whych armes he berys
quarterde with hys in the furste quarter. He sayd that Master Garter lycensed
hym so to do, and he gave Mr. Garter an angell noble, but he gave me nothing,
nor made me no good cher, but gave me prowde words." Certes *he* was a very
naughty and '*un*gentyll Esqwyr.'

[2] It frequently happened in those days, as well as at the present time, that
parties used arms for which they had no authority either from grant or antient
usage. These were publicly disclaimed by the heralds who made visitation. In
a copy of the Visitation of Wiltshire, in 1623, are the names of no less than fifty-
four persons so disclaimed at Salisbury. (Montagu's Guide, p. 21.)

When a family from any circumstance did not bear arms, a coat was readily granted by the kings, who received fees proportioned to the rank of the parties; for example:

A bishop paid £10.

A dean £6 13s. 4d.

A gentleman of 100 marks per annum, in land, £6 13s. 4d.

A gentleman of inferior revenue £6.

The passion for emblazoning the arms of the nobility and gentry upon glass, in the windows of churches and halls, imposed considerable employment, and brought no small emolument, to the officers of arms, who undertook to marshal and arrange them, as well as often to draw up short pedigrees of such families, which were set forth in the gloomy chancel or the sombre hall of the long-descended patron or lord of the mansion, exemplified with the shield rich in quarterings.[1]

Henry VIII was a great admirer of the " pomp and circumstance" of chivalry. During his reign the College was in high estimation and full employment. At home and abroad he was constantly attended by his heralds, some of whom were often despatched to foreign courts, to assist in negociations, to declare war, to accompany armies, to summon garrisons, to deliver the ensign of the order of St. George (the Garter) to foreign potentates, to attend ban-

[1] Noble, p. 105. In these heraldric displays the arms of the sovereign generally found a conspicuous place. "The royal arms placed over doors or upon buildings was an antient mode of denoting that they were under the protection of the sovereign. When some troops of a tyrant were ravaging the estates of the Chartreuse de Montrieu, the monks had recourse to the antient remedy. They put up the arms of the king over the gate of the house; but the depredators laughed at it, saying that it might have been efficacious in times past (que cela étoit bon autrefois) and persecuted them with more severity." (Mem. de Petrarque, quoted by Fosbroke.)

quets, jousts, and tournaments, and to serve upon every
great occasion of state. "There was nothing performed,"
says Noble,[1] "of a public nature, but what the heralds were
employed in."

The history of this reign teems with curious anecdotes
touching the dignity and prerogatives of the heralds. So
great was the regard entertained by the 'bluff' monarch
for the officers of arms, that he treated even those of foreign
sovereigns, who came to his court to deliver hostile messages,
with all the courtesy inculcated by the laws of chivalry, and
even gave them bountiful largesses. For example, when in
1513 'Lord Lyon, King at Arms,' came to him at Tours
upon an errand of a very disagreeable character from the
Scottish court, his majesty sent Garter with him to his tent,
commanding him to give him 'good cheer;' and when his
reply to the message was framed he dismissed him cour-
teously, with a gift of one hundred angels.[2] Although the
persons of the heralds, in their ambassadorial capacity, were
generally regarded as sacred, they sometimes received very
rough treatment from desperate enemies. On one occasion,
Ponde, Somerset herald, going to Scotland with a message
to James V, was slain in his tabard—a violation of the laws
of honour which was only compensated by the death of the
bailiff of Lowth and two others, who were publicly executed
at Tyburn in the summer of 1543.

"It is singular," says Noble, "that in this reign it was
usual to give to pieces of ordnance the same names as those
appropriated to the members of the college; names, we must
presume, dear to the sovereign and cherished by the people."[3]

At the Field of the Cloth of Gold, in 1520, the heraldic

[1] Hist. Coll. Arms, 102.   [2] Ib. 102.   [3] Ib. 107.

corporation attended in magnificent array. It then consisted
of the following members :

KINGS.   Garter, Clarenceux, Norroy.

HERALDS.   Windsor, Richmond, York, Lancaster,
  Carlisle, Montorgueil, Somerset.

PURSUIVANTS IN ORDINARY.   Rouge-Cross, Blue-
  Mantle, Portcullis, and Rouge-Dragon.

PURSUIVANTS EXTRAORDINARY.   Calais, Risebank,
  Guisnes, and Hampnes.   These four took their
  titles from places in France within the English pale.

The armorial bearings devised in this reign had little of
the chaste simplicity of those of an earlier date. Those
coats which contain a great variety of charges may be generally referred to this period, and they are familiarly styled
' *Henry-the-Eighth* coats.' Such arms have been humorously
compared to " garrisons, *well stocked* with fish, flesh, and
fowl."[1]

Edward VI bestowed upon the heralds many additional
immunities and privileges; and Mary, his successor, by
charter dated 1554, granted them Derby House for the
purpose of depositing their rolls and other records.

---

[1] Mr. Woodham, in his tract (No. 4 of the publications of the Cambridge
Antiq. Soc.) says, " The styles of blazonry admit of classification like those of
Gothic Architecture. The bare deviceless ordinaries agree with the sturdy pier
and flat buttress of the *Norman* age ; the progress of ornament uniting still with
chasteness of design may be called *Early English;* the fourteenth century exhibits
the perfection of both sciences, as displayed in the highest degree of *Decoration*
consistent with purity ; and the mannerism of Henry VIII's time, with its crowded
field and accumulated charges, is as essentially *Florid* and flamboyant as any
panelling or tracery in the kingdom." (p. 11.)

Elizabeth inherited from her father the spirit of chivalry, and its concomitant fondness for pageantry. Hence she necessarily patronized the officers of arms. In this reign the quarrels which for some time previously had been hatching between various members of the body touching their individual rights, broke out with great virulence. "Their accusations against each other," Noble remarks, "would fill a volume." Broke, or Brokesmouth, York Herald, whose animosities against the great and justly venerated Camden have given to his name a celebrity which it does not deserve, was foremost amongst the litigants.[1]

A new order of gentry had sprung up in the two or three preceding reigns, some of whom had enriched themselves by commercial enterprise, while others had acquired broad lands at the dissolution of the monasteries. These *novi homines* were very ambitious of heraldric honours, and accordingly made numerous applications for grants of arms. Cooke, Clarenceux, granted upwards of five hundred coats, and the two Dethicks twice that number in this reign, Great pains were taken by the sovereign to preserve inviolate the rights of the college; yet notwithstanding there were some adventurers who, for the sake of lucre, devised arms and forged pedigrees for persons of mean family, to the no small umbrage of the antient gentry, and the pecuniary loss of the corporation. One W. Dawkeyns compiled nearly a hundred of these spurious genealogies for families in Essex, Herts, and Cambridgeshire, an offence for which he was visited with the pillory; but though he stood "earless on high," he seems to have been "unabashed;" for after an interval of twenty years he was found 'at his olde trickes againe,' and

---

[1] See Chapter XII.

again fell under the lash of the earl-marshal. The warrant for his second apprehension is dated Dec. 31st, 1597.

James I advanced the regular salaries of the heralds, and indirectly promoted their interests, further, by a lavish distribution of new titular honours. In this reign occurs an instance of the antient custom of degrading a knight. Sir Frances Michel having been convicted of grievous exactions was sentenced, in 1621, to a 'degradation of honour.' Being brought by the sheriff of London to Westminster-Hall, in the presence of the commissioners who then executed the office of earl-marshal and the kings of arms, the sentence of parliament was openly read by Philipot, a pursuivant, when the servants of the marshall hacked off his spurs, broke his sword over his head, and threw away the pieces, and the first commissioner proclaimed with uplifted voice, that he was "𝔫𝔬 𝔩𝔬𝔫𝔤𝔢𝔯 𝔨𝔫𝔦𝔤𝔥𝔱, 𝔟𝔲𝔱 𝔞 𝔰𝔠𝔬𝔲𝔫𝔡𝔯𝔢𝔩-𝔨𝔫𝔞𝔟𝔢!"

The disputes in the College concerning the duties and prerogatives of its members, and their jealousies respecting preferments continued unabated. Broke (or Brokesmouth), York, and Treswell, Somerset, carried their effrontery so far as to defy the authority of their superiors in office, for which offence, added to contempt of the earl-marshal, they were committed to prison. The house was 'divided against itself,' and consequently could not 'stand,' at least in the respect and estimation of the public. Francis Thynne, a herald of the period, speaks of the poverty of the College as compared with its antient condition; complains that 'the heralds are not esteemed,' and that 'every one withdraweth his favour from them;' and prays the superior powers to repair their 'ruined state.'

Of Charles I it has been truly said, that he was

not more arbitrary in his government than several of his
predecessors had been. His mistake was, that he did not
march with the times, but wished, amid the increased en-
lightenment of the 17th century, to exercise the monarchical
prerogatives of the middle ages. Most of the acts which
led to his downfall were not greater violations of the fun-
damental principles of the constitution than had been committed by earlier monarchs; but the time was now come when
they could no longer be tolerated by a free and generous
nation. In relation to heraldic usages Charles only copied
the acts of former sovereigns; yet they added not a little to
his unpopularity. One of his commissions directed to the
provincial kings of arms, authorized them to visit all churches,
mansions, public halls, and other places, to inspect any arms,
cognizances, or crests, set up therein; and, if found faulty
in regard of proof, to pull down and deface the same. It
further empowered them to reprove, control, and *make in-
famous, by proclamation at courts of assize,* all persons who
had without sufficient warrant assumed the title of esquire or
gentleman; to forbid the use of velvet palls at the funerals
of persons of insufficient rank; and to prevent any painter,
glazier, engraver, or mason, from representing any armorial
ensigns, except under their sanction and direction. All de-
linquents were to be cited into the earl-marshal's Court of
Chivalry, an institution almost as arbitrary and unconstitu-
tional as the court of Star-Chamber itself. Nothing perhaps,
as Noble observes, injured the Heralds' College more than
this shameful tribunal, which proceeded to fine and imprisonment for mere words spoken against the gentility of
the plaintiff. "Had it only decided upon what usually ends
in duels it would have been a most praiseworthy institution."
But it went further, and its severity became deservedly odious

to the nation. Mr. Hyde (afterwards Lord Clarendon) de-
precated its insolence and said, "the youngest man remembered the beginning of it, and he hoped the oldest might
see the end of it."—"A citizen of good quality," said he, " a
merchant, was by that court ruined in his estate and his
body imprisoned, *for calling a swan a goose !*"

It is needless to say that the Court of Chivalry was swept
away along with other grievances of a like nature in the revolution which succeeded. It was revived, however, at the
restoration of Charles II, and continued, though rather
feebly, to execute its functions until the year 1732. Some
of its proceedings, as recited by Dallaway, are very curious.
I give an abstract of a case or two.

29th May, 1598. The earl-marshal, assisted by several
peers and knights, held a court of chivalry to decide on a quarrel between Anthony Felton, Esq., and Edmund Withepool,
Esq. It appears that a dispute had occurred between these
two gentlemen at the town of Ipswich, when Withepool
so far forgot himself as to bastinado the other, for which the
latter summoned him into this court. The decree of the
earl-marshal was that Withepool should confess to his pro-
secutor " that he knew him to be a gentleman unfitt to be
stroken," and promise that he would hereafter maintain
Mr. Felton's reputation against all slanderous persons. The
delinquent submitted to this judgment, and the proceedings
were at an end. Pity it is that a similar court of honour,
voluntarily supported, should not now exist for the purpose
of settling those quarrels among the aristocracy, which are
generally adjudicated by the stupid, illegal, and wicked ordeal of the bullet.[1] Let it form part of every gentleman's
code of honour to bow to the decision of a tribunal so con-

[1] A 'Society for the Suppression of Duelling,' lately established, enrols among its
members many of the greatest and best men of our times. All success to it !

stituted, and duelling—that purest relic of mediæval barbarism, which has descended to our time—would be numbered among the absurdities of the past.

1638.   Fowke contra Barnfield. Walter Fowke of Ganston, co. Stafford, prosecuted Richard Barnfield of Wolverhampton for a libel, for that he had said 'that complainant was never a soldier or captain before the Isle of Rhe voyage, when he was made a captain, and afterwards ran away; and that he dared the said W. F. to go to a fencing-school to fight it out with him, &c.' The decree of the court was, that Barnfield should make submission, find security for his good behaviour towards Fowke, and pay a fine of £10 to the king, £10 to the complainant, and 20 marks costs; and, in default, be committed to prison.

The assumption of the arms of a family, by persons bearing the same name, though unauthorized by family connexion, brought many causes into this court.

West, Lord Delawarr, against West.   A man who had been a famous wrestler, and bore the sobriquet of ' Jack in the West,' acquiring a fortune by keeping a public-house, assumed the regular surname of West, and the arms of Lord Delawarr's family.   In support of this double assumption he got some venal member[1] of the College of Arms to furnish

[1] That the College at this period comprised several officers of unimpeachable integrity cannot be doubted, while it is equally certain (at least, according to popular opinion) that others were less scrupulous. " An herald," says Butler :

" An herald
Can make a gentleman scarce a year old
To be descended of a race
Of antient kings in a small space."

And,

" For a piece of coin,
Twist any name into the line."

*e may have been deserved at the time—it was a corrupt age; but I am

him with a pedigree, deducing his descent, through three or four generations, from the fourth son of one of the Lords Delawarr. His son, who had been bred in the Inns of Court, and was resident in Hampshire, presuming, upon the strength of his pedigree, to take precedence of some of his neighbours, they instigated Lord Delawarr to prosecute him in the Court of Honour. At the hearing, the defendant produced his patent from the heralds; but, unfortunately for his pretensions, an antient gentleman of the house of West, who had been long abroad and was believed to be dead, and whom our innkeeper's son had claimed as his father's father, returned at this juncture to England, and 'dashed the whole business.'[1] The would-be West was fined £500, and commanded 'never more to write himself gentleman.'

On the breaking out of the civil wars the heralds espoused opposing interests. The three kings of arms, with a few of their subordinates, adhered to *their brother monarch:* the others sided with the Parliament.

When, in 1642, Charles was compelled to take up his residence at Oxford, several of the officers of arms were in attendance upon him; and it affords very high testimony of their respectability and learning that some of them were admitted to the first distinctions the university could bestow. The afterwards famous Dugdale (then Rouge Croix) and Edmund Walker, Chester, were created masters of arts, and Sir William le Neve, Clarenceux, was admitted to the dignity of LL.D. In 1643 and 1644, George Owen, York, John Philipot, Somerset, Sir John Borrough, Garter, and his

not sure that the reputation of the College has not suffered, even to our days, from this biting sarcasm, which is as far from the truth, as applied to the learned and respectable body now composing it, as Hudibras is from poetry.

[1] Rushworth.

successor, Sir Henry St. George, were also honoured with
the last-mentioned degree.

It is singular that an institution so immediately connected
with royalty as was the College of Arms, should have been
permitted to exist during the Commonwealth; and still more
so that while the republicans carried their hatred to the
very name of king so far as to alter the designation of the
King's Bench, and to strike the word *kingdom* out of their
vocabulary, that the principal functionaries of the College
should have been allowed to retain their antient titles of
kings of arms.   The royal arms, of course, disappeared from
the herald's tabard, though it does not very clearly appear
what was substituted; probably the state arms, namely, two
shields conjoined in fesse; dexter, the cross of St. George,
and, sinister, the Irish harp.[1]

Oliver Cromwell was, as Noble justly remarks, " a splendid
prince, keeping a most stately and magnificent court." Hence
the heralds could by no means be dispensed with. They
attended at his proclamation, and on all subsequent state
occasions.   The Protector's funeral was a pageant of more
than regal magnificence, and cost the extravagant sum of
£28,000.[2] But, notwithstanding the patronage of Cromwell,
the College was far from prosperous at this period, for the
visitations were discontinued, and the nobility and antient
gentry, awaiting in moody silence the issue of the system of

---

[1] In the churchwardens' accounts of Great Marlow are the following entries:

    " 1650, Sept. 29.   For defacing of the King's Arms £0 „ 1 „ 0.

    " 1651. Paid to the painter for setting up the State's Arms £0 „ 16 „ 0."

Three years earlier there is an entry of 5 s. ' payd the ringers when the king came
thorowe the towne !'

[2] Dallaway.

government then in operation, paid little attention to heraldric
honours, which were disregarded by the nation at large, or,
if recognized at all, only to be associated (as they have too
often since been[1]) with the idea of an insolent and overbear-
ing aristocracy.

The College of Arms, like all other public bodies, was put
into very great disorder by the return of the exiled Charles.
Several of the officers who had been ejected on account of
their loyalty to his father were restored to their former posts;
those who had changed with the times were degraded to the
inferior offices; while those who had been appointed during
the Commonwealth and Protectorate were expelled. In
Scotland the heralds were restored to their former privileges.
Sir Andrew Durham, created Lyon king of arms in 1662, had,
at his investment, a crown of gold placed upon his head in
full Parliament, and was harangued by the Chancellor and
the Lord Register on the duties and importance of the office
conferred upon him.

The great fire of 1666 destroyed the buildings of the
College of Arms; but fortunately all the records and books
were rescued from the flames and deposited at Whitehall,
whence they were afterwards removed to an apartment in the
palace at Westminster. The College was rebuilt some years
subsequently; a small portion of the necessary funds having
been raised by subscription; but by far the greater part was

---

[1] Witness the French Revolution, a period at which these distinctions of gentry
were temporarily abolished, as if, forsooth, bends and fesses and lions-rampant
had conduced to the previous misgovernment of the nation! From the blow which
heraldry received in France during that bloody struggle it has never recovered;
although, from some recent movements, it appears evident that heraldric honours
will, ere long, receive that attention which they deserve in every antient and
well-constituted state in Christendom.

contributed by the officers themselves.[1]   At its completion
in 1683 it was considered ' one of the handsomest brick buildings in London.'   The income of the heralds was, at this
time, little more than nominal; but they were principally
persons of good family, who possessed private property.

County Visitations were revived soon after the Restoration, but (with the exception of those of Sir William Dugdale,
which are amongst the best in the College) they do not
appear to have been conducted with so much strictness as in
former times; and at the Revolution of 1688 they were
entirely abandoned.   During the intolerant proceedings
against the nonconformists under Charles II, the pursuivants
were occasionally employed in that disagreeable duty of their
office from which they originally borrowed their designation,
(POURSUIVRE, Fr. v. a. to pursue), that of bringing suspected
persons up to London.   Noble gives (from Calamy) some
instances of their being despatched to apprehend nonconformists in Cheshire.

James II " affected great state, and was the last of our
monarchs who kept up the regal state in its full splendour."[2]
The investiture of some new officers of arms in this reign was
probably more splendid than any that had previously taken
place.   But all the benefits they received from the sovereign
were countervailed by his insisting upon their attending him
to the Catholic worship on all high days and holidays, a proceeding which very much disgusted them.

Nothing of particular importance relating to the College
occurs in the reign of William and Mary, except the refusal
of the usual commissions to hold visitations, as a practice

---

[1] The expense of the N.W. corner was defrayed by Dugdale, then Norroy.

[2] Noble.

discordant with the spirit of the times. Under the antient system, a broad line of demarcation had separated the nobility and gentry from the common people; but gradually the commercial interests of the nation introduced that intermediate rank recognized as the middle classes of society, and these, by means of the wealth acquired in merchandise and trade, often eclipsed in the elegancies of life many of the antient gentry.. Hence the Heraldic Visitations, had they been continued to our times, would have necessarily led to much invidiousness of distinction on the part of the heralds, and probably to much ill feeling. between the representatives of far-descended houses and the upstarts of a day.

At the union with Scotland, temp. Anne, it was determined that Lyon, the Scottish king of arms, should rank in dignity next after Garter, the principal English king.[1]

The reign of George I presents us with two incidents deserving of notice. The first is the ceremony of the degradation of the Duke of Ormond, attainted of treason, from the order of the Garter, which was performed with the

[1] The present heraldic establishment of Scotland consists of Lyon, king of arms; six heralds, Albany, Rothsay, Snowdoun, Marchmont, Yla, and Ross; and six pursuivants, Unicorn, Kintire, Bute, Dingwall, Ormond and Carrick. The Scottish College, as Noble observes, has not been much distinguished for literature; there is, however, one example, a name familiar to the readers of Marmion:

" Sir David Lyndsay of the Mount,
Lord Lyon king at arms,"

who was author of 'The Dreme,' 'The Complaynt,' and other politico-moral poems; also of ' The Three Estates,' a satirical piece of great humour; his most popular work was ' The History of Squire Meldrum,' which " is considered as the last poem that in any degree partakes of the character of the metrical romance." The principal functionary for Ireland is styled Ulster, king of arms: under him are two heralds, Cork and Dublin, and one pursuivant, Athlone.

usual ceremonials at Windsor, in 1716. The other I give in the words of Noble :

" In the year 1727, an impostor, of the name of Robert Harman, pretending to be a herald, was prosecuted for the offence by the College of Arms, at the quarter-sessions for the county of Suffolk, held at Beccles, and being convicted of the offence, was sentenced to be placed in the pillory in several market-towns on public market-days, and afterwards to be imprisoned and pay a fine, which sentence was' accordingly executed, proving that the impudent and designing were not to encroach upon the rights of the College with impunity."[1]

When war with Spain was proclaimed in the thirteenth year of George II, the proclamation was made in the metropolis by the officers of arms, according to antient usage. They also attended at the trial of the three Scottish rebel lords in Westminster-Hall, in 1746. Fourteen standards taken from the adherents of the Pretender were publicly burnt at Edinburgh, by the common hangman. " The prince's own standard was carried by the executioner, each of the others by *chimney-sweepers* (!) The former was first committed to the flames, with three flourishes of the trumpets, amidst repeated acclamations of a vast concourse of people. The same was done with each of the other colours separately ; the *heralds* always proclaiming the names of the ' rebel traitors to whom they belonged.' "[2]

" After the battle of Dettingen, fought in 1743, his Majesty revived the order of Knights-Bannerets, the last of whom had been Sir John Smith, created a banneret by Charles I at the battle of Edgehill, the first in the fatal civil war. The form of treating them formerly was, the candidate

---

[1] Hist. Coll. Arms, p. 352.   [2] Ibid. p. 372.

presented his standard or pennon to the sovereign or his general, who cutting off the skirt or tail of it made it square, when it was returned: hence they are sometimes called knights of the square banner. They precede all knights, not of the Garter or Bath, of England, and even baronets, being reputed next to the nobility after those preceding orders."[1] They have the privilege of using supporters to their arms; but, as the honour is not hereditary, their descendants cannot claim it.

In 1732 an unsuccessful attempt was made to revive the Court of Chivalry. The earl-marshal's deputy and his assistant lords and the officers of arms being present, the king's advocate exhibited complaints, *First*, against Mrs. Radburne, for using divers ensigns at the funeral of her husband not pertaining to his condition; *secondly*, against the executors of a Mr. Ladbrook for using, on a similar occasion, arms not legally belonging to the defunct; and, *thirdly*, against Sir John Blunt, Bart. for assuming, without right, the arms of the antient family of Blount of Sodington. This gentleman had been a scrivener, and was one of the projectors of the well-known South-Sea Scheme or 'Bubble,' which ended in the total ruin of so many respectable families. But "the whole business was imprudently begun, and unskilfully conducted; the lawyers who were consulted laughed at it;"[2] and, though the court proceeded so far as to fine some of the parties, it was unable to carry its decisions into effect; and we hear no more of the Court of Chivalry.

It would be tedious, and beyond the design of the present hasty sketch, to notice all the great occasions on which the heralds were in requisition during the reigns of the three predecessors of her present Majesty. During this

[1] Noble, p. 372.   [2] Noble.

period several members of the College have shed lustre on
their office, and on the antiquarian literature of England.
These will come under review in my next chapter; and it
will only be necessary here to add a few particulars relating
to the present state of the College.

The building, which stands upon the site of the *Derby
House* before referred to, is approached by an archway on
St. Benet's Hill, and has a sombre appearance perfectly in
keeping with the purposes to which it is devoted.   It com-
prises the great hall, the library, consisting of two rooms;
the outer one of the time of Charles II, fitted with dark
carved-oak panels, and containing a beautifully executed
chimney-piece, said to be the work of Sibborn; the inner,
a spacious and lofty octangular apartment, recently erected
and rendered fire-proof, for the safer preservation of the
records and more valuable documents; and besides these
rooms there are separate apartments appropriated to the use
of the several officers.   The great hall, where the Courts of
Chivalry were antiently held, and where the 'Chapters' of
the heralds still take place, remains almost *in statu quo*,
with its high-backed throne for the earl-marshal, surrounded
with balustrades, and retaining somewhat of the awe-striking
solemnity of the tribunal.   The panelling has recently been
decorated with shields of the several lords and earls-marshal
from the origin of that office till the present time.   The
library, it is scarcely necessary to state, contains a large
and extremely valuable collection of original visitation books,
records of the arms and pedigrees of families, funeral certificates of the nobility and gentry, antient tournament and
other rolls of great curiosity; the sword, dagger, and ring of
King James IV, of Scotland; and probably every work illustrative, in any degree, of heraldry and genealogy, that has

issued from the press of this country, together with many foreign works on those subjects. Of the great value of this inexhaustible mine of information the historian and the antiquary are well aware, and there is scarcely any work in their respective departments that has not received some addition from this library.

The following is a list of the Corporation of the College as it now exists:

Earl-Marshal and Hereditary Marshal of England.
Henry-Charles, Duke of Norfolk, &c. &c. &c.

Kings of Arms.

GARTER. Sir Charles George Young, Knt., F.S.A.
CLARENCEUX. Joseph Hawker, Esq., F.S.A.
NORROY. Francis Martin, Esq., F.S.A.

Heralds.

SOMERSET. James Cathrow Disney, Esq.
CHESTER. Walter Aston Blount, Esq. Genealogist and Blanc-Coursier Herald, of the Order of the Bath.
RICHMOND. James Pulman Esq., F.S.A. Registrar of the College of Arms, and Yeoman-Usher of the Black Rod to the House of Lords.
WINDSOR. Robert Laurie, Esq.
LANCASTER. Albert William Woods, Esq. Gentleman-Usher of the Red Rod, and Brunswick Herald of the Order of the Bath.
YORK. Edward Howard Gibbon, Esq., Secretary to the Earl-Marshal.

𝕻ursuíbants.

BLUEMANTLE.   George Harrison Rogers Harrison, Esq.,
    F.S.A.

ROUGE-DRAGON.   Thomas William King, Esq., F.S.A.

ROUGE-CROIX.   William Courthope, Esq.

PORTCULLIS.   George William Collen, Esq.

CHAPTER XII.

Distinguished Heralds and Heraldric Writers.

IN the earliest ages after the introduction of Heraldry the laws of the science must have been orally taught to novitiate heralds: but when the regulations of chivalry were framed into a code they began to be committed to writing, and among the earliest MSS. are some on this subject.[1] But these generally have reference rather to feats of arms than to the technicalities of blazon.

The first author, of any note, on this subject is Doctor Nicholas Upton, a native of Devonshire, who was honoured A.D. 1441. with the patronage of Humphrey, "the good" Duke of Gloucester, temp. Henry IV, by whose influence he became canon of Sarum, Wells, and St. Paul's. Previously to obtaining these preferments he had served in the French wars under Thomas de Montacute, earl of Salisbury; and it was during those campaigns he wrote a Latin treatise, entitled 'De Studio Militari,' MS. copies of which are preserved in the College of Arms, and elsewhere.[2]

---

[1] Dallaway.

[2] It was printed in 1654 by Sir Edward Bysshe, Garter.

It consists of five books; viz. 1, Of officers of Arms; 2, Of Veterans, now styled Heralds; 3, Of Duels; 4, Of Colours; 5, Of Figures; forming altogether a systematic grammar of Heraldry. The latinity of Upton is considered very classical for the age in which he flourished.

One of the earliest treatises on Heraldry, as well as one of the first productions of the press in this country, is contained in the highly-celebrated 𝕭𝖔𝖐𝖊 𝖔𝖋 𝕾𝖙. 𝕬𝖑𝖇𝖆𝖓𝖘, printed within the precincts of the monastery from which it is designated, in the year 1486. This singular work contains tracts on hawking, hunting, and ' coot-armuris'—the last constituting the greater portion of the volume. It is printed in a type resembling the text-hand written at the period, and with all the abbreviations employed in manuscript. The margin contains exemplifications of the arms described in the text, stained with coloured inks. This edition, like others of that early date, is now exceedingly scarce, there being probably not more than five or six copies extant. Another edition was published in 1496 by Wm. Copeland, and a single copy occurs of the same date with the imprint of Wynkyn de Worde: these were probably of the same impression with different title-pages. A new edition appeared in 1550; and another was included in Gervase Markham's ' Gentleman's Academie,' in 1595.[1] The entire work was attributed, for the first three centuries after its publication, to Dame Julyan Berners,[2] prioress of Sopewell, and sister of Richard, Lord Berners, a woman of great personal and mental endowments.[3] That a woman, and especially the

---

[1] That portion of the original edition which relates to arms is reprinted in the Appendix to Dallaway.

[2] Or, by corruption, Barnes.

[3] Bale, de Script. Brit. viij. 33.

superior of a religious sisterhood, should have devoted her pen to the secular subjects of heraldry and field-sports, at first sight, seems singular; but the rude complexion of the times in which she lived renders little apology necessary for this apparent violation of propriety; and we may fairly venerate the memory of this gentle lady as a promoter of English literature. Dallaway is the first, and, as far as I am aware, with the exception of Mr. Haslewood, the only author who questions the pretensions of Dame Juliana to the authorship of the whole work; and he founds his doubts upon the difference observable between the style of the heraldric essay and the previous ones. He considers the former as the work of some anonymous monk of St. Albans. But as several almost contemporary authors ascribe it to her, and there is no positive proof to the contrary, far be from me that want of gallantry which would despoil the worthy prioress of the honour of having indited this goodly tractate, this 'nobull werke!' [1]

If the reader has never seen the Boke of Saint Albans, and feels only half as much curiosity to become acquainted with its contents as I did before I had the good fortune to meet with it, I am sure he will not consider the following choice bits of Old English, extracted from it, impertinently introduced.

---

[1] It is worthy of remark, as sustaining the claim of Dame Julyan to the authorship of the heraldric portion of the Boke, that at the end of the treatise on arms there is a passage in which evident recurrence is made to her former and undisputed essays. Speaking of the necessity of attending to precise rules in the study of heraldry she adds in conclusion, "Nee ye may not overryn swyftly the forsayd rules, bot dyligently have theym in yowr mind, and be not to full of consaitis. For he that will hunt ij haris in oon howre, or oon while oon, another while another, lightly he losys both."

Dame Julyan Berners merits honourable notice as one of
the earliest of English poetesses. The treatise on hunting
is in rhyme, and consists of 606 verses. The style is didactic.
Take a specimen :

> " *Bestys of venery.*

> "Whersoever ye fall by fryth or by fell,
>   My dere chylde take heed how Tristrom dooth you tell,
>   How many maner beestys of venery ther were,
>   Lysten to your dame and then schall you lere,
>   Ffour maner beestys of venery there are ;
>   The first of them is the hert—the secunde is the hare,
>   The boore is oon of them—the woolff and not oon moe."

> " *How ye schal break an hert.*

> "Then take out the suet that it be not lefte,
>   For that my child is good for lechecrafte (medicine),
>   And in the myddest of the herte a boon shall ye fynde,
>   Loke ye geve hit to a lord—and chylde be kynde.
>   For it is kynd for many maladies."

In subsequent parts of the poem, 'the namys of diverse
maner houndys,' 'the propertees of a good hors,' 'the company of bestys and fowles,' and other sporting subjects are
discussed, and interspersed with proverbs of a somewhat
caustic description. The composition very oddly concludes
with an enumeration of " all the shyeris and the bishopryckes
of the realme of England."

From the heraldrical portion of the Boke many short extracts have already been given. Some others follow :

" *Note here well who shall gyue cotarmures :*

" Ther shall none of the IV. orduris of regalite bot all onli
the soueregne kyng geue cootarmur. for that is to hym im-

properid by lawe of armys.[1] And yit the kyng shall nott make a knyght with owte a cootarmure byfore.

"Ev'y knyght cheftayn i the felde mai make a cootarmur knight.

" *In how many places a knyght may be made :*

" A knyght is made in IV. dyuerse placis. in musturing in lond of werys. In semblyng under baneris. In listys of the bath and at the sepulcur.

" *A gentylman spirituall :*

" Ther is a gentylman a churls sone a preste to be made and that is a spirituall gentylman to god and not of blode. Butt if a gentylmannys sone be made a preste he is a gentilman both spirituall and temperall. Criste was a gentylman of his moder's behalue and bare cotarmure of aunseturis. The iiij Euangelists berith wittenese of Cristis workys in the gospell with all thappostilles. They were Jewys and of gentylmen come by the right lyne of that worthy conqueroure Judas Machabeus but that by succession of tyme the kynrade fell to pouerty, after the destruction of Judas Machabeus, and then they fell to laboris and ware calde no gentilmen. and the iiij doctores of holi church Seynt Jerom Ambrose Augustyn and Gregori war gentilmen of blode and of cotarmures !"

The following are specimens of her directions for ' blasing of armys,' the most important part of the work :

" Off armys palit crokyt and sharpe now I will speke.

" Loke and beholde how mony maner of wyse thes palit armys be borne dyuersli, as it is shewyt in thys boke, and theis armys now shewyt here [referring to the exemplification in the margin] be calde palit, crokyt and sharpe, for in theys armys ij coloris paly ar put togethir : oon into another

---

[1] Here the good Dame contradicts her own assertion; vide p. 36.

crokytly and sharpe. Therefore it shall be sayd of hi' the wich beris thes armis in thys wyse, first in latyn thus. Portat arma palata tortuosa acuto de nigro et argento. Gallice sic: Il port pale daunsete de sable et dargent. Anglice sic: He berith pale crokyt and sharpe of sable and syluer."

" Off armys the wich ar calde frectis (Frets) here now I will speke:

"A certain nobull baron that is to say the lorde awdeley of the reame of England baar in his armys a frecte, the wich certain frectis in mony armys of dyurse gentillmen ar founde, other while reede other while golde, and other while blac oderwhile simple and oderwhile double otherwhile tripull and other while it is multepliet ou' (over) all the sheld as here it apperith, and ye most vnderstande on gret differans bytwix armys bendit and theis armys the wich be made with the forsayd frettys, wherefore it is to be markyt that in bendyt armys the colouris contenyt equally ar dyuydit. Bot in this frectis the felde alwai abydys hool as here, and this forsayd lorde Audeley beris thus in latyn. Portat arma frectata de auro in campo rubreo. Et gallice sic. Il por de gowles vng frecte dor. Anglice sic. He berith gowles and a frecte of golde."

The next author of any note on the subject of Heraldry is GERARD LEGH, whose 'Accedens of Armorie' be-
1562
came, as Anthony à Wood phrases it, 'the pattern or platform of those who came after." This gentleman was son of Henry Legh, of London, an illegitimate scion of a Cheshire family, who, according to the proverb, were "as plenty as fleas." He was educated at Oxford, and died in 1563, the year after the first appearance of his work. The 'Accedens' obtained a degree of popularity not usual at that ·d, and reached a fifth edition within half a century.

It was the text-book on the science until Guillim's ' Displaie' superseded it. The author, in his preface, acknowledges the aid he had received from a work " on the whole subject," by one Nicholas Warde, concerning whom nothing further is known. He likewise acknowledges his obligations to eight other authors, but somewhat singularly omits to mention the Boke of St. Albans, the method of which he follows, and the very words of which he frequently borrows. After the literary fashion of his times, his work is cast in the form of a dialogue, the speakers being Gerard and Legh, his own christian name and surname. The style is highly pedantic, yet withal sufficiently amusing, and the illustrative woodcuts are executed with great spirit. Specimens of his composition have already been cited.[1]

JOHN BOSSEWELL, gentleman, of whose personal history little or nothing is known, next appears in the field of heraldric literature. His ' Workes of Armorie, de-
1572
vyded into three bookes,' reached a second edition in 1597. His design was an improvement upon the treatise of Legh, in which he partly succeeded; but the admixture of the antient mythology, the moral virtues, the marvellous attributes and fictitious anecdotes of animals, and other foreign topics, with the more immediate subject of his work, renders it, like that of his predecessor, almost unreadable, except to the initiated. The following short extract will serve as a specimen of Bossewell's lucubrations:

" The field is of the Saphire, on a chiefe Pearle, a Musion . . . . Ermines. This beaste is called a Musion, for that he is enimie to Myse and

---

[1] Vide pp. 108, 109, 116, 117, &c. &c.

Rattes . . . he is slye and wittie and . . . seeth so sharpely that he ouercommeth darknes of the nighte by the shyninge lyghte of his eyne. In shape of body he is like vnto a Leoparde, and hathe a great mouth. He dothe delighte that he enioyeth his libertie; and in his youthe he is swifte, plyante, and merye. He maketh a rufull noyse and a gastefull when he profereth to fighte with an other. He is a cruell beaste, when he is wilde, and falleth on his owne feete from moste highe places: and vneth is hurte therewith. When he hathe a fayre skinne, he is, as it were, prowde thereof, and then he goeth faste aboute to be seene."[1]

Need the reader be informed that this beast of the 'rufull noyse,' which falleth from 'highe places on his *owne* feete,' is the common house CAT?

An anonymous quarto, which reached a fourth edition, made its appearance in 1573, bearing the modest title of 'A very proper Treatise, &c.' and it shows the attention paid to heraldrical 'tricking and painting' in the time of queen Elizabeth, when an art which is now limited to herald-painters was deemed a fitting accomplishment for 'gentlemenne.'

Among a host of small works on subjects connected with heraldry which appeared about this time, one may be mentioned as a great curiosity. This is a funeral sermon on the death of Walter, earl of Essex, to which are prefixed copies of verses on his lordship's pedigree in Latin, *Hebrew*, Welsh,

[1] Armorie of Honour, fo. 56.

and French! The author of this tract was ' Richard Davis, Bishoppe of Saint Davys.'

SIR JOHN FERNE, Knight, descended from a good family in Leicestershire, and connected, on his mother's side, with the noble house of Sheffield, is believed to have studied at Oxford, though he never graduated. Great part of his life was spent as a member of the Inner Temple. King James gave him the office of secretary and keeper of the signet for the northern parts, then established at York. He died about 1610. Henry Ferne, his eighth son, was the loyalist bishop of Chester, and a writer of some note.

1586

His ' Blazon of Gentric,' published in 1586, is divided into two parts, ' The Glorie of Gencrositie,' and 'Lacie's Nobilitie;' the former treating of blazon, and the latter of the genealogy of the family of Lacy, with a view to disprove the claim of affinity to it set up by Albertus a Lasco, Count-Palatine of Syradia, which is very successfully refuted. Of this learned work, which our author tells us is " compiled for the instruction of all gentlemen, bearers of arms, whom and none else it concerneth," Peacham speaks as " indeed very rare, and sought after as a jewell." Dallaway describes it as " a continued dialogue, alternately supported by six interlocutors, who discuss the original principles of nobility and the due gradations of the other ranks in-society, adjust military distinctions, describe orders of knighthood, and adduce proofs of certain symbols and devices, concluding with high commendations of heraldic investigation. To Ferne the rank of a classic in heraldry will not be denied. His studies were directed to the investigation of the laws of chivalry, and he has transfused into his work the spirit of the voluminous codes now forgotten, which he delighted to consult. It may be considered therefore as the most complete epitome of them now extant. But we must allow that he writes more for the amusement of the learned than for the instruction of novices, and that he deals much more in criticism than rudiments."

The interlocutors are ' Paradinus, the herald; Torquatus, a knight; Theologus, a deuine; Bartholus, a lawier; Berosus, an antiquary; and Columell, a plowman,' who converses in the dialect of Somerset. "There is somewhat of a dramatic spirit in this dialogue; the characters are supported by sentiments appropriate to each, particularly the clown, who speaks freely both the language and opinions of the yeomanry at that time; nor are the strong prejudices of the knight and herald described with less force."

As a copy of this "rare jewell" lies before me, I should certainly be to blame if I did not present my reader with a specimen of its brilliancy. The topic of discourse is the " blasing of armes."

"*Torq.* I pray you *pose* me once again.

"*Parad.* Goe to then: you shall begin with a coate of easie charge to be discried. Therefore, I pray you begin, and tell your soueraigne, what coat-armour this knight beareth (for I tell you, it is the coate of a knight), that your soueraine might know him by his signes of honour, sith that perchaunce you know not his name.

"*Torq.* Me thinkes hee beareth Sable, a Musion [1] passaunt

The cutter hath not done his duety. [2]

Ignorance bringeth rash judgements of Armes, and signes honourable.

gardaunt Or, oppressed with a frett gules, of eight parts, nayles d'argent.

"*Columel.* Iesa zir: call you this Armes? Now by my vaye, chad thought Armes should not have been of zutche trifling

---

[1] The heraldric term for a *cat;* vide p. 252, ante.   [2] The nails are omitted.

thinges. Why, this is euen the cat in the milke-house window. Full ill will her dayrie thriue, giffe she put zutch a vermine beast in trust to keepe it.

"*Torq.* I am iust of thy minde : for thou hast reasoned as profoundly as might be upon so bad a deuise.

"*Parad.* I perceaue (*Torq.*) as clearkly as you seem to be in armory yet are you far to seeke and must still be taught. This payssaunt's glosse is euen comparable with your blazon : for bad is the best.

"*Torq.* I suppose my blazon cannot be amended.

"*Parad.* Yes, it shall be amended, and your errour also corrected. Did you euer see a fret thus formed before (I mean nayled ?) To correct your blazon, learne by this :

The true bla-zon of the for-mer coat. Hee beareth Sable, a Musion, Or, oppressed with a Troillis G. cloué dargent ; for this, which you call a fret, is a lattice, a thing well knowne to poore prisoners and distressed captiues, which are forced to receaue their breath from heauen at such holes for want of more pleasant windowes, &c."

Sir William Segar is, I believe, the first of our heralds who published on the subject. His 'Book of Honor and Armes,' enlarged and republished in 1602, 1590. under the title of 'Honor Military and Ciuill,' relates as its designation implies, not to the art of blazon, but to dignities. His zeal for antiquity, like that of his contemporaries, outruns historical truth, as a proof of which it may be mentioned that he deduces the origin of knight-hood from the fabulous Round Table of King Arthur. His work possesses, however, great merit, and exhibits much learning and profound research. Many of his unpublished MSS., genealogical and otherwise, are still extant.

Segar, who was of Dutch extraction, was bred a scrivener,

and obtained his introduction to the College through the interest of Sir T. Heneage, vice-chamberlain to Queen Elizabeth. Here, at length, his talents raised him to the post of Garter, the *ne plus ultra* of heraldic ambition. He died in 1633.

WILLIAM WYRLEY, author of 'The Trve Vse of Armorie,' is the next heraldric author who had any official connexion with the College of Arms, in which establishment he rose, however, no higher than the degree of a pursuivant.

1592.

He was a gentleman by birth, a native of Staffordshire, and died in 1618. He did not confine his attention to heraldry, but studied antiquities at large : his collections he bequeathed to the College. The ' Trve Vse,' his only published work, is a scarce quarto of 162 pages, and is freer from the irrelevant rubbish which blemishes most of the treatises of this century than any one which preceded it, or any one which for a long time subsequently issued from the press. Sir W. Dugdale makes great use of this work in his ' Ancient Usage of bearing Arms,' 1681, and in return somewhat ungratefully, robs Wyrley of the honour of its authorship, ascribing it, upon hearsay evidence, to Sampson Erdeswicke, the historian of Staffordshire.

We now come to a name which has shed more lustre upon the office of the herald and the science of heraldry than any other our country has produced—that of the justly-celebrated WILLIAM CAMDEN. Any biographical notice, however brief, of so eminent a personage seems almost uncalled for in these narrow pages. It will be sufficient, for the sake of uniformity, merely to mention a few particulars respecting him. This laborious antiquary and historian was born in London in 1551, and received his education first at Christ's Hospital and St. Paul's School, and afterwards at

Oxford. He quitted the University in 1570, and made the tour of England. At the early age of twenty-four he became second master of Westminster School; and while performing the duties of that office devoted his leisure to the study of British antiquities. Here, after ten years' labour, he matured his great work, the 'Britannia,' which was first published in 1586. Four years previously to its publication he visited many of the eastern and northern counties, for the purpose of making a personal investigation of their antiquities. The 'Britannia' immediately brought him into notice, and he lived to enjoy the proud gratification of seeing it in its sixth edition. It was written in elegant Latin, and in that language passed through several of its earlier editions, the first English version having been made, probably with the author's assistance, by Dr. Philemon Holland, in 1610. This great national performance, which Bishop Nicholson quaintly styles "the common sun whereat our modern writers have all lighted their little torches," has been so highly esteemed in all subsequent times, that it has been many times reprinted. The last edition is the greatly enlarged one of Gough. In 1589 the bishop of Salisbury presented him with a prebend in his cathedral, which he retained till his death; and in 1597, the office of Clarenceux king of arms becoming vacant, he was advanced to that dignity.

After his establishment in the College he published several emended editions of The 'Britannia,' 'The Annals of the Reign of Queen Elizabeth,' 'An Account of the celebrated Persons interred in Westminster Abbey,' and that very interesting little volume, 'Remaines concerning Britaine,' which, as he tells us, was composed of the fragments of a projected work of greater extent, which his want of leisure

17

prevented his executing. All these works, except the last, were written in Latin, a language for which he had so great a predilection, that he even compiled pedigrees in it. As an antiquary, Camden deserves the highest praise; as an historian, he is charged with partiality towards the character of the virgin queen; and as a herald, he was confessedly unequal to some of his contemporaries. In the latter capacity he was much indebted to Francis Thynne, or Botteville, Blanch Lion pursuivant, and afterwards Lancaster herald, of whom Anthony a Wood gives a high character. Camden was concerned with that delightful old chronicler, Holinshed, in the production of his famous work. He was mainly instrumental in the formation of the original Society of Antiquaries, whose discourses have been printed by Hearne. He was a great admirer of the father of English poetry, and contributed many additions to Speght's edition of his works. He left many unpublished MSS. amongst which was a ' Discourse of Armes,' addressed to Lord Burghley. The last years of his life were spent in retirement at the village of Chislehurst, co. Kent, where he died in 1623, in the 73d year of his age.

RALPH BROOKE, Rouge Croix pursuivant, and York herald, was contemporary with Camden and his violent adversary. His skill as a herald has rarely been questioned, but his whole career exhibits the character of a petulant, envious, mean, and dishonest person. He pretended to be a descendant of the antient family of Brooke of Cheshire; but it is unfortunate for his pretensions that his father's name was not Brooke, but *Brokesmouth*. He was bred to the trade of a painter-stainer, and became free of that company in 1576. How he obtained his introduction to the College does not appear, though it is certain that it would have been better, both for himself and that body, had he never entered it. Noble characterizes him as "so extremely worthless and perverse that his whole mind seemed bent to malice and wickedness : unawed by virtue or by station, none were secure from his unmerited attacks. His enmity towards Camden arose out of the circumstance of the antiquary's having been appointed, on the demise of Richard Lee, to the office of Clarenceux, to which, from a long connexion with the College, and greater professional knowledge, he considered himself entitled; and it is but justice to admit that he certainly had some ground for complaint, though the mode in which he chose to give vent to his spleen cannot be defended. Camden's great work, the 'Britannia,' had passed through several editions unimpeached as to its general accuracy, when Brooke endeavoured to bring its well-deserved popularity into contempt by a work entitled 'A Discoverie of certaine Errours published in print in the much-commended Britannia,' a production overflowing with personal invective. To this spiteful book Camden replied in Latin, treating his opponent with the scorn he deserved, exposing his illiteracy, and at the same time adroitly waiving such of the charges as were really well founded. Never was reviewer more severely reviewed. 'A second Discoverie of Errours' followed, and, as it remained unanswered, Brooke might in some sort have claimed a triumph, particularly as Camden, recognizing the maxim "Fas est ab hoste doceri," availed himself, in the subsequent editions of the 'Britannia,' of his adversary's corrections.

In 1619 Brooke published a 'Catalogue and Succession of Kings, Princes, and Nobilitie since the Norman Conquest,' a work of considerable merit, though it did not escape censure, for Vincent, Rouge Croix, an adherent of Camden, in a ' Discovery of Errors,' printed three years afterwards, controverted many of its statements. Brooke still continued his paltry and litigious proceedings, and was twice suspended from his office; and it was even attempted to expel him from the College.[1]   He closed his unenviable life in 1625, and was buried in the twin-towered church of Reculver, co. Kent, where a mural monument informs us that

> " quit of worldly miseries,
> Ralph Brooke, Esq., late York herald, lies.
> Fifteenth October he was last alive,
> One thousand six hundred and twenty-five
> Seaventy three years bore he fortune's harmes,
> And forty-five an officer of armes," &c.

[1] Bishop Gibson records a piece of malicious revenge practised by Brooke which alone would be sufficient to stamp his character with opprobrium. Having a private pique against one of the College he employed a person to carry to him a ready-drawn coat of arms, purporting to be that of one Gregory Brandon, a gentleman of London then sojourning in Spain, desiring him to attest it with his hand and seal of office, and bidding the messenger return with it immediately, as the vessel by which it was to be transmitted was on the point of sailing. The officer, little suspecting Brooke's design, did what was required of him, received the customary fee, and dismissed the bearer. Brooke immediately posted to the Earl of Arundel, one of the commissioners for the office of earl-marshal, exhibited the arms, which were no other than *the royal bearings of Spain*, and assured his lordship that Brandon, the supposed grantee, was a man of plebeian condition, no way entitled to the honour. The Earl laid the matter before the king, who ordered the herald to be cited into the court of Star Chamber, to answer for the insult offered to the court of Spain. He, having no alternative, submitted himself to the mercy of the court, only pleading, in extenuation of his offence, that he had acted without his usual circumspection in the business, in consequence of Brooke's urgency, on the pretence that delay was impossible. Brooke was compelled to admit his own knavery in the transaction, and the consequence was that both himself and the other herald were committed to prison, himself for treachery, and the other for negligence.

ROBERT GLOVER, Somerset, temp. Elizabeth, wrote a treatise entitled 'Nobilitas Politica vel Civilis,' which was posthumously published in 1608, the author having died in 1588. He was a most learned and industrious herald, and his authority in genealogy and heraldry is much relied on by the officers of arms of the present day. His MSS. are in the library of the College.

In 1610 appeared 'The Catalogue of Honour, or Treasury of true Nobility peculiar and proper to the Isle of Great Britaine,' by Thomas Milles, esq. of Davington-hall, co. Kent. This large folio of eleven hundred pages is professedly a compilation from the MSS. of Glover, to whom Mr. Milles was nephew; and although reliance is not to be placed upon all its statements, it constitutes a remarkable monument of the persevering labour and research of that herald.

EDMUND BOLTON, a retainer of Villiers, duke of Buckingham, was author of several works. His principal heraldric composition is a small volume entitled the 'Elements of Armouries,' to which are prefixed commendatory epistles by Segar and Camden, honourable testimonies of its merit. In his remarks upon the lines of partition, &c. he displays more geometrical than heraldric knowledge. His religious opinions are discovered by his wish for a new crusade. His style is highly pedantic, and the reader would scarcely thank me for a specimen.

JOHN GUILLIM (Rouge Dragon pursuivant in 1617, in which office he died in 1621,) was of Welsh extraction, and a native of Herefordshire. His 'Display of Heraldrie,' one of the most popular of heraldric treatises, has passed through numerous editions. Anthony a Wood asserts that the real author of it was John Barkham, rector of Bocking in Kent, who composed it in the early part of his life, and afterwards thinking it somewhat inconsistent with his profession to publish a work on arms, communicated the manuscript to Guillim, who gave it to the world with his own name. What authority Wood had for this assertion does not appear, but from the erudition displayed in the work, it is evidently not the production of a very young man; and besides this, in the dedication to the king, Guillim himself does not hesitate to claim the merit of originality, for he says "I am the first who brought a method into this heroic art." It is remarkable that three of the most celebrated books on our science, namely those of Dame J. Berners, William Wyrley, and John Guillim, should have been ascribed to other parties than those under whose names they have gone forth to the world. The highly complimentary verses prefixed to this volume by Guillim's seniors in office can hardly be supposed to have been written to sanction a fiction in allowing him the merit of another's labours.[1] The eulogium of one G. Belcher not only commends the work in the highest terms, but, after enumerating the several authors who had written on the same subject, namely Wynkenthewordius,[2] Leghus, Boswell, Fernus, and Wyrleius, adds

"At tu præ cæteris *Guillime*."

The 'Display' may fairly claim to be considered the first methodical and intelligent view of heraldry published in England; and the addition of the name of the family to every coat of arms cited as an example (which in all earlier treatises is wanting) has conduced as much as its intrinsic merit to give to Guillim's book the popularity it enjoys.[3]

[1] Moule.

[2] Referring to the edition of the Boke of S. A., printed by Wynkyn de Worde.

[3] For extracts from it see several of the preceding chapters.

HENRY PEACHAM (whose name is more familiar to the non-heraldric reader than those of most other armorists of early date, in consequence of Dr. Johnson, in his Dictionary, referring exclusively to him as an authority for terms of blazonry,) wrote 'The Compleat Gentleman,' which professes to treat of every necessary accomplishment befitting that character, and of course, among other things, "of armorie or the blazon of armes." The 13th chapter, devoted to this subject, is a compendious and scientific production. 'The Compleat Gentleman' was one of the most popular books of its time, and between 1622 and 1661 passed through six editions. In 1630 Peacham published another work called 'The Gentleman's Exercise, or an exquisite practise as well for drawing all manner of beasts in their true portraitures, as also the making of all kinds of colours to be used in lymming, painting, tricking and blazon of coates and armes, with diuers others most delightfull and pleasurable obseruations for all yong Gentlemen and others."

The two MARKHAMS, Gervase and Francis, were brothers, and flourished in the early part of this century. The former republished the Boke of St. Albans, under the title of 'The Gentleman's Academy;' and the latter wrote a 'Booke of Honour,' one of the dullest of books upon a very dull subject.

The 'Titles of Honour' of the celebrated SELDEN demands for him a place among heraldric authors.[1]

[1] In this hasty glance at writers on the subject of armory it would be unjust to omit the names of several heralds and others who are either almost unknown to the general student of English literature, or are recognized in some other character than that of illustrators of our science. In the former class may be noticed Sir Edward Bysshe, Garter, (who published the 'De Studio Militari,' and another treatise of Upton, and the 'Aspilogia' of Sir H. Spelman;) John Philipot,

Hitherto, a review of our sixteenth and seventeenth century armorists presents us with the names of men of erudition
or of professional heralds, but another class of authors now
occasionally demands, each in his turn, a passing remark.
This is composed of the persons, who, possessed of few qualifications beyond a knowledge of the technicalities of blazon
and an ardent zeal in the pursuit, have ventured to add to
the already extensive stock of heraldric lore.   The earliest
writer of the class alluded to is JAMES YORKE, the Black-
smith of Lincoln, who in 1640 published ‘The Union of
Honovr,’ containing the arms, matches, and descents of the
nobility from the Conquest.   Appended to it are the arms
of the gentry of Lincolnshire, and an account of all the
battles fought by the English.   It is dedicated to Charles I;
and there is also an epistle dedicatory to Henry, son and heir
of Thomas, earl of Arundel, earl-marshal, in which Yorke very
candidly avows his lack of erudition.   “My education,”
says he, “hath made me but just so much a Scholler as to
feele and know my want of learning.”   He hopes, however,
that his noble patron will find the work “decent.”   “I
undertooke it not for vaine-glory, nor assume the credit of
mine authours to my selfe, onely am proud nature inclin’d
me to so Noble a study: *long was I forging and hammering
it to this perfection,* and now present it to your Lordship, as
a *master-piece, not yet matched by any of my trade.*”   In
his address to the courteous reader he expresses his appre-
hensions that “some will *smutch* his labours with a scorne of
his profession.”   There was, however, little to fear on this
head, for the book is really a very ‘*decent*’ production.

Somerset, and his son Thomas; Thomas Gore; John Gibbon, Bluemantle; and
Matthew Carter, author of ‘Honor Redivivus;’ and among the latter Speed,
Weever, Heylyn, and Stowe.

Fuller includes Yorke among the 'Worthies' of Lincoln-shire, and gives the following quaint account of him and his work :—" James Yorke, a blacksmith of Lincoln, and an excellent workman in his profession, insomuch that if Pegasus himself would wear shoes, this man alone is fit to make them, contriving them so thin and light, as that they would be no burden to him. But he is a servant as well of Apollo as Vulcan, turning his Stiddy into a Study, having lately set forth a Book of Heraldry, called the *Union of Honour, &c.* and although there be some mistakes (no hand so steady as always *to hit the nail on the head*) yet it is of singular use, and industriously performed, being set forth *anno* 1640."

The plain common-sense of our unlettered blacksmith presents a singular contrast to the inflated and bombastic style of EDWARD WATERHOUSE, a gentleman, and a man of education, who, twenty years later, published 'A Discourse and Defense of Armory.' Anthony a Wood speaks of this writer and of his works in terms of the highest contempt, characterizing the former as " a cock-brained man," and the latter as " rhapsodical, indigested and whimsical." Dallaway says, " The most severe satyrist whose intention might be to bring the study of heraldry into contempt could not have succeeded better than this author, who strove to render it fashionable by connecting it with the most crude conceits and endless absurdities." Waterhouse is supposed to have contributed the principal portion of the two works published under the name of SYLVANUS MORGAN, an arms-painter of London.

The character of this last-named author must have been already inferred from the quotations I have made from his works. The ponderous volume, entitled 'The Sphere of Gentry,' and its successor, 'Armilogia, or the Language of

Armes,' may be safely.pronounced two of the most absurd productions of the English press. That the former contains much useful information is proved by the eagerness with which it is sought after in the formation of an heraldrical library; but this is so overlaid with crude, unconnected, and irrelevant jargon, that although I have had the volume many times upon my table, I never could muster the patience to read three consecutive pages of it. Of the 'Armilogia,' we are told on the title-page that it is *"a work never yet extant!"* This volume has the imprimatur of Sir E. Walker and Sir W. Dugdale, kings of arms; but, singularly enough, the terms of the license are so disparaging that the printer has very judiciously placed it on the last page; for had it been on the first, no *judicious* reader would have proceeded beyond it. "In this book are such strange conceits and wild fancies,. that I do not know of what advantage the printing of it can be to any that soberly desires to be instructed in the true knowledge of arms,"—is one of the severe things said of it by Dugdale.

Morgan died in 1693, at the age of 73. He seems to have been countenanced by the members of the College of Arms. Gibbon, Bluemantle, who knew him well, describes him as "a witty man, full of fancy [too full], very agreeable company . . . . and the prince of arms-painters." [1]

Almost equal to Camden, in a literary point of view, and perhaps his superior in his qualifications as a herald, stands the name of SIR WILLIAM DUGDALE. Independently of his great works, 'The Baronage of England,' and the 'Monasticon,' his 'Antiquities of Warwickshire,' and 'History of St. Paul's Cathedral,' would have served to hand down his name to posterity among the literary worthies of his.

[1] Moule.

country. Sir William died in 1685, at the age of 80 years, nearly thirty-two of which he was a member of the College of Arms, having passed through all the gradations of office to the post of Garter, king of arms. It would be supererogatory, even if I had space, to give the simplest outline of his life, by no means an uneventful one; as his memoirs have been often written, and are accessible to every reader.

ELIAS ASHMOLE (1617-1692), the friend and son-in-law of Dugdale, was the son of a tradesman of Litchfield. His talents, which were of the most versatile order,[1] raised him into notice and procured him many offices of honour and trust, among which was that of Windsor herald. This situation he obtained at the restoration of Charles II, and resigned, from motives of jealousy, in 1676. His great work is the 'History of the Order of the Garter.' He was an eminent collector of rarities, and founded the Museum at Oxford which bears his name.

FRANCIS SANDFORD, Esq., Lancaster, published, besides several other works of great value, 'A Genealogical History of the Kings of England,' one of the most lordly tomes that ever appeared in connexion with our subject. It was originally published in 1677, and was reprinted in 1707. It is well executed, and Charles II pronounced it "a very useful book." The fine plates, by Hollar and others, of the royal arms, seals, and monuments, with which it is embellished, give it charms to a larger circle than that which includes the mere students of heraldry.

In 1688 appeared decidedly the most curious heraldric

---

[1] He was a musician, a lawyer, an alchemist, a herald, a naturalist, an historian, an antiquary, an astrologer, and to use the encomium of his friend, the notorious Lilly, "the greatest virtuoso and curioso that was ever known or read of in England."

treatise ever printed. I mean Randle Holme's 'Academie of Armory, or a Storehouse of Armory and Blazon.' Mr. Moule characterizes it as "a most heterogeneous and extraordinary composition, which may be well denominated a Pantalogia. The author was not a learned man, nor has he adopted any systematic arrangement of its multifarious contents, but he has contrived to amass in this *storehouse* a vast fund of curious information upon every branch of human knowledge, such as is not to be found in any other work, and of a nature peculiarly adapted to the illustration of the manners and customs of our predecessors, from the highest rank to the lowest menial."

It is one of the scarcest of books, there being, according to Mr. Moule, not more than fifty copies in the kingdom.

It will be interesting to the general reader to know that "Dr. Johnson confessed, with much candour, that the Address to the Reader at the end of this book suggested the idea of his own inimitable preface to his Dictionary."[1]

The volume, a large folio, is illustrated by numerous plates of objects borne as charges in arms, as well as many that never entered the field of heraldry. "The author's object," says Mr. Ormerod, "appears to have been the formation of a kind of encyclopædia in an heraldic form."[2] To give the merest outline of the subjects treated would occupy many pages; suffice it to say that every imaginable created being, spiritual and corporeal; every science and pseudo-science; every gradation of rank, from the 'emperour' with the ceremonies of his coronation, to the butcher and barber, with the implements of their trades; hunters' terms

---

[1] Beloe's Anecdotes of Literature, vi, 342.
[2] Hist. of Cheshire.

and the seven deadly sins; palmistry and the seven cardinal virtues; grammar and cockfighting; poverty and the sybils; an essay on time, and bricklayers' tools; glass-painting and billiards; architecture and wrestling; languages and surgery; tennis and theology, all find a place in this compendium, and are all adorned with "very proper cuts," in copper.

I have had the good fortune to procure a copy of this amusing work. It has, opposite the title, an engraving containing the external ornaments of a coat of arms, the coat and crest being neatly inserted in pen-drawing. Beneath is the following in letter-press, except the line in italics, which is MS.:

"The Coat and Crest of

The ever Honoured and Highly Esteemed

S͏ᴿ. James Poole of Poole, Baronett:

To whom this First Volume of the Book Entituled The Academy of Armory is most humbly Dedicated and presented, from him who is devoted yours

RANDLE HOLME."

This was probably a compliment paid to every subscriber, and it displays, as Mr. Moule observes, the finest illustration extant of the "œconomy of flattery."

The following extract will give an idea of a large proportion of the contents of this famous 'Storehouse,' which, like many other storehouses, holds much that is of very little value. Honest Randle blazons one of his fictitious bearings for the purpose of introducing the names of the implements and terms employed by that useful personage the barber.

"LVII. He beareth Argent a 𝕭𝖆𝖗𝖇𝖊𝖗 𝖇𝖆𝖗𝖊 𝕳𝖊𝖆𝖉𝖊𝖉, with a 𝖕𝖆𝖎𝖗 𝖔𝖋 𝕮𝖎𝖘𝖊𝖗𝖘 in his right hand, and a 𝕮𝖔𝖒𝖇 in his left, 𝖈𝖑𝖔𝖆𝖙𝖍𝖊𝖉 in Russet, his 𝕬𝖕𝖗𝖔𝖓 𝕮𝖍𝖊𝖖𝖚𝖊' of the first and Azure, &c.

" Instruments of a Barber.

The instrument case, in which are placed these following things in their several divisions :

The glass or seeing glass.

A set of horn combs, with teeth on one side, and wide.

A set of box combs.

A set of ivory combs with fine teeth, and toothed on both sides.

An ivory beard comb.

A four square bottle with a screw'd head for sweet water, or Benjamin water, &c.

The like bottle with sweet powder in ; but this is now not used.

A row of razors, &c. &c."

Then follow

"TERMS OF ART *used in Barbing and Shaving* (! ! !)

Take the chair, is for the person to be trimmed to sit down.

Clear the neck, is to unbutton and turn down the collar of the man's neck.

Cloath him, is to put a trimming cloth before him, and to fasten it about his neck.

Powder the hair, is to puff sweet powder into it.

Walk your combs, is to use two combs, in each hand one, and so comb the hair with one after the other.

Quever the combs, is to use them as if they were scratting on each side the temples.

Curle up the hair, is to rowle it about a pair of curling or beard irons, and thrust it under the cap.

Lather the face, is to wash the beard with the suds which the ball maketh by chaffing it in the warm water.

Hand the razor, set it in a right order between the thumb and fingers.

Shave the beard, is to take off superfluous hairs.

Hold him the glass, to see his new made face, and to give the barber instruction where it is amiss.

Take off the linnens.

Brush his cloaths.

Present him with his hat, and according to his hire, he makes a bow, with your humble servant, Sir."[1].

But, although the 'Academy of Armory' abounds in passages equally useless and totally irrelevant of the subject of arms, it must be acknowledged to contain a great body of information which, at a time when Encyclopædias were unknown, must have been of considerable utility.[2]

---

[1] Book III, Chap. iii.

[2] The Holmes of which our author was a member were a remarkable family. They were of gentle origin, their ancestors having been seated at the manor of Tranmere in the Hundred of Wirral, in Cheshire.

WILLIAM HOLME, of Tranmere.

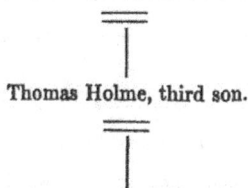

Thomas Holme, third son.

(1.) Randle Holme, 1st son, deputy to the Coll. of Arms for Cheshire, Shropshire, and North Wales; paid a fine of £10 for contempt in refusing to attend

ALEXANDER NISBET, Gent. appears at the beginning of the 18th century as an heraldric writer. In 1702 he published 'An Essay on Additional Figures and Marks of Cadency;' in 1718, 'An Essay on the Ancient and Modern Use of Armories;' and in 1722, 'A System of Heraldry,' which are all characterized by great intelligence and research. In the preface to his 'System' he tells us, in a style bordering upon the egotistical, yet in perfect accordance with truth, "Though I have not been able to overtake some things in the system of Heraldry as I first intended, yet I have explained the true art of Blazon in a more ample, regular, and distinct manner than anything I have ever yet seen on the subject."

the Coronation of Chas. I. Mayor of Chester 1634 ; married the widow of Thos. Chaloner, Ulster King of Arms. Died 1655.

(2.) Randle Holme, a warm royalist, Mayor of Chester in 1643, during the siege. Died 12 Charles II.

(3.) Randle Holme, author of the 'Academy,' Sewer of the Chamber in extraordinary to Chas. II. He followed the employment of his father and grandfather as deputy to the Kings of Arms. Died 1700, and was suceeded in office by his eldest son.

(4.) Randle Holme. Died in 1707, in reduced circumstances.

(5.) Randle Holme and his sisters died before their father.

The heraldric collections of the first four Randle Holmes, relating chiefly to their native county, are in the British Museum. Ormerod's Cheshire ; Moule's Bibliotheca, p. 240 et seq.

Nisbet's illustrations are principally drawn from Scottish heraldry, and he must be acknowledged to occupy a very high, if not the first, place among his countrymen in this department of literature.

JOHN ANSTIS, a gentleman of fortune, was born at St. Neot's, co. Cornwall. He sat for St. Germains in the first parliament of Queen Anne, and was afterwards elected for Launceston. He was a strenuous Tory, and, being attached to heraldrical pursuits, obtained a reversionary patent for the office of Garter, king of arms. On the accession of George I, he was imprisoned under the suspicion of a design to restore the Stuarts. At this critical time the office of Garter becoming vacant, he petitioned for it in 1717, and received his appointment the following year. He wrote many works relating to heraldry, and edited ' The Register of the Garter,' with an introduction and notes. " In him," says Noble, " were joined the learning of Camden, and the industry, without the inaccuracy, of Dugdale; he was a most indefatigable and able Herald, and though he lived to the age of seventy-six, yet we wonder at the greatness of his productions."[1] He died in 1744.

Glover, Brooke, Vincent, Dugdale, and others had long since paid much attention to the genealogy of the noble families of this country, when ARTHUR COLLINS, Esq. projected a more complete account of existing houses in his afterwards celebrated ' Peerage.' This work, which first appeared in 1709 in a single octavo of 470 pages, was augmented in successive editions, until the last, edited by Sir Egerton Brydges in 1812, reached the goodly number of nine volumes. This work is too well known to require the

[1] Hist. Coll. Arms, p. 377.

slightest eulogium. In 1720 he published the first edition of his valuable 'Baronetage,' and subsequently one volume of a 'Baronage,' and several independent family histories. Upon the whole, Collins was one of the most laborious of writers; and none but those who have paid some attention to the construction of genealogies can fully appreciate his industry and research. Collins was born in 1682, and died in 1760.

The reigns of the first two Georges produced many other writers on subjects connected with heraldry and titular honours, including (i) Kent and Coats, and (ii) Crawfurd on the 'Peerage of Scotland,' Wotton on the 'English Baronetage,' the learned Madox on 'Land-honours and Baronies,' and the indefatigable *Mr. Salmon.* During the same period also appeared innumerable volumes on the genealogies of our royal and noble families.

JOSEPH EDMONDSON, F.S.A. (author of 'Baronagium Genealogicum,' 1764, and 'A Complete Body of Heraldry,' 1780,) was of humble parentage. Becoming a herald-painter, that pursuit led his naturally inquisitive genius to the study of heraldry and family history, and the two works referred to are sufficient monuments of his assiduity in both. His merits raised him to the office of Mowbray Herald Extraordinary, but even after his appointment to that honour, he continued his business as a coach-painter, thus uniting the seemingly discordant avocations, science and trade. He died in 1786. The 'Baronagium' consists of five folio volumes, and contains the pedigrees of the peers, originally drawn up by Sir W. Segar, enlarged and continued to 1764. The 'Complete Body' is in two volumes folio, and must be regarded as the great standard work on the subject of English heraldry. It contains numerous dissertations on the origin and history of the science, on the great offices of state, on the heralds, on knighthood, on the arms of corporate bodies, on blazon in all its departments, an alphabet of 50,000 coats of arms, and various other interesting matters. The celebrated Sir Joseph Ayloffe assisted the author in both these works. Edmondson possessed what was somewhat rare in his day—*good taste* on the subject of blazon. He animadverts with becoming asperity on the ridiculous landscape-painting which disfigures some modern arms and augmentations, and justly remarks that the "several charges they contain, puts it out of the power of a very good herald to draw new arms from their blazons." On the subject of crests he adds, "Crests are objects intended to strike the beholder at a distance," and then produces the instance of a crest lately granted to the family of Titlow: "a book, on the book a silver penny! and on the penny the Lord's Prayer!! and on the top of the book a dove, holding in its beak a crow-quill pen!!!"[1]

FRANCIS GROSE, Esq., F.S.A., held the office of Richmond herald, but resigned it in 1763 to become paymaster of the Hampshire militia. His numerous antiquarian works are well known; but I am not aware that he contributed anything towards the advancement of heraldric literature.

RALPH BIGLAND, Esq., Somerset, and at length Garter, published in 1764 a very curious and useful book on Parochial Registers. He made large collections for a History of Gloucestershire, which were posthumously published by his son. He died in 1784.

The Rev. JAMES DALLAWAY, A.M. F.S.A., &c. obtained a well-deserved celebrity as the author of 'Inquiries into the

[1] Moule, 435.

Origin and Progress of Heraldry in England,' published in
1793.   This learned and elegant work traces the history of
our science from its source in the feudal ages to his own
times; and has the merit of having made attractive to the
general reader a subject from which he had hitherto turned
away in disgust.   Moule compares its style to that of
Tacitus.   A new edition, with additional literary illustrations and more appropriate embellishments, appears to me to
be a desideratum.

The Rev. MARK NOBLE, F.S.A., rector of Barming, co.
Kent, wrote, besides several other works, 'Memoirs of the
House of Cromwell,' and 'A History of the College of
Arms,' with lives of all the officers from Richard III to the
year 1805.   The value of the latter production is generally
acknowledged, though Mr. Moule accuses the author of partiality in the biographical department.   To this work I am
under great obligations, particularly for many of the materials
of Chapter XI of this volume.

THOMAS BRYDSON, F.S.A., Edinburgh, published in 1795
'A Summary View of Heraldry, in reference to the usages
of chivalry and the general economy of the feudal system,'—
an agreeable and intelligent work, which will be read with
much interest by those who study our science *historically*.
About the same time, a lady—for the first time I think
since the days of Dame Julyan Berners—makes her appearance in the field of heraldric literature: 'Historical Anecdotes
of Heraldry and Chivalry, by a Lady.'   This work, which
was published at Worcester, is generally attributed to a
Mrs. Dobson, and abounds with curious information relative
to the acquisition of particular coats of arms.[1]

[1] The following works appeared between the years 1760 and 1800.   Douglas's
Scotch Peerage, 1764, (reprinted in 1813).   Kimber's Peerage and his Baronetage.

SIR EGERTON BRYDGES, Bart., wrote several works on the peerage, particularly 'A Biographical Peerage of Great Britain,' and edited Collins's voluminous and popular work.

The anonymous volume on the 'Historical and Allusive Arms' of British Families, noticed at page 162, is ascribed to Colonel De la Motte. It appeared in 1803.

The Rev. W. BETHAM, of Stonham-Aspall, Suffolk, published 'Genealogical Tables' of the sovereigns of the world, and an elaborate 'Baronetage,' in five volumes, 4to, (1805.) T. C. BANKS, Esq., between 1807 and 1816, produced several works of great importance, particularly 'The Dormant and Extinct Baronage of England,' an elaborate and spiritedly-written work. In 1809 appeared that most voluminous work, 'British Family Antiquity,' a genealogical view of the titled classes of the United Kingdom, in nine vols. 4to, by W. PLAYFAIR, Esq. JOSEPH HASLEWOOD, Esq., celebrated for his vast bibliographical knowledge, reprinted in 1810 the treatises on hawking, hunting, coat-armour, &c., known as the 'Boke of St. Albans,' from the edition of W. de Worde, 1496. Mr. Haslewood's edition is printed in black letter with fac-simile cuts, and is designated by Mr. Moule " one of the choicest specimens of printing which have issued from the modern press." Mr. W. BERRY, the compiler of several minor works, published in 1825, and following years, his

---

Jacob's Peerage, 3 vols. fol. Almon's Peerages; these afterwards went under the name of Debrett; Peerages by Barlow, Archdall, Catton and Kearsley. Many of these compilations bear the names of the publishers. Two popular elementary treatises also appeared, viz. 'The Elements of Heraldry,' by Mark Antony Porny, French Master at Eton, several editions; and Hugh Clark's 'Introduction to Heraldry,' the 13th edition of which, lately published, is one of the prettiest little manuals ever published on the subject. Clark also published 'A Concise History of Knighthood,' 2 vols. 8vo.

'Encyclopædia Heraldica,' 4 vols. 4to, including dictionaries of the technical terms of heraldry and of family bearings. Of the latter there are 90,000 examples. Mr. Berry has subsequently published a series of volumes containing tabular pedigrees of the principal families (contributed in part by the resident gentry) of Kent, Sussex, Hants, Surrey, Bucks, Berks, Essex, and Herts, under the general title of 'County Genealogies.' Some severe criticisms on one of the early volumes of this work, in the 'Gentleman's Magazine,' induced the editor to commence proceedings in the Court of King's Bench against the conductor of that periodical for a libel. In 1830 appeared another large compilation, entitled Robson's 'British Herald.' It was published at Sunderland, in three vols. 4to. It contains the arms of many of the gentry of Scotland and the Northern Counties of England, which are not to be found in any previous work. In 1822, THOMAS MOULE, Esq., published 'Bibliotheca Heraldica,' a catalogue of all the works that have appeared on heraldry and kindred subjects in this country. To this highly useful publication I am greatly indebted. In 1842 Mr. Moule published a beautiful and interesting volume entitled 'The Heraldry of Fish,' containing notices of all the charges "with fin or shell" which occur in the arms of English families, with excellent illustrations on wood.

"Within the last twenty years," observes Mr. Montagu, "there have been published some of the very best works that have ever appeared, connected with the subject of heraldry, and its kindred science, genealogy." I much regret my inability to do justice to living and to recently deceased authors in this department of literary effort. In this book-teeming age it would be laborious merely to name all the persons who have written on the subject within the last few years. It will suffice for my purpose to mention some of those who stand *præ cæteris*, either in the intrinsic merit or the magnitude of their productions.

SIR HARRIS NICOLAS has rendered essential service to the heraldric student by the publication of several rolls of arms of early date and unquestionable authenticity; namely, those of temp. Henry III, Edw. I (Carlaverok), Edw. II, and Edw. III; and a splendid ' History of the Orders of Knighthood of the British Empire,' in four 4to volumes. The late G. F. BELTZ, Esq., Lancaster Herald, a gentleman of extensive antiquarian research, published an interesting work, entitled ' Memorials of the Order of the Garter.'

THOMAS WILLEMENT, Esq. who combines with the research of the antiquary the skill of the artist, has produced, 'Regal Heraldry,' 'Heraldic Notices of Canterbury Cathedral,' and some additional rolls of arms, viz. temp. Rich. II and Hen. VIII.   Mr. MONTAGU'S ' Guide to the Study of Heraldry,' evinces a profound knowledge of the subject, and is elegantly written.

In addition to these works of general reference, several volumes of great local interest have appeared, particularly several county visitations; among which may be noticed the Visitations of Durham, 1575 and 1615 ; the former edited by N. J. Philipson, Esq., F.S.A., and the latter by Sir Cuthbert Sharp and J. B. Taylor, Esq.; and Middlesex, 1663, printed at the expense of Sir Thomas Phillipps, Bart.   Sir Thomas has also printed, at his own press at Middle Hill, those of Wiltshire, 1623; Somersetshire, 1623; and Cambridgeshire, 1619.

In the genealogical department two classes of works of modern date possess great value, namely, *County Histories*, such as Baker's Northamptonshire, Surtees's Durham,

Clutterbuck's Hertfordshire, and Ormerod's Cheshire; and
Family Histories, of which Rowland's History of the House
of Neville, and Shirley's ' Stemmata Shirleiana,' are splendid
examples.   Mr. Drummond's ' Histories of Noble Families'
bids fair to do honour to the author, the subject, and the
age.   That the Messrs. Burke are indefatigable in the heraldric field, their Existing and Extinct Peerages, Baronetages,
' History of the Landed Gentry,' ' General Armory,' &c. give
ample proof.   Of other books of reference relating to the
titled orders, the press is annually pouring out a quantity
which sufficiently proves the estimation in which the aristocracy of this country is held.   In fine, the ' Archæologia,'
the ' Collectanea Topographica et Genealogica,' and that
veteran periodical, the ' Gentleman's Magazine,' contain
innumerable papers of great interest and value to the
student of genealogy.

CHAPTER XIII.

Genealogy.

"I must not give up my attachment to Genealogy, and everything relating to it, because it is the greatest spur to noble and gallant actions."

Rev. Mark Noble.

"It is a reverend thing to see an ancient castle or building not in decay; or to see a fair timber-tree sound and perfect; how much more to behold an ancient noble Family which hath stood against the waves and weathers of time?"

Bacon. Of Nobility.

A PASSION for deducing a descent from the most remote progenitor of a family appears to be inherent in mankind; for we trace its existence in all ages, and in almost every state of society. The Hebrews, the oldest historical people in the world, entertained this feeling in a degree perhaps unparalleled in any nation. The Egyptians, Greeks, Scythians, Phrygians, and Romans claimed a very high, though probably a very much exaggerated, antiquity. Alexander claimed descent from Jupiter Ammon; Cæsar's pedigree was traced without an hiatus to Venus; Arthur's to Brutus; Hengist's to Woden! The English peer views with complacency the muster-roll of departed generations, which connects him with Charlemagne or the Plantagenets. The democratic

American is proud if perchance he bears the name of a stock renowned in the annals of Fatherland; and even the plebeian Berkeley or Neville of busy London walks a little more erect as he tells you that his great-grandfather came from the same county where dwells the coronetted aristocrat who bears his patronymic! The love of a distinguished ancestry is universal.

The credibility of genealogy depends, like that of every thing else, upon the nature of the evidence by which it is supported. I have met with persons who could not trace their lineage beyond their grandfather; but such instances are rare; for the oral traditions of a family, even in middle life, generally ascend to about the fifth generation, or a century and a half: beyond that all is obscurity. If we go to documents, such as parish registers, monumental inscriptions, and court-rolls, numerous families may be traced 300 years with absolute certainty. An hereditary title or an entailed patrimony carries families of higher pretensions still further; and antient wills, genealogical tables, and the public records lead an exclusive few back to the glorious days of Cressy, to the Norman Conquest, or even to the times of the Edreds and the Edwys. That this antiquity is of the utmost rarity will appear from the data given below.

"At present," observes Mr. Grimaldi,[1] "there are few English families who pretend to a higher antiquity than the Norman Invasion; and it is probable that not many of these can authenticate their pretensions." The claim to such an honour, as has just been intimated, is well founded in some families. The Ashburnham pedigree, for instance, is carried two generations higher than 1066; and the family still re-

---

[1] Orig. Gen. p. 4.

side on the spot from whence, at the commencement of the eleventh century, their great ancestor derived his surname. The Shirleys have dwelt upon their estate of Lower Eatington, co. Warwick, uninterruptedly for eight centuries from the time of Edward the Confessor. In Collins's Peerage (edit. Brydges[1]) there is an abstract of the antiquity of the nobility, from which it appears that out of the 249 peers, 35 could trace their descent beyond the Conquest:

49 beyond the year	1100
29 „ „	1200
32 „ „	1300
26 „ „	1400
17 „ „	1500
26 „ „	1600
30 ,. „	1700

Mr. Grimaldi has ably illustrated the sources from which, and from which only, the genealogies of English families can be derived, in his 'Origines Genealogicæ,' and any one who will take the pains to consult that curious work may easily convince himself of the futility of attempting to trace pedigrees beyond the periods adverted to. Yet there was a time when the most ridiculous notions prevailed respecting the antiquity of some of our great houses. The royal family were traced in a direct line to the fabulous Brutus, a thousand years before the Christian era; the Cecils pretended to be of Roman origin, and the house of Vaux deduced themselves from the kings of the Visigoths. Many Welsh families went farther, and carried up their pedigree as far as it could well

[1] 1812.

be carried, namely, to Adam! The Scottish and Irish families pretended to an equal antiquity. This taste in the nations descending from a common Celtic stock was probably derived from the bards of antient times, whose office consisted in the recital of the heroic deeds of mighty ancestors. The splendid history of the family of Grace, drawn from a great variety of antient sources, by Sheffield Grace, Esq., F.S.A., contains some of the finest possible specimens of fictitious genealogy. The family is traced, in the male line, to the time of Alfred, and through some female lines to the founder of the human race himself. The pedigree of O'More begins with " God the Father, &c., who was from all eternity [and who] did, in the beginning of time, of nothing create red earth, and of red earth framed Adam, and of a rib out of the side of Adam fashioned Eve; after which creation, plasmatation and formation succeeded generation." The pedigree is regularly deduced through Adam, Noah, Nilus, and the kings of Scythia to Milesius, who conquered Spain and settled in Ireland. Thence through Cu Chogry O'More, king of Seix, and M'Murrough, king of Leinster, in the time of our Henry II, to Anthony O'More, dynast or sovereign of Seix, whose daughter married Sir Oliver Grace about the year 1450!

Considering the vast number of individuals who in the course of a few ages proceed from a common parent, and taking into account the mutations to which families are subject, it is not surprising that the " high" are often found to be " descended from the low, and, contrariwise, the low from the high." I know a comparatively obscure country gentleman who can (by the most undeniable evidences) prove his descent through three different lines from William the Conqueror, and consequently from the Northman Rollo, the founder of the duchy of Normandy in the tenth century. Two hundred years ago we find some descendants of the line of the Paleologi, emperors of the East, residing in privacy in the little village of Landulph, in Cornwall. In the church of that place there is a small monument to the memory of "Theodoro Paleologus, of Pesaro in Italye, descended from ye imperial line of ye late Christian emperors of Greece, being the sonne of Camilio, the son of Prosper, the sonne of Theodoro, the sonne of John, ye sonne of Thomas, second brother of Constantine Paleologus, the 8th of that name, and last of y^t line y^t rayned in Constantinople until subdved by the Turks ; who married w^t. Mary, ye daughter of William Balls, of Hadlye in Souffolke, Gent., and had issue 5 children, Theodoro, John, Ferdinando, Maria, and Dorothy, and departed this life at Clyfton, ye 21st. of Janu. 1636." Some female descendants of this individual married persons of humble condition in the immediate vicinity of Landulph, and hence, as Mr. Gilbert observes, the imperial blood may still flow in the veins of the bargemen of Cargreen![1] On the other hand, many of our peers descend from tradesmen, and other persons of plebeian condition. Not to meddle with the pedigrees of some of our *Novi Domini*, the earl of Dartmouth descends from a worthy London skinner of the fourteenth century; the earl of Coventry from a mercer of the fifteenth; and Lord Dudley from a goldsmith of the seventeenth.

"Genealogy," says Sir Egerton Brydges, "is of little value, unless it discloses matter which teaches the causes of the decay or prosperity of families, and furnishes a lesson of moral wisdom for the direction of those who succeed. When

---

[1] A village on the western bank of the Tamar in the parish of Landulph.

we reflect how soon the fortunes of a house are ruined, not only by vice or folly, but by the least deficience in that cold prudence with which highly endowed minds are so seldom gifted, the long continuance of any race of nobility or gentry seems to take place almost in defiance of probabilities."[1]

Persons not conversant with antiquarian researches often express surprise at the possibility of tracing the annals of a family through the long period of five, six, or seven centuries. It may therefore be interesting to mention the principal sources from which genealogical materials are derived.

1. The several records which go under the general name of *Doomsday Books* constitute, collectively, one of the most valuable monuments possessed by any nation. They contain the name of every landowner, with the value of his estate, and frequently refer to earlier proprietors antecedently to the Conquest. The ' Great Doomsday Book' in the Chapter House, the ' Exon Doomsday,' and the ' Inquisitio Eliensis,' were compiled between 1066 and 1086; the 'Winton Doomsday,' temp. Hen. I; and the ' Boldon Book' in 1183.
2. The next documents in point of antiquity are *Monastic Records*, such as Chartularies, Leiger-Books, Chronicles, Obituaries, Registers of Marriages and Burials, and Abbey Rolls. These usually contain much information for the genealogist, particularly in relation to the founders and bene-factors of the respective establishments. Of Abbey Rolls the ' Roll of Battel Abbey' is an eminent example. Its authen-ticity, however, is extremely doubtful, and we have the authority of Camden for declaring that, "Whosoever con-sidereth it well shall find it always to be forged."[2]

---

[1] Desultoria, p. 6.

[2] This roll professes to give the names of the distinguished personages who accompanied William the Conqueror in his invasion; but it is a fact strongly

It has been asserted that many records of great value were destroyed at the dissolution of the religious houses, and there is probably truth in the allegation; for John Bale, a contemporary observer, writes, that the library books of [some of] the monasteries were reserved by the purchasers of those houses to scour their candlesticks, to rub their boots, and even for still viler uses. Some again, he says, were sold to grocers and soap-sellers, or sent over sea to the bookbinders. A merchant bought two noble libraries for forty shillings. Peacham, in his 'Compleat Gentleman,'[1] and several other authors declare that Polydore Vergil, the historian, *burnt* many of the best and most antient records he could find in the conventual and cathedral libraries;[2] but the learned Italian has been most ably defended against this heavy charge.[3] 3. *Antient Charters* and Deeds transferring lands, &c. are most excellent authorities for genealogical particulars. Such documents are immensely numerous. By series of these in the muniment-rooms of our nobility and gentry, and other places, both family lines and territorial descent may be clearly established for a great length of time. 4. *Monumental Inscriptions* are documents of great interest. Many of them are of very high antiquity. That of King Arthur, described by Camden, is, if genuine, more than thirteen centuries old. The legend is, "HIC JACET SEPVLTVS IN-CLYTVS REX ARTVRIVS IN INSVLA AVALONIA."

militating against its genuineness that many of the names occurring in it are not to be found in the Doomsday books.

[1] 1622, p. 51.

[2] The reason assigned by Peacham for Polydore's thus playing ' *old gooseberry*' with the records is that " his owne historie might passe for *currant!*"

[3] Vide Sir H. Ellis's Polydore Vergil, printed for the Camden Soc. 1844. Preface.

There are several remains of this description belonging to
the Norman period whose genuineness is not questioned.
There are two in my own locality; namely, the epitaph on
Gundred, wife of William de Warren, and daughter of William
the Conqueror (ob. 1085), in the church of Southover, Lewes,
and that on Mangnus, a Danish prince of the eleventh or
twelfth century, in the wall of St. John sub Castro.[1] Unfortunately *most* of the monuments of those early times have
no inscriptions; so that, without the evidence of concurrent
tradition, they can scarcely be regarded as monuments at all.
Monumental *brasses*, a most interesting class of memorials,
occur from the thirteenth century to the era of the mural
tablets now in use. Regular genealogical series of them are
sometimes to be found in our country churches. 5. The
Public Records, many of which have been printed at the
national expense, contain an inexhaustible mine for the
genealogist and historian. Particulars relating to knights'
fees and other feudal matters are found in the 'Black and
Red Books of the Exchequer,' the 'Testa de Neville,' the
'Nomina Villarum,' and the 'Hundred Rolls.' These are
all of very early date. The fine, charter, close, patent, nona,
and numerous other rolls, and particularly the Inquisitiones
post mortem[2] and Escheat rolls are rich in materials for pedigrees. Lists of English gentry for certain counties occur
temp. Edw. II; and the celebrated list of temp. Hen. VI
purports to contain the names of all the gentry in thirty
counties. 6. The *Wills* proved in the Prerogative Court of
Canterbury at Doctors' Commons commence so early as

---

[1] Vide notices of each in Horsfield's Lewes, vol. i.

[2] " The proof of pedigrees has become so much more difficult since Inquisitiones
post mortem have been disused, that it is easier to establish one for 500 years
before the time of Charles II than for 100 years since." (Lord C. J. Mansfield.)

1383, and those in several of the local registries are of considerable, though not of equal, antiquity. These are of all documents the most confidently to be relied on, containing as they do much information respecting the family-connexions of the testators. From a single will a descent of four generations can frequently be traced. 7. The *Heraldic Records*, gathered from documents no longer extant, are most valuable. The Visitation-books, extending from 1528 to 1687, are in the College of Arms; and there are numerous other collections of pedigrees in public and private MS. libraries. The funeral certificates of the nobility and gentry preserved at the College are most authentic and useful documents, though apparently little known even amongst antiquaries. The following is a specimen:

" 1578. Sire John Gefferay, knyght, Lord Chief Baron of the quenes majesties exchequer Died at his house in London on Twesday the xiij daye of Maye, and from thense was conveyed to his Maner house at Chettingligh in the County of Sussex & was buryed at the p[ar]ishe churche of Chettingligh the xxij[th] daye of the same monthe A? 1578, he maryed to his fierst wiff Alis doughte[r] & heire aperante to John Apesley of London, gent. & by her had yssue Elizabethe his only doughte[r] and heire; secondly he maryed Mary doughter to George Goringe of Lewis in the county of Sussex, esquier, & by her had no yssue. The offycers of armes that se[r]vid their was Ric. Turpyn alias Windsor and Edmond Knyght alias Chester, herauldes. In Witnes of the truthe of this certyfycatt these pties hereunder writen have subscribed their names the xxiij[th] daye of Maye a° 1578.

(Sign'd) GEORGE GORINGE.
W[m] APSLEY . RICHARD JEFFERAY." [1]

[1] I, 10, p. 91, in Coll. Arm.

19

8. Last, though not least, among the aids in tracing pedigrees, are *Parish Registers.* The dispersion of the monks, who had previously been the great register-keepers, gave rise to the necessity of these local records. A mandate was issued in 1538, by Thomas Cromwell, the king's vicar-general, for the keeping, in every parish, of registers of baptisms, marriages, and burials. Many of the existing registers begin with that year, but more generally they commence in 1558, the first year of Elizabeth.[1]

Parish registers, when carefully kept, are amongst the most useful of public records. In the sixteenth and seventeenth centuries, and in the earlier part of the eighteenth, they are in many instances a sort of chronicles not only of the rites of baptism, marriage, and burial, but also of interesting parochial events; such as fires, unusual mortalities, storms, alterations in the churches, and short remarks on the baptisms or burials of distinguished persons. The following extracts from various registers may not be unamusing to the reader :

"*Mr.* Henry Hastings, son & heir of Mr. Francis Hastings, was born on St. Nicholas' even, April 24, between the hours of 10 & 11 of the clock at night. Sign. Sagit. secund. die pleni-lunii Marte in Taurum intrato die precedente, & was christened May 17." *Eaton, co. Rutland.*

"1597. M^m forgotten until now, that Edmond Denmark & Alice Smyth were married the 24th. of May, 1584." *Thorington, Essex.*

---

[1] The register of Alfriston, co. Sussex, begins with marriages if I mistake not, in the year 1512, but as all the entries up to 1538, or later, were evidently written at one time, they were doubtless copied from a *private* register kept by the incumbent prior to the mandate of the Government. I mention this fact because I never heard of another parish register of equal antiquity.

"1618. License to Lady Barbara Hastings to eat flesh in Lent, on account of her great age." *St. Mary, Leicester.*

"1643. Richard Snatchall, a stout yong man, a curious black-smith, died of y° small-pox." *Chiddingly, co. Sussex.*

"1656. A time of mortality upon the Dicker.

Richard Luccas, wthout any buriall was buried!" *Ibid.*

It would be difficult to say how this was managed. Some of the entries are occasionally very loose.

"1658. Buried. Wickens, a lame boy. 1659. A maide of N. M. A maide of R. B." *Ibid.*

"An infant crisaned!"—Burials. "A mayde from the mill." "Black John." "A prentice of M^r. Kirford." "A Tinker of Berye in Suffolk." Vide *Grimaldi's Orig. Geneal.*

"Richard Cole and *his wife* were marryed the xixth. of May 1612. Symon Fuller was marryed the 3rd. of October, 1612." *Alfriston, co. Sussex.*

"The son of a mason, buried x Feb. 1593."

"Mother Fowler buried 18th. Nov. 1603."

"Goody Hilton bur. April 7. 1699." *Ibid.*

During the protectorate of Cromwell marriages were solemnized by justices of the peace. The following entry of such a marriage, cited by Mr. Grimaldi, is a curious specimen of magisterial literature:

"*Marriadges.*
Begone the 30. September, 1653.

John Ridgway, *Bricklar* and Mary Chart *widdow* according to *a* Act of Parliament *baringe* date the 24. August 1653, *was* three several times *publissed* in the market-place, and afterwards *maried* by *mee* upon Tuesday, the *six* of December, 1653.

"THOMAS ATKIN."

"1707. Married William Thunder and Eliz. Horscraft as is reputed but not certainly known *Anab:. Chiddingly.*

"1718. M.ʳ Thomas Shirley, a young Gentleman of great hopes, who in all probability had he lived longer would have been very useful to his country and neighbours." *Ibid.*

"1722. This day were married by M.ʳ Holloway, *I think,* a couple *whose names I could never learn,* for he allowed them to carry away the license." *Lincoln's Inn Chapel.*

"1705. Buried M.ʳ Matt. Hutchinson, vicar of Gilling, worth £50 a year. 1706. M.ⁿ Ursula Allen worth £600." *Richmond, co. York.*

Many of the entries respecting local events are very curious; but as they belong still less than the foregoing to my subject, I must resist the temptation to transcribe any of them.

To these several principal sources of genealogical materials may be added the private memoranda preserved in many families, correspondence, entries in family bibles, and others which it is unnecessary to mention.

There are some persons who cannot discriminate between the taste for pedigree and the pride of ancestry. Now these two feelings, though they often combine in one individual, have no necessary connexion with each other. Man is said to be a hunting animal. Some hunt for foxes; others for fame or fortune. Others hunt in the intellectual field; some for the arcana of nature and of mind; some for the roots of words or the origin of things. I am fond of hunting out a pedigree. *Parva decent parvum.*

Family pride, abstractedly considered, is one of the coarsest feelings of which our nature is susceptible.

"Those who on glorious ancestors enlarge,
      Produce their debt instead of their discharge."

A great and wise man among the antients said

"——Genus, et proavos, et quæ non fecimus ipsi,
      Vix ea nostra voco."

"The glory of ancestors," says Caius Marius, "casts a light indeed upon their posterity, but it only serves to show what the descendants are. It alike exhibits to full view their degeneracy and their worth."

> "Boast not the titles of your ancestours,
> Brave youths! They're *their* possessions, none of *yours;*
> When your own virtues equall'd have their names,
> 'Twill be but fair to lean upon their fames,
> For they are strong supporters; but, till then,
> The greatest are but growing gentlemen." *Ben Jonson.*

I do not know that I can more appropriately close this last chapter of my essay than by citing a passage from Lord Lindsay's introduction to his 'Lives of the Lindsays,' a passage which entitles its author to as high a place among "virtue's own noblemen" as he deservedly occupies among the great ones of man's creation.

" Be grateful, then, for your descent from religious as well as noble ancestors: it is your duty to be so, and this is the only worthy tribute you can now pay to their ashes. Yet, at the same time be most jealously on your guard lest this lawful satisfaction degenerate into arrogance, or a fancied superiority over those nobles of God's creation, who, endowed in other respects with every exalted quality, cannot point to a long line of ancestry. Pride is of all sins the most hateful in the sight of God; and of the proud, who is so mean, who so despicable as he who values himself on the merits of others? And were they all so meritorious, these boasted ancestors? were they all Christians? Remember, remember, if some of them have deserved praise, others have equally merited censure; if there have been " stainless knights," never yet was there a stainless family since Adam's fall.

Where, then, is boasting? for we would not I hope glory in
iniquity.

> ' Only the actions of the Just
> Smell sweet and blossom in the dust.'

"One word more. Times are changed, and in many respects
we are blessed with knowledge beyond our fathers, yet we
must not on that account deem our hearts purer, or our lives
holier, than theirs were.   Nor, on the other hand, should we
for a moment assent to the proposition, so often hazarded,
that the virtues of chivalry are necessarily extinct with the
system they adorned.   Chivalry, in her purity, was a holy
and lovely maiden, and many were the hearts refined and
ennobled by her influence; yet she proclaims to us not one
virtue that is not derived from and summed up in Christianity.
The age of chivalry may be past—the knight may no more
be seen issuing from the embattled portal-arch on his barbed
charger, his lance glittering in the sun, his banner streaming
to the breeze,—but the spirit of chivalry can never die; through
every change of external circumstances, through faction and
tumult, through trial and suffering, through good report and
evil report, still that spirit burns like love, the brighter and
purer;—still, even in the nineteenth century, lights up its
holiest shrine, the heart of that champion of the widow, that
father of the fatherless, that liegeman of his God, his king,
and his country, the noble-hearted but lowly-minded Christian
gentleman of England."

APPENDIX.

Differences, Abatements, Grant of Arms, etc. etc.

Appendix A.

DIFFERENCES.

A FEW remarks upon this interesting branch of Heraldry have been made at p. 43 et seq. This subject is ably discussed by Wyrley, Camden, Dallaway, and others, in their published works, but the following treatise, I have good reason to believe, has never before appeared in print. It is the production of Sir Edward Dering, a representative of the great family of that name in Kent: the author, who enjoyed the friendship of Sir William Dugdale, was knighted 22 Jan. 1618, and created a Baronet 1st Feb. 1626.

The only copy of this essay I have seen occurs in a copy of the Visitation of Kent, 1619, transcribed from a MS. of Peter Le Neve, by Hasted, the Kentish Historian, and now in the possession of Mr. J. R. Smith.

"VARIATIONS OF THE ARMS IN THE FAMILY OF DERING, BY SIR EDWARD DERING, KNT. AND BART.

The differences of Arms by adding small and minute figures as of Crescents, Mullets, Martlets, etc. is neither antient nor could be so: For 300 years since every man of note and family carried in the wars his shield carved and coloured, and his armour painted suitable, and his coat of arms to cover his armour embroidered of the same; besides the caparison of his horse, if so be he served on horseback; you shall have it by example as follows:—

[A rude sketch of a brass of a man in armour with his surcoat of arms is here given, and beneath it—
" This was copied from Pluckley Church, from the gravestone of John Dering, Esq., who dyed August 1550."]

The use of all this art was to distinguish and notify the party, and soe his valorous atchievements might be seen and known, when his face was not. The further off and the easier this view could be made, the better; for that concurred to the end for which these signs were taken. Now these petty variations were not to be seen, but when near at hand, requiring a clear light and near approach to make them, and so consequently, the bearers of them, discoverable.

In the last battle fought by the famous Earl of Warwicke for K. Henry 6th against K. Edward the 4th, the day grew hopefull for Warwick by the valor of the Earl of Oxford: Oxford's soldiery had his star, or rather mullet, embroidered on their coats—K. Edward's men, saith Speed, the sun; but it was indeed a little white rose, with the rayes of the sun-beams pointing round about it. The day was overcast and foggy; Oxford had made such impression upon the Yorkists, that many fled from the field at Barnet to London, giving out the news that the day was Warwick's. Warwick, intending to perfect the victory over that part of K. Edward's army, came up to Oxford, when, the light being dull with mists, rendered Oxford's badge as big as the king's, the difference in form and colours being but little; so that Warwick's men by mistake let fly at those of Oxford. They seeing Warwick's ragged staff and bear making havock at their backs, whilst they were pressing forward on K. Edward's sun-beams, not knowing or guessing the cause and Error, cryed out, " Treason ! Treason ! we are all betrayed." Hereupon the Earl of Oxford, with 800 men fled the field, and the Yorkists prevailed, with the death of the great Warwick and his brother the Marquis of Montacute.

Other examples have been two; in Wyrley. one, of the

two Baliols—the other of the French Lord of Chine, who laying up the Lord Courcy's banner, the English of Sir Hugh Calvely's company, reputing them friends, were thereby unfortunately slain, and the Lord Courcy had thereupon dishonour spoken of him, though absent as far as Austrich.

> " This Chine did raise Lord Courcy's fair Devìse,
>   Which was 6 Bars of vairy and of red ;
> This way the same or difference small so nice
> And slender that 'mongst them they error bred,
> Which now were either taken slain or fled.
> All men of younger house which banners bear
> Should have their difference glist'ning large and fair."

Capital de Bur, p. 151.

These minute differences, as they were antiently dangerous and insufficient, so in manner as they are now used they were then unknown ; neither is there art enough by any of our heralds' rules, though much refined of late, to guide one so as to know which of the Crescent-bearers was the uncle or which the nephew, and for Crescent upon Crescent, Mullet upon Mullet, etc. in a pedigree of no great largeness, perspective-glasses and spectacles cannot help you ; but you must have Lyncean eyes, or his that could write Homer's Iliads, and fold them into a nutshell.

There was an elder way of differencing in former ages, and very good, though at no time regularly prescribed, yet it was much practised, as by bordures, bars, bends, chiefs, etc. and something upon special motives of relinquishing the whole devise and assuming another ; all which are eminently known in the families of Nevil, Howard, Berkeley, Beauchamp, Stafford, Chaworth, Latymer, Grey and Bassett, Willoughby, etc. You shall have an example of two in Kent leaving the chevron-bearers in imitation of the great Lords of Clare and Criol, the ten variations and imitations of Leyborne's Lions ; and of Sandwich's indentings in like number, I will here instance in Say and Cobham.

Sir Wm. de Say. (1)   Sir R. de Huntingfield. (2)   Sir Ibron de Huntingfield. (3)   Sir Alex. de Cheney. (4)   ....Huntingfield. (5)

Sir Ralph de Perington. (6)   St. Nicholas. (7)   Parrocke.[1] (8)

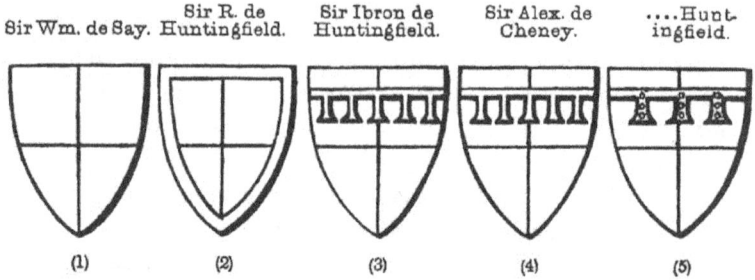

There are more examples, but these are in Kent.

Now for an instance in the family of Cobham.

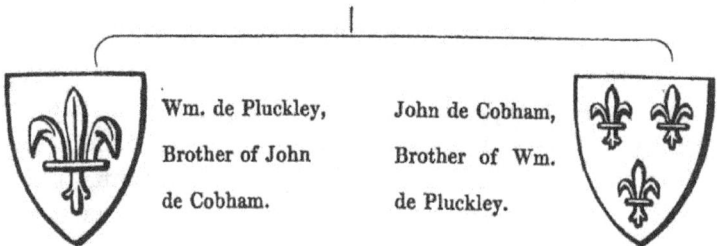

Wm. de Pluckley, Brother of John de Cobham.

John de Cobham, Brother of Wm. de Pluckley.

---

[1] In the MS. the tinctures of these shields are shown in the usual manner by lines, &c. Nos. 1, 2, 3, 4, 5, and 6, are quarterly, or and gules. The bordure of No. 2 is sable; the label of No. 3 is sable; that of No. 4 purpure; and that of No. 5 sable, charged with plates; the charge of No. 6 is a plate; the chief of No. 7 is quarterly, or and gules; and that of No. 8 gules and or. The coat No. 7 is identical with that of Peckham of Kent and Sussex.

Vide Book of Differences, p. 177. Henry Cobham, great grandchild of this John, and Joane, da. and heir of de Bokeland.

John de Cobham, son of Henry and Joane Bokeland, put his father's fleurs de lizs upon his mother's cheveron, and had issue three sons, who did each constitute a several family, and varied their arms.

Henry Cobham, the eldest son, married Joane, sister and heir of Step^n de Pencester.	John, the 2d son, to whom his father gave the manor of Cobham, and from whom the Lords Cobham descended.	Reginald, the 3d, de Orkesden, from whom the Cobhams of Sterborough are descended.

This Henry by the great heir, his wife, was father of three sons, who all of them followed the copy of their Mother's Arms, whereof

1. Stephen de Cobham, Lord of Shorne, who leaving the paternal coat, took his Mother's Arms.	2. John de Toneford, where he dwelt, a place in Chartham.	3. Stephen de Cobham, father of Henry, Lord of Dunstall.

This elder Stephen was father of Sir John de Cobham of Rundale, and of Robert de Cobham, which Sir John was father of Sir Thomas Cobham de Rundale, and of John de Hever, who had the manor of Hever, and thence his name.

Robert de Cobham.   John de Hever of Hever.

John de Cobham, aforesaid, who bore the three lions on his cheveron, was father of Henry Lord Cobham, and of John Cobham de Blackburg, in co. Devon. Henry Lord Cobham was father of Henry Lord Cobham and of Thomas Cobham, of Chafford in Kent. This Henry Lord Cobham was father of John Lord Cobham and of Thomas Cobham, owner of Belunele and Pipards-clive, who had issue two sons, Thomas and Henry; now all these younger Cobhams varied their Arms as under.

John Cobham de Blackburg.   Thos. Cobham de Chafford.   Thos. Cobham de Belunele.   Henry Cobham de Pypard's Clive.[1]

In like manner the family of Dering, though not so eminent, (yet as antient, and more numerous, for aught yet appears,) did, as the use and necessity of those former ages required, vary their arms upon several occasions, which need not here be repeated, being more visible in the descent,[2] it

[1] These shields are all, as to the fields, gules; as to the cheverons, or; and as to the charges, sable.

[2] Id est, in the family pedigree. *Ed.*

shall therefore be enough in this place to set down the
several shields borne anciently and at present by this name
and the several branches thereof, by seals, monuments, old
rolls, windows, &c.   The antient paternal coat of this family
was (if tradition may persuade us) only the blue fesse in a
white field, until, say they, one of our ancestors being slain
in the king's wars, his shield was found to have three great
bloody spots in place where now the roundels are.   I cannot
justify such far-fetcht storys; yet two things have a propor-
tionate correspondence with this tradition.

First, it is certain that Norman Fitz-Dering was sheriff of
Kent, as shall be evident in the part of the genealogical
history which concerns him.   2dly. The Arms of William
de Wrotham, Constable of Dover castle, and one of this
family, were by old rolls the fesse without the roundells,
which may confirm the report, because he was descended
from Godred, brother to Norman, who was slain as aforesaid, and not of the body of the said Norman.

The concurrence whereof has induced me to assign that
coat unto all before the said Norman Fitz-Dering.

So then the several shields borne by the several persons
of this family have been as follows, setting them down as
they have first been in antiquity used, and so in order successively.

Sired Fitz-Dering,
   t. W. Conqr.

De la Hell, 'T'. R.
   Steph ao. 1.

Deerman ao. 1,
   Hen. 2d.'

W. de Wrotham.
   1 R. Johis.

Hamo de Pirefeld,
   T. R. 1.

Norman Fitz-Der-
ing, 1 Hen. I and
   T. R. Steph.

Arnaldus de Cuck-
eston, t. H. 2.

Wm. de Cheriton,
   T. H. 3.

Normannus de Ash-
de Fraxino—and
de Fresne. Miles,
T. R. 1 et H. 2.[1]

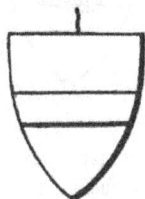

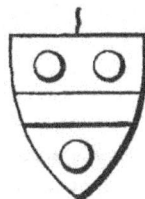

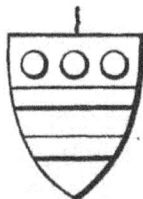

[1] The shields are all argent, the fesses azure, and the roundels, gules.

Wm. de Perington Miles, T. Hen. 3.[1]

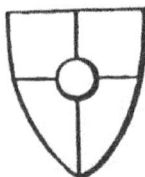

Wimond Fi*z-Wi-mond, T. Hen. 3. Hamo Wimond. filius ejus, T. Ed. I[2]

Ricus Fitz-Dering, qui obiit il Ed. L[3]

Henry Dering, frater junior Ricardi.[4]

John Dering, Dns. de Evering-acre in Pluckley, ao 1 Hen. 5 et Ricus filius ejus, occis apd. Bosworth.[5]

Wm. Dering de Petworth in co. Sussex, et de Lisse in co. Hants, Arm. T Hen. 7.[6]

To these ten may be added two very antient, whose order gave them a diversification, being Knights-Templers, and three other moderne, assigned by Sir Wm. Segar, Garter.

Dns. Robtus Dering, Miles ordinis militiae sci. Templi ad dissolut. ejus ap^d. Ewell.

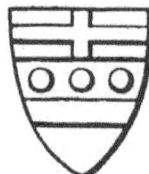

[1] Quarterly, or and gules, a plate.

[4] Ditto, with a chief gules.

[2] Argent, a fesse azure between six torteaux. [5] Gules, three bucks' heads, or.

[3] Or, a saltire sable. [6] Or, a saltire sable, a canton gules.

[7] The first of these two is or, a saltire sable, the second argent, a fesse azure, in chief three torteaux; the chiefs are both gules, a cross argent.

The three modern ones assigned by Sir Wm. Segar are as follows:

Anthony Der-
ing, of Char-
ing, Esq.

John Dering,
of Egerton,
Esq.

Xtopher Der-
ing, of Wick-
ins.[1]

So in old chartularies of abbeys I have often observed that one and the same man varied his own name of addition by the change of places where he made his abode.

Besides the variations of arms, here is much change of sirname to be observed, which among antiquaries is nothing new. Here are Dering, Wimond, Dereman, De la Hell, Wrotham, Cuckeston, Pevington, Pirefield, Cheriton, Ash, and de Fraxino, whereof the first three are assumed from forenames or Xtian names, as have done the families of Herding, Herbert, Aucher, Bagot, Bardolph, Hasting, Durand, Hubert, Oughtred, Leonard, and very many more; all the others here were assumed by reason of lands possessed of that name. Norman Fitz-Dering being Lord of Ash was called Norman de Fraxino, de Fresne, and de Ash. Arnold, a son of another Norman Fitz-Dering, being Lord of Cuckeston, was called Arnold de Cuckeston, whose grandchildren were Wm. de Pevington and Wm. de Cheriton, and so the rest had their surnames appropriated from their habitation and possession. In the family of Cobham you have Toneford and Hever of the same blood. Mortimer and Warren were brothers, and the sons of Walter de St. Martin. De Frydon, de Pantley, and de Albdy, were three brothers, the sons of Hugh de Saddington. Wm. Belward, lord of the moiety of Malpas, in Chester, had issue David and Richard; from David came three sons, Wm. de Malpas, Philip Gogh, David Golborne;

---

[1] These three are alike, or, a saltire sable, the differences being in the chief; the first is sable, the second gules, and the third azure. As the MS. bears evident marks of haste, the reader is desired not to depend upon the blazon here given.

20

and from them Egerton and Goodman—Richard, son of
Wm. Belward, had issue Thomas de Cotgreve, Wm. de Weston,
and Richard Little, father of N. Keneclerk and of John Richardson, (who would conceive without good proof that Malpas,
Gough, Golborne, Egerton, Goodman, Cotgrave, Weston, Little,
Kenclerk, and Richardson were all in short time the issue
of Wm. Belward.)   Nay, to make the instance of better impression, the antient earls of Norfolk having also Suffolk
within their earldom did write themselves of Norfolk, of
Suffolk, and sometimes of Norwich, indifferently, according to the place where they signed or subscribed, or were
in any instrument named.   The like did the old earls of
Dorset and Somerset, using either title indifferently.   Four
earls of Chester had several sirnames successively one after
another—Randolph Meschines had issue Randolph Gemers,
father of Hugh Kivilicke, whose son was Randolph Blundeville.
If yet you wish a more full president, you have it in Lucas
de Hardres, who . . . .
   [N. B. The rest is wanting, or rather seems never to have
been attempted by the author.]

   The distinctions of arms to be borne by the several
branches of the family of Dering, according to Sir Edward
Dering, knight and baronet.   The younger sons of the
eldest house to give these differences instead of the crescent,
mullet, martlet, etc. :
   The 2d son a bordure sable.
   The 3d son a bordure gules.
   The 4th son a bordure purflewe, argent and azure.
   The 5th son a bordure azure.
   Likewise the collar of the buck, their crest, was of the
same colour as their bordure.

Younger houses :
   The 2d house a chief sable.
   The 3d house a chief gules.
   The 4th house . . . . . .
   The 5th house a chief azure.

Likewise the collar of the buck's head, the crest, the same
colour as the chief.

Younger sons of younger houses give the minute difference in the crest besides the great one in the arms: as
Nichs. Dering, of Charing, gives a mullet on the buck's
neck.

Note. Nich⁵ Dering quarters both Lambert's arms and
Home's, tho' descended but from one of them; whereas
Finch Dering and his son, Brent Dering, leave out the
Home's.

Anthony Dering, son of Anthony by a second venter,[1]
gives the fleur de liz upon the buck's neck. The wreath
on which the crest stands is in all houses Or and sable. . . .

---

[1] *Venter,* [a law term] a mother. *Bailey.*

Appendix B.

A VERY curious illustration of some antient heraldric usages is furnished by an examination of the armorial bearings of families connected with the county of Cornwall.

1. The arms of the county of Cornwall are SABLE, FIFTEEN BEZANTS—5. 4. 3. 2 AND 1., with two lions as supporters, and the motto 'One and all.'[1] This coat is pretended to be derived from Cadoc, or Cradock, earl or duke of Cornwall in the fifth century.

2. The families of Moreton and De Dunstanville, successively earls of Cornwall after the Norman Conquest, bore personal arms totally different from these; yet on the marriage of Roger Valetorte with Joan, daughter of Reginald de Dunstanville, he surrounded his paternal arms (argent, three bendlets gules,) with a bordure sable bezantee.

3. Whalesborough of Cornwall, temp. Henry III, bore the same arms, with the bordure sable bezantee, whence he is presumed to have been a cadet of Valetorte.

4. Henry II took the earldom into his own hands, and gave it to his youngest son John, and John, on coming to the throne, gave it to his second son, Richard, afterwards king of

---

[1] In general the arms assigned to a county are those of one of its chief, or most antient, boroughs. Thus the arms of Sussex are identical with those of East Grinstead, once the county town; (although within the last 10 years, for some unexplained reason, the *fictitious* bearings ascribed to the South-Saxon kings have been employed as the official arms of the county.) But the arms of Cornwall are those of its antient feu, attached to the territory, and not to any particular family.

the Romans and earl of Poictou. "Richard, 2nd son of king John, in the 9th year of king Henry III, his brother, being crowned king of the Romans, writ himself *Semper Augustus*, and had his arms carved on the breast of the Roman 𝕖𝕒𝕘𝕝𝕖. He bare 𝖆𝖗𝖌𝖊𝖓𝖙, 𝖆 𝖑𝖞𝖔𝖓 𝖗𝖆𝖒𝖕𝖆𝖓𝖙 𝖌𝖚𝖑𝖊𝖘, crowned or, within a 𝖇𝖔𝖗𝖉𝖚𝖗𝖊 𝖘𝖆𝖇𝖑𝖊 𝖇𝖊𝖟𝖆𝖓𝖙𝖊𝖊." [1] "He had," says Nisbet, "nothing of his father's royal ensigns [his arms being] composed of his two noble Feus, viz. Argent, a lion rampant gules, crowned or (the arms of Poictiers), surrounded with a border sable bezantée, or, (the arms of Cornwall,) and which were on his seal of arms appended to instruments, anno 1226." [2]

5. Edmund, his son and successor, bore the same arms, only omitting the imperial supporter.

6. The same arms are borne as the ensigns of the borough of Grampound. Boroughs usually took the arms of their over-lords.

7. Walter de Cornwall, knight of the shire in 1311, an illegitimate descendant of one of the earls of Cornwall, bore the same arms. [3]

8. Sir Geoffrey Cornwall having taken prisoner the duke of Brittany, received in reward that nobleman's arms, viz. Ermine, which he made the field of his own, retaining the lion gules, &c. [4]

The descendants of the bastard offshoot of the earls of Cornwall became widely scattered, and; according to the practice of antient times, varied their arms in every house. For example :

9. De Cornewall, and Cornwall of Oxfordshire, bore the 𝖗𝖊𝖉 𝖑𝖎𝖔𝖓 of Poictou, debruised by a bend 𝖘𝖆𝖇𝖑𝖊, charged with three 𝖇𝖊𝖟𝖆𝖓𝖙𝖘.

[1] Morgan's Armilogia, p. 158.

[2] Armories, p. 39.

[3] Sandford's Geneal. Hist. gives Richard, king of the Romans, two natural sons, viz. Richard de Cornwall, ancestor of the knightly family commonly called Barons of Burford, and Walter de Cornwall, to whom he gave lands in Branel. Walter de Cornwall mentioned in the text was probably descended from the latter.

[4] Nisbet, 37.

10. Cornwall of Devon omitted all traces of Poictou, but retained the characteristics of Cornwall, viz., On a cross patée 𝔰𝔞𝔟𝔩𝔢 five 𝔟𝔢𝔧𝔞𝔫𝔱𝔰.

11. Cornwall of Essex bore the 𝔯𝔢𝔡 𝔩𝔦𝔬𝔫 of Poictou, the ermine of Burgundy, and the 𝔰𝔞𝔟𝔩𝔢 𝔟𝔬𝔯𝔡𝔲𝔯𝔢 𝔟𝔢𝔧𝔞𝔫𝔱𝔢𝔢 of Cornwall.

12. Cornwall of Salop bore the same, except that he made his lion reguardant. His descent from the princely stock of Cornwall is hinted at in his crest, which is a *Cornish Chough.*

In Glover's 'Ordinary' are these two:

13. Cornwayle, Argent, on a fesse 𝔰𝔞𝔟𝔩𝔢, three 𝔟𝔢𝔧𝔞𝔫𝔱𝔰.

14. Cornwall, Argent, on a cross-patonce 𝔰𝔞𝔟𝔩𝔢, five 𝔟𝔢𝔧𝔞𝔫𝔱𝔰.

Many other coats borne by this name are given in various works of reference. Nearly the whole of them retain one or other of the charges and tinctures of the coat from which they were primarily borrowed. Similar arms are also borne by other names connected with the county.

15. Chamberlayne, M.P. for Liskeard, temp. Edw. III, bore, Argent on a bend 𝔰𝔞𝔟𝔩𝔢, five 𝔟𝔢𝔧𝔞𝔫𝔱𝔰. It seems exceedingly probable that this gentleman, or one of his ancestors, held the office (unde nomen) of Chamberlain to the earls of Cornwall, who paid him for his services with a few of their bezants.

16. Killegrew of Cornwall bore, Argent, an 𝔢𝔞𝔤𝔩𝔢 displayed with two heads 𝔰𝔞𝔟𝔩𝔢, within a 𝔟𝔬𝔯𝔡𝔲𝔯𝔢 𝔰𝔞𝔟𝔩𝔢 𝔟𝔢𝔧𝔞𝔫𝔱𝔢𝔢. Crest. A demi-𝔩𝔶𝔬𝔫 rampant, 𝔤𝔲𝔩𝔢𝔰, charged on the flank with two 𝔟𝔢𝔧𝔞𝔫𝔱𝔰. I cannot trace any connexion between this family (which was of great antiquity) and the earls of Cornwall; but the similarity between these bearings and those of the king of the Romans is too striking to admit a doubt of some connexion.

17. Cole of Cornwall bears, inter alia, a 𝔟𝔬𝔯𝔡𝔲𝔯𝔢 𝔰𝔞𝔟𝔩𝔢, charged alternately with 𝔟𝔢𝔧𝔞𝔫𝔱𝔰 and annulets.

18. Carlyon of Cornwall bore 𝔰𝔞𝔟𝔩𝔢, between three towers . . . . a 𝔟𝔢𝔧𝔞𝔫𝔱. Query. Did the founder of this family hold the office of castellan to the earls of Cornwall?

Many Cornish families bear double-headed 𝖊𝖆𝖌𝖑𝖊𝖘, and the number bearing 𝖇𝖊𝖟𝖆𝖓𝖙𝖘 is really astonishing.   In the foregoing enumeration I have confined myself to such of the latter as are borne upon sable.

It is probable that if the arms of other districts were examined they would produce a similar result; and I doubt not that, carrying out a large series of such investigations, the majority of our armorial bearings might be traced to a comparatively small number of antient baronial coats.

Appendix C.

ABATEMENTS.

AN Abatement of Honour is defined as a mark introduced into the paternal coat to indicate some base or ungentlemanlike behaviour on the part of the bearer. The number of these figures is, as usual, *nine,* and they are all tinctured of the *stainant* or disgraceful colours, tenné and sanguine. The first is the delf tenné, assigned to him who revokes his challenge. 2. The escocheon reversed sanguine, occupying the middle point of the arms, is the sign of disgrace proper to him who offends the chastity of virgin, wife, or widow, or flies from his sovereign's banner. 3. The point-dexter parted tenné is for him who boasts of valiant actions he never performed. 4. The point-in-point sanguine is the badge of a coward. 5. The point champaine tenné attaches to him who breaks the laws of chivalry by slaying a prisoner after he has demanded quarter. 6. The liar should bear the plain-point sanguine. 7. The gore sinister tenné is the punishment of the soldier who acts in a cowardly manner towards his enemy. 8. The gusset sanguine, if on the right side, denotes adultery, and if on the left, drunkenness. 9. The last and greatest 'abatement of honour' is the reversing or turning upside down of the whole shield: this belongs to the traitor. From these abatements originates the expression—" He has a *blot* in his scutcheon."

It is scarcely necessary to state that 'abatements of honour' exist only in theory. Who ever did or would voluntarily bear a badge of disgrace? Every one deserving either of them would sooner relinquish all claim to the bearing of arms than continue it with such a stigma.

Leigh, Guillim, and other old writers are sufficiently prolix on this subject, which would seem to belong exclusively to English heraldry; for Menestrier calls them *English fooleries* ('Sottises Anglaises,') and Montagu thinks " we shall seek in vain for a more appropriate designation."

A singular mistake prevails among the vulgar respecting the " bloody hand," borne in the arms of Baronets. I have been very seriously and *confidentially* told, that murders had been committed by the ancestors of such and such families, and that the descendants were compelled to bear this dreadful emblem in consequence. According to the same sapient authorities, it can only be got rid of by the bearer's submitting, either in his own person or by proxy, *to pass seven years in a cave, without either speaking or cutting his nails and beard for that length of time!* The intelligent reader needs not be informed that this supposed badge of infamy is really a mark of honour, derived from the arms of the province of Ulster in Ireland, the defence and colonization of which was the specious plea upon which the order of Baronets was created by James I.

Appendix D.

GRANT OF ARMS.

(Referred to at p. 35, note.)

A TOUTS pn̄ts et advenir qui ces pn̄ts lettres verront ou
orront Thomais Trowte autrement dit Norrey roy
d'armes du norst de cestuy royalme d'Angleterre salut et
dilection avec humble recomendacion : Equitie veult et
raison ordonne que les hom̄es vertueulx et de noble courage
soient per leurs merites par renommee remunerez et non
par seulment leurs personnes en ceste vie mortelle tant
breife & transitoire mes apres euls ceulx qui de leurs corpes
ystront et serront procreez soient en touts placs degraund
honneur perpetuellem^t devant autres luisans par certaines
ensignes et de monstrances d'honneur et gentillesse. C'est
ascavoir de blason heaillme & tymbre a fine que a leur
example autres plus sefforcent de ƥseverement user leurs
joures en faitz d'armes et ouvres verteuces pour acquirer la
renowme d'auncienne gentillesse en leurs lignes & posterité :
Et pource Je Norrey roy d'armes desusdit que non pas
seulm^t. par commune renoume mais aussi par le report et
testemoigne d'autres nobles hom̄es dignes de fois suy pour
vray adverty et enforme que Alan Trowte natef de la counte
de Norff. a longem^t. poursuey les faicts de vertues et tant en
ce quen autres ces affayres s'est porte vertuesment et honnor
ablement gouverne tellement q'ill a bien deservy et est bien
digne que doresnavannt perpetuellement lui et sa posterite

soyent en touts placs honurables admits, renomeez, countez, nombrez, et receivez en nombre et en la campaigne dez autreiz auncients gentils et nobleis hommes : et pour la remembrance du celle sagentilesse par sa vertue del authorite et povoir annexes et attribues a men dit office de roy d'armes Jay devise, ordonne et assignee au dit Alan Trowte par luy et sa dite posterite le blason, heaulme et tymbre, en la maniere qui sensuit c'est ascavoir ung escu d'or ung cheveron de purpure troys testes moriens de sable crounes de troyes trovels d'argent : le timbre sur le heaulme ung teste morien assis dedans ung torse entre deux eliez pale du Champ et du cheveron & emant elle de sables sommees de cinq foyles doublee d'or si come le picture en le merge cy devant le demonstre : A voyir et tenir par luy et sa dit posterite et eux on revestir a tous journais. En testemoiging de ce Je Norrey roy d'armes desus nomée ay signe de ma main et selle de mon seale ces p'senteis fait et donne a Londrez le viij jour de novēbre l'an de n̄re seig^n Jesus Christ mccclxxvj et l'an de n̄re seig^n roy Edwarde le Tierce apres le conquest xvj.

> This Patent was examined with the Record in the College of Arms by Charles Townley, York Herald, 29. Apr. 1745.

N. B. There is a mistake in the date, either in the year of Our Lord, or of the King.

Appendix E.

THAT the curious relic of brass found at Lewes (alluded to at p. 39[1]), was the sword-pommel of Prince Richard, King of the Romans, was an easy and natural inference from its rounded form, so similar to that observed on ancient swords, and from its being found where that Prince is known to have been engaged in the great battle of 1264. Further examination, however, proves this supposition to be erroneous, and by reference to page 589, in vol. xxv of 'Archæologia,' it

---

[1] It is now in the possession of Mr. Wm. Davey of Lewes. The engraving (from a drawing by Mr. Wm. Figg,) is of the actual size of the object.

will be seen so closely to resemble, in form, material, workmanship, and heraldic bearings, the two ancient steelyard
weights found in Norfolk, and there represented, that its
identity with their former use must be at once recognized.
The Lewes relic is smaller than the two other weights, and
is deficient in the upper part, through which the suspending
hook was passed, but, as it now weighs 18½ oz., it was probably, when perfect, a 2 lbs. weight.   It is remarkable that
all these weights, thus found at distant localities, and all
evidently of the same era, the thirteenth century, should
bear the arms of the King of the Romans,[1] though in each
instance intentionally varied, in order, probably, to signify
more readily to the eye the intended amount of each weight
when in use.   Sandford (Geneal. Hist., p. 95) says that the
King of the Romans did not bear the arms of his father,
King John, but on the larger Norfolk specimen the three
royal lions are exhibited passant, sinisterwise, a remarkable
difference, of which only one other similar example is known,
on the ancient stamped tiles of Horsted-Keynes Church, co.
Sussex, where the Prince's arms, as earl of Cornwall, are
also extant.   This Prince had a grant of the stanneries and·
mines of Cornwall, held by service of five knights' fees, (vide
Dugdale's Baronage,) and Sandford says that "he got much
money by farming the mint," but he would not appear to
derive from these sources any peculiar right to stamp
with his own arms all the weights of the kingdom.   He
is also mentioned (Madox, Hist. Exch.) as sitting with
others of the king's council in the Court of Exchequer in
14° and 54° of Henry III: there was an ancient officer of
that court, called a Pesour, Ponderator, or Weigher, but
the family of Windesore held this office for four generations
by hereditary serjeantry, during the reigns of kings John
and Henry III.   It would seem more probable, therefore,

---

[1] The charges on the shields are conjectured to be, 1, The lion-rampant of
Poictou; 2, The double-headed eagle of the King of the Romans; and 3, The lion
of Poictou, surrounded by the bezantée bordure of Cornwall, (vide p. 310.) The
workmanship is so extremely rude that the bezants are scarcely perceptible.

that these weights were stamped with his arms,[1] by the king of the Romans, in the ordinary exercise of his baronial rights, for the common use of his own officers in his widely extended domains, and especially for those of his own personal household, in order efficiently to check the entries and deliveries of the stores of food and forage necessary for the supply of his numerous retinue. The contemporary accounts of his sister, the Princess Eleanor, wife of the great Simon, earl of Leicester, in 1265 (recently published by the Roxburghe Club), show with what minute detail and accuracy such expenses in a large household were regulated, and superintended by the steward of a great personage. The steward of the king of the Romans may have been thus busily employed at Lewes in measuring out with this identical weight their scanty rations to his Cornish troops, until surprised by the hurry of the fatal battle, in which— for human bones were found with the weight near the Castle gateway—he may have continued to clutch it faithfully, even in death. Prince Richard embarked at Yarmouth in 1253, on his way to his coronation as king, at Aix-la-Chapelle, and he went to Cologne in 1267, to marry his German bride, Beatrice. On one of these occasions, when he would have been accompanied by a large suite, or on some other passage through Norfolk, which was a customary route to Germany, the two interesting weights found there may have been accidentally dropped.

[1] A similar example of ancient measures thus guaranteed by Heraldry exists in the market-place of Aisme, a small town in Piedmont, where a large marble block is adapted by four excavations of different sizes for corn measures from half a bushel to two bushels. On the front of this are two heater shields, apparently of the thirteenth century, with the arms of Savoy and Val Tarentaise. (Vide p. 32, vol. xviii, N. S. Gent. Mag.)

C. AND J. ADLARD, PRINTERS, BARTHOLOMEW CLOSE.

www.armorial-register.com

www.ingramcontent.com/pod-product-compliance
Lightning Source LLC
Chambersburg PA
CBHW060327100426
42812CB00003B/900